Occupying Subjectivity

This book explores a variety of forms of radical political subjectivity. It takes its cue from the 2011 uprisings in the Middle East and North Africa, the Occupy Movement, and the European Anti-Austerity Movement – alongside the wider opposition to authoritarian and neoliberal forms of governance from which they sprang – in order to ask an urgent series of questions about the subject of radical politics: Who or what is it that engages in resistance? Who or what should they be? And how are we to negotiate the many complexities of that second question? The contributions, drawing on a wide range of theoretical traditions, offer a rich series of provocations towards new ways of conceptualising, evaluating, and imagining radical political praxis. They engage different kinds of subjects, including protestors, dancers, self-burners, academics, settlers, and humans, in order to think through the ways in which contemporary subjects are constituted within and work to unsettle dominant relations of power. Together, the chapters open up spaces to think about how political and intellectual commitment to social change can be enlivened through attention to the subject of radical politics. This book was published as a special issue of *Globalizations*.

Chris Rossdale lectures in PAIS at the University of Warwick. His research focuses on international political theory and the political philosophy of resistance, with a particular focus on militarism and anti-militarism. He has published in *International Political Sociology, Millennium: Journal of International Studies, Global Society*, and *Globalizations*, and in 2014 was awarded the BISA Michael Nicolson Thesis Prize.

Rethinking Globalizations

Edited by Barry K. Gills,
University of Helsinki, Finland and Kevin Gray, University of Sussex, UK.

This series is designed to break new ground in the literature on globalization and its academic and popular understanding. Rather than perpetuating or simply reacting to the economic understanding of globalization, this series seeks to capture the term and broaden its meaning to encompass a wide range of issues and disciplines and convey a sense of alternative possibilities for the future.

1. **Whither Globalization?**
   The vortex of knowledge and globalization
   James H. Mittelman

2. **Globalization and Global History**
   *Edited by Barry K. Gills and
   William R. Thompson*

3. **Rethinking Civilization**
   Communication and terror in the global village
   Majid Tehranian

4. **Globalization and Contestation**
   The new great counter-movement
   Ronaldo Munck

5. **Global Activism**
   Ruth Reitan

6. **Globalization, the City and Civil Society in Pacific Asia**
   *Edited by Mike Douglass, K.C. Ho and
   Giok Ling Ooi*

7. **Challenging Euro-America's Politics of Identity**
   The return of the native
   Jorge Luis Andrade Fernandes

8. **The Global Politics of Globalization**
   "Empire" vs "Cosmopolis"
   Edited by Barry K. Gills

9. **The Globalization of Environmental Crisis**
   *Edited by Jan Oosthoek and
   Barry K. Gills*

10. **Globalization as Evolutionary Process**
    Modeling global change
    *Edited by Geroge Modelski,
    Tessaleno Devezas and
    William R. Thompson*

11. **The Political Economy of Global Security**
    War, future crises and changes in global governance
    Heikki Patomäki

12. **Cultures of Globalization**
    Coherence, hybridity, contestation
    *Edited by Kevin Archer,
    M. Martin Bosman, M. Mark Amen
    and Ella Schmidt*

13. **Globalization and the Global Politics of Justice**
    Edited by Barry K. Gills

14. **Global Economy Contested**
    Power and conflict across the international division of labor
    Edited by Marcus Taylor

15. **Rethinking Insecurity, War and Violence**
Beyond savage globalization?
Edited by Damian Grenfell and
Paul James

16. **Recognition and Redistribution**
Beyond international development
Edited by Heloise Weber and
Mark T. Berger

17. **The Social Economy**
Working alternatives in a globalizing era
Edited by Hasmet M. Uluorta

18. **The Global Governance of Food**
Edited by Sara R. Curran, April Linton,
Abigail Cooke and Andrew Schrank

19. **Global Poverty, Ethics and Human Rights**
The role of multilateral organisations
Desmond McNeill and Asunción Lera
St. Clair

20. **LGlobalization and Popular Sovereignty**
Democracy's transnational dilemma
Adam Lupel

21. **Limits to Globalization**
North-South divergence
William R. Thompson and Rafael Reuveny

22. **Globalisation, Knowledge and Labour**
Education for solidarity within spaces of
resistance
Edited by Mario Novelli and
Anibel Ferus-Comelo

23. **Dying Empire**
U.S. imperialism and global resistance
Francis Shor

24. **Alternative Globalizations**
An integrative approach to studying
dissident knowledge in the global justice
movement
S. A. Hamed Hosseini

25. **Global Restructuring, Labour and the Challenges for Transnational Solidarity**
Edited by Andreas Bieler and
Ingemar Lindberg

26. **Global South to the Rescue**
Emerging humanitarian superpowers and
globalizing rescue industries
Edited by Paul Amar

27. **Global Ideologies and Urban Landscapes**
Edited by Manfred B. Steger and
Anne McNevin

28. **Power and Transnational Activism**
Edited by Thomas Olesen

29. **Globalization and Crisis**
Edited by Barry K. Gills

30. **Andre Gunder Frank and Global Development**
Visions, remembrances and explorations
Edited by Patrick Manning and
Barry K. Gills

31. **Global Social Justice**
Edited by Heather Widdows and
Nicola J. Smith

32. **Globalization, Labor Export and Resistance**
A study of Filipino migrant domestic
workers in global cities.
Ligaya Lindio-McGovern

33. **Situating Global Resistance**
Between Discipline and Dissent
Edited by Lara Montesinos Coleman and
Karen Tucker

34. **A History of World Order and Resistance**
The Making and Unmaking of Global
Subjects
André C. Drainville

35. **Migration, Work and Citizenship in the New Global Order**
Edited by Ronaldo Munck,
Carl-Ulrik Schierup and
Raúl Delgado Wise

36. **Edges of Global Justice**
The World Social Forum and Its 'Others'
Janet Conway

37. **Land Grabbing and Global Governance**
Edited by Matias E. Margulis,
Nora McKeon and Saturnino Borras Jr.

38. **Dialectics in World Politics**
Edited by Shannon Brincat

39. **Crisis, Movement, Management: Globalising Dynamics**
Edited by James Goodman and Jonathan Paul Marshall

40. **China's Development**
Capitalism and Empire
Michel Aglietta and Guo Bai

41. **Global Governance and NGO Participation**
Charlotte Dany

42. **Arab Revolutions and World Transformations**
Edited by Anna M. Agathangelou and Nevzat Soguk

43. **Global Movement**
Edited by Ruth Reitan

44. **Free Trade and the Transnational Labour Movement**
Edited by Andreas Bieler, Bruno Ciccaglione, John Hilary and Ingemar Lindberg

45. **Counter-Globalization and Socialism in the 21st Century**
The Bolivarian Alliance for the Peoples of our America
Thomas Muhr

46. **Global Civil Society and Transversal Hegemony**
The Globalization-Contestation Nexus
Karen M. Buckley

47. **Contentious Agency and Natural Resource Politics**
Markus Kröger

48. **Social Movements, the Poor and the New Politics of the Americas**
Edited by Håvard Haarstad, Mark Amen and Asuncion Lera St Clair

49. **Development in an Era of Neoliberal Globalization**
Edited by Henry Veltmeyer

50. **The State–Capital Nexus in the Global Crisis**
Rebound of the Capitalist State
Edited by Bastiaan van Apeldoorn, Naná de Graaff and Henk W. Overbeek

51. **From Empires to Imperialism**
The State and the Rise of Bourgeois Civilisation
Boris Kagarlitsky, translated by Renfrey Clarke

52. **Global Justice and the Politics of Information**
The Struggle over Knowledge
Sky Croeser

53. **Labour and Development in East Asia**
Social Forces and Passive Revolution
Kevin Gray

54. **Global Capitalism and Transnational Class Formation**
Edited by Jason Struna

55. **Rethinking Border Control for a Globalizing World**
A Preferred Future
Edited by Leanne Weber

56. **Global Governance, Legitimacy and Legitimation**
Edited by Magdalena Bexell

57. **Critical Rationalism and Globalisation**
Towards the Sociology of the Open Global Society
Edited by Masoud Mohammadi Alamuti

58. **Globalisation Development and Social Justice**
A Propositional Political Approach
Edited by Ann El-Khoury

59. **Globalization: The Career of a Concept**
Edited by Manfred Steger and Paul James

60. **Globalization and Capitalist Geopolitics**
Sovereignty and state power in a
multipolar world
Daniel Woodley

61. **Dialectics in World Politics**
Edited by Shannon Brincat

62. **The Redesign of the Global Financial Architecture**
The Return of State Authority
Stuart P.M. Mackintosh

63. **Markets and Development**
Civil Society, Citizens and the Politics of
Neoliberalism
*Edited by Toby Carroll and
Darryl S.L. Jarvis*

64. **Occupying Subjectivity**
Being and Becoming Radical in the
21st Century
Edited by Chris Rossdale

Occupying Subjectivity
Being and becoming radical in the 21st century

Edited by
Chris Rossdale

LONDON AND NEW YORK

First published 2016
by Routledge
2 Park Square, Milton Park, Abingdon, Oxon, OX14 4RN, UK

and by Routledge
711 Third Avenue, New York, NY 10017, USA

Routledge is an imprint of the Taylor & Francis Group, an informa business

© 2016 Taylor & Francis

All rights reserved. No part of this book may be reprinted or reproduced
or utilised in any form or by any electronic, mechanical, or other means,
now known or hereafter invented, including photocopying and recording,
or in any information storage or retrieval system, without permission in
writing from the publishers.

Trademark notice: Product or corporate names may be trademarks or
registered trademarks, and are used only for identification and
explanation without intent to infringe.

British Library Cataloguing in Publication Data
A catalogue record for this book is available from the British Library

ISBN 13: 978-1-138-12506-3

Typeset in Times New Roman
by RefineCatch Limited, Bungay, Suffolk

Publisher's Note
The publisher accepts responsibility for any inconsistencies that may have
arisen during the conversion of this book from journal articles to book chapters,
namely the possible inclusion of journal terminology.

Disclaimer
Every effort has been made to contact copyright holders for their permission to
reprint material in this book. The publishers would be grateful to hear from any
copyright holder who is not here acknowledged and will undertake to rectify
any errors or omissions in future editions of this book.

Contents

Citation Information		xi
Notes on Contributors		xiii

1. Occupying Subjectivity: Being and Becoming Radical in the Twenty-First Century: Introduction   1
   Chris Rossdale

2. Derrida and Political Resistance: The Radical Potential of Deconstruction   6
   Aggie Hirst

3. Paradoxical Peace: A Scholar-activist's Auto-ethnography on Religious Pacifism and Anti-capitalism   25
   Ruth Halaj Reitan

4. 'A Direct Act of Resurgence, a Direct Act of Sovereignty': Reflections on Idle No More, Indigenous Activism, and Canadian Settler Colonialism   43
   Adam J. Barker

5. Real Politics in Occupy: Transcending the Rules of the Day   66
   Anna Szolucha

6. The Political Subject of Self-immolation   82
   Nicholas Michelsen

7. Maze of Resistance: Crowd, Space and the Politics of Resisting Subjectivity   100
   Andreja Zevnik

8. Dancing Ourselves to Death: The Subject of Emma Goldman's Nietzschean Anarchism   115
   Chris Rossdale

9. Liberation for Straw Dogs? Old Materialism, New Materialism, and the Challenge of an Emancipatory Posthumanism   133
   Erika Cudworth and Stephen Hobden

Index   147

Citation Information

The chapters in this book were originally published in *Globalizations*, volume 12, issue 1 (January 2015). When citing this material, please use the original page numbering for each article, as follows:

Chapter 1
Occupying Subjectivity: Being and Becoming Radical in the Twenty-First Century: Introduction
Chris Rossdale
Globalizations, volume 12, issue 1 (January 2015) pp. 1–5

Chapter 2
Derrida and Political Resistance: The Radical Potential of Deconstruction
Aggie Hirst
Globalizations, volume 12, issue 1 (January 2015) pp. 6–24

Chapter 3
Paradoxical Peace: A Scholar-activist's Auto-ethnography on Religious Pacifism and Anti-capitalism
Ruth Halaj Reitan
Globalizations, volume 12, issue 1 (January 2015) pp. 25–42

Chapter 4
'A Direct Act of Resurgence, a Direct Act of Sovereignty': Reflections on Idle No More, Indigenous Activism, and Canadian Settler Colonialism
Adam J. Barker
Globalizations, volume 12, issue 1 (January 2015) pp. 43–65

Chapter 5
Real Politics in Occupy: Transcending the Rules of the Day
Anna Szolucha
Globalizations, volume 12, issue 1 (January 2015) pp. 66–82

Chapter 6
The Political Subject of Self-immolation
Nicholas Michelsen
Globalizations, volume 12, issue 1 (January 2015) pp. 83–100

CITATION INFORMATION

Chapter 7

Maze of Resistance: Crowd, Space and the Politics of Resisting Subjectivity
Andreja Zevnik
Globalizations, volume 12, issue 1 (January 2015) pp. 101–115

Chapter 8

Dancing Ourselves to Death: The Subject of Emma Goldman's Nietzschean Anarchism
Chris Rossdale
Globalizations, volume 12, issue 1 (January 2015) pp. 116–133

Chapter 9

*Liberation for Straw Dogs? Old Materialism, New Materialism, and the Challenge of an
Emancipatory Posthumanism*
Erika Cudworth and Stephen Hobden
Globalizations, volume 12, issue 1 (January 2015) pp. 134–148

For any permission-related enquiries please visit:
http://www.tandfonline.com/page/help/permissions

Notes on Contributors

Adam J. Barker is a social and cultural geographer, activist, and Teaching Fellow at the University of Leicester. He holds a PhD in Human Geography, is a managing editor of the journal *Settler Colonial Studies*, and teaches and researches on settler colonialism, decolonisation, and movements for radical social change.

Erika Cudworth is Professor in the School of Social Sciences at the University of East London, UK. Her research interests include complexity theory, gender, and human relations with non-human animals, particularly theoretical and political challenges to exclusive humanism. She is author of *Environment and Society* (Routledge, 2003), *Developing Ecofeminist Theory: the Complexity of Difference* (Palgrave, 2005), and *Social Lives with Other Animals: Tales of Sex, Death and Love* (Palgrave, 2011). Erika has co-authored *The Modern State: Theories and Ideologies* (Edinburgh University Press, 2007) and *Posthuman International Relations: Complexity, Ecologism and International Politics* (Zed, 2011); and co-edited *Technology, Society and Inequality: New Horizons and Contested Futures* (Peter Lang, 2013) and *Anarchism and Animal Liberation: Essays on Complementary Elements of Total Liberation* (McFarland, 2015). Erika's current projects are on animal companions, animals and war, and posthuman emancipation.

Aggie Hirst is Lecturer in International Politics at City University London. Her research interests are situated in critical International Relations theory, radical political philosophy, and US foreign policy. She is author of *Leo Strauss and the invasion of Iraq: Encountering the Abyss* (Routledge, 2013) and co-organiser of a *Millennium: Journal of International Studies* forum entitled 'International Politics and the "Death of God"' (42 (1), 2013). She is currently developing a new research project exploring the relationship between drone operation and war videogaming.

Stephen Hobden is Principal Lecturer in International Politics at the University of East London, UK, where he teaches courses on International Relations theory and China in world politics. Previous publications include *Historical Sociology and International Relations* (Routledge, 1998) and a volume edited with John Hobson, *Historical Sociology of International Relations* (Cambridge University Press, 2002).

Nicholas Michelsen is Lecturer in the Department of War Studies, Kings College, London. He was awarded his undergraduate degree in International Relations and Philosophy by the University of Sussex, holds an MA in International Conflict Studies, an MRes in War Studies, and a PhD from King's College, London. He is the author of *Politics and Suicide: The philosophy of political self-destruction* (Routledge, 2016).

NOTES ON CONTRIBUTORS

Ruth Halaj Reitan is a filmmaker, instructor, and graduate fellow in the University of Miami's Department of Cinema and Interactive Media. She currently teaches the history of international film, gender and American cinema, and Italian cinema and the urban environment, and previously taught in the International Studies Department at UM. She has a PhD in International Relations from American University in Washington, DC.

Chris Rossdale lectures in PAIS at the University of Warwick. His research focuses on international political theory and the political philosophy of resistance, with a particular focus on militarism and anti-militarism. He has published in *International Political Sociology, Millennium: Journal of International Studies, Global Society* and *Globalizations*, and in 2014 was awarded the BISA Michael Nicolson Thesis Prize.

Anna Szolucha is a Marie Sklodowska-Curie fellow at the University of Bergen, Norway. She has a keen interest, both personally and professionally, in social movements and community groups that use direct action and direct democracy. Her PhD thesis analysed direct democratic processes in the Occupy movement in Ireland and the San Francisco Bay Area. She has published inter alia in *Interface: An International Journal for and about Social Movements* and *Research in Social Movements, Conflicts, and Change*.

Andreja Zevnik is a Lecturer in International Politics at the University of Manchester. Her work is interdisciplinary and focuses on questions of resistance, violence, political subjectivity, and aesthetic politics. She is an author of a monograph entitled 'Lacan, Deleuze and World Politics' and co-editor of *Jacques Lacan between politics and psychoanalysis* (Routledge, 2015). She convenes the Critical Global Politics research cluster at the University of Manchester and is head of a project 'Politics in Times of Anxiety'.

Occupying Subjectivity: Being and Becoming Radical in the Twenty-First Century: Introduction

CHRIS ROSSDALE

Royal Holloway, University of London, London, UK

ABSTRACT   *Critical theory has long concerned itself with the exploration of radical political subjectivities, of the various ways in which social movements, revolutionary classes and everyday communities reshape themselves and their relations in order to survive, transform or defeat oppressive forces. This special issue brings together a series of articles examining different forms (and spaces) of contemporary radical subjectivities, situating them in a global context. This short editorial introduction highlights the major themes of the special issue (placing particular attention on the relationship between theory and the subject), and outlines the eight pieces that follow.*

In the wake of the political, social and economic devastation caused by the 2008 financial crisis, we have seen a resurgence of resistance and revolution of many kinds across the globe. Whether in response to neoliberal austerity and the dismantling of welfare states, to increasingly securitised borders, autocratic leaders, unchecked movements of financial capital or the ever increasing militarisation of both liberal and illiberal societies, a new generation of disobedient subjects have captured the public attention in recent years. Particular sites of revolutionary and radical struggle, such as the uprisings in the Middle East and North Africa and the Occupy movement, have become the headline news stories of their time, and continue to have major social and geopolitical ramifications. These resistances have brought together disparate subjects across political and theoretical landscapes, who have found collective expression in forms of protest and resistance which borrow from previous generations while finding new articulation. This special issue does not begin from the premise that there is something in common about these processes, some new collective subject in-and-against authority/neoliberalism/capitalism, nor does it attempt to theorise the causes and effects of this latest wave in an ever-extending history of rebellion. It does, however, take them as a starting point to ask an urgent (though not by any means new) series of questions about the subject of radical politics; that is, who or what is it that engages in radical politics? Who or what should they be? And how are we to negotiate the many complexities of that second question?

These questions are expressed across much of critical or radical political thought. Despite substantial differences (many of which are expressed within this issue), the various theoretical traditions which comprise critical thought hold in common a desire to explore the character of (supposedly) revolutionary subjects. This has included ideas of the mass, of the revolutionary class, the rebel, the nomad, queer subjects, the multitude, and more. More specific identifications have found form in the international proletariat, the peasantry, women, blacks, the colonised, mestizas, etc. Whilst the insistence upon and search for a universal revolutionary subject has, at least to some extent, been discarded as the forms of domination that exercised themselves through such images has been continually and convincingly unveiled, the need to consider, explore, experiment and deconstruct expressions of radical subjectivity remains crucial. This special issue collects together a series of papers which seek to do just this. While the papers employ a diverse range of theoretical and empirical reference points, they all seek to identify and think through ways in which subjects have, are, and might possibly orient themselves in and against particular configurations of power.

The articles in this issue all recognise radical political action as a project of becoming otherwise, of contending with the ways in which subjectivities are produced by and implicated in their social context and of seeking to embody some forms of alternative. Visions of social change that ignore such dynamics are destined to reproduce that with which they contend. More importantly, the articles also grapple with the ways in which such abstract ideals of counter-subjectivities and creative alternatives are not easily realised, nor are they free from their own contradictions and violences. All of the articles, in different ways, shine light on how an intimate encounter with radical subjectivities reveals not a straightforward confrontation between alternative systems, but a web of contestations, a colossal loss of innocence, and a plethora of creative possibilities.

This last point, perhaps the major theme uniting the papers, divides into two sub-themes that run throughout the issue. I will outline each briefly, before introducing the pieces that follow. The first is an appreciation of the complex relationship between the practice of theory and the nature of subjectivity. The authors here use a range of theoretical traditions and conceptual tools to explore the ways in which different forms of radical subjectivity reflect, reinforce, displace, subvert or otherwise interrelate with entrenched social relations. Throughout the issue we are reminded that sweeping assignations of revolutionary content (whether in the form of ideas, subjects, projects or states of affairs) all too frequently mask the complex challenges and reperformances at play. Theory is mobilised as a tool for (de)constructing the politics of radical becoming. It can also work to recognise the ways in which attempts to resist and create alternatives to existing states of affairs might be understood as theoretical exercises in their own right—that is, must not be simply reduced to objects of curiosity or critique. In their (frequently frustrated) moves to reshape the world, disobedient or radical subjects reveal lines of friction, force and possibility which are of urgent relevance to anyone seeking to investigate the workings of power. However, the practice of theory can also close down explorations of radical subjectivity, delimiting who or what can be properly understood as radical (or, for that matter, political), and in what ways, and when. All of the articles pursue at least one of these questions. What emerges is a theoretical project which, whilst grappling with questions of significant social importance, situates theory as a deeply personal exercise. In asking whether and how we should read the politicality of particular subjects, be they political activists, humans, protest collectives, academics, settlers or those who have engaged in protest self-burning, the authors fashion revolutionary questions into intimate encounters.

Beginning from this point, the second major sub-theme is a common encounter with what we might loosely term revolutionary sentiment, albeit in a determinedly ambiguous form. Whilst the papers are all firmly seized of the non-innocent nature of professedly radical subjects, and of the consequent dangers of sentimentalisation, they also display optimisms, creativities and exhortations which pull their sceptical and critical investigations into a restless series of contestations. There are no heroes, nor critiques from a position of purism—instead, we have experiments, confessions, challenges and reflections which lay a plethora of critiques but which invite and excite further moves. They call to mind Foucault's reflections on judgment, in which he responds to the common criticism that his work invites political apathy by stating that

> my point is not that everything is bad, but that everything is dangerous, which is not exactly the same as bad. If everything is dangerous, then we always have something to do. So my position leads not to apathy but to a hyper- and pessimistic activism. (1997, p. 256)

The papers, even as they criticise, point towards a multitude of possibilities.

The issue begins with Aggie Hirsts' important moves to bring the interconnected but often separated concepts of deconstruction and resistance into dialogue. Leading off from the argument that both Gramscian and Foucaudian conceptions of resistance within international politics serve, at particular junctures, to leave the question of politics (and the subject) untouched, she suggests that, far from being apolitical or motivating a form of immobilisation, Jacque Derrida's mobilisation of deconstruction can provoke a form of resistance which resists reinscription into prevailing forms of global ordering. We then turn to Ruth Reitan's reflections on her experience as a scholar-activist navigating the tensions and even contradictions between her position as a non-violent Buddhist and as an anarchist activist. Engaging in an autoethnographic process which weaves together poetry and diary pieces, and which charts the many, everyday and often quite incidental moments which have made her who she is, Reitan gently breaks down grand revolutionary narratives and identities without sacrificing either respect or generosity for the more contested and ambiguous routes through which radical subjectivities are produced (and sustained).

Adam Barker's contribution focuses on the Idle No More movement, which emerged in 2012 as a significant moment in the ongoing resistance to settler-colonialism on the part of Indigenous populations in Canada. He argues that the protests in late-2012 and early 2013 represent the assertion of a specifically indigenous form of sovereignty, which, though emerging from movements with histories extending back hundreds of years, found particular expression through new forms of communication and new ways of conceptualising space. He also argues that some attempts on the part of settler Canadians to express solidarity with the campaign counterproductively threatened to pull the movement back into political terms defined by settlers, blunting the more radical priorities of Indigenous populations. His arguments are important both insofar as they highlight the significant struggles on the part of first-nation peoples to assert themselves politically *on their own terms*, and insofar as they demonstrate the ways in which even well-meaning gestures of solidarity can serve to reinscribe colonial relations when expressed without attention to those structures which determine the terms of political contestation.

Anna Szolucha explores the ways in which attempts to realise alternative ways of being were negotiated within the Occupy movement of 2011 and 2012. Based on extensive fieldwork in both the USA and Ireland, her account of the contradictions at work within the movement moves beyond most treatments by taking seriously the aporetic nature of appeals to democracy, equality and so forth. Occupy matters not because it offered the space for an ideal embodiment of alternatives, but because it allowed participants to recognise and explore the limits of contemporary systems, and to learn some of the ways in which politics does not involve flight to a utopian outside, but precisely a politicisation and negotiation of these limits. Her mobilisation of Derrida and Jacques Lacan as theorists relevant to such a project does much to refute the suggestion that these thinkers have no purchase for radical politics. As Szolucha highlights the limitations of looking for particular and/or stable subjectivities in the context of radical political praxis, Nicholas Michelsen in his piece argues that the assignations of political content to revolutionary acts can obscure the more fundamental challenges at play. Specifically, he explores the political subject of self-burning, asking what it means to understand such subjects (and acts) as political. By considering the case study of Mohammed Bouazizi's self-burning, commonly recognised as the tipping point for the Tunisian revolution of 2010, Michelsen suggests that conceptualising such acts as 'self-sacrifices' places focus only on the retrospective interpretation by other actors—an interpretation that, whilst not unimportant, obscures the more originary or divine violence at the heart of such actions. The political subject of self-burning, in Michelsen's reading, constitutes a far more substantial challenge to the sovereign order than is generally acknowledged.

Andreja Zevnik suggests that the sovereign order is precisely what has been challenged in the assemblage of subjects that have constituted the core of many contemporary movements against austerity and authority. Looking across protests in Egypt, Tunisia, Greece and more, she argues that we can see the emergence of a new form of subjectivity that does not repeat the calls for new forms of authority ('new masters', in Lacan's formulation) in the manner common to previous periods of upheaval. She suggests that, rather than the multitude, we can see the emerging power of 'the crowd', which signifies collective and affective experiences of grievance, exclusion and violence, which asserts certain rights centred around ideas of the common, and which does not establish common claims tied to particular identities and subject positions. My own piece explores concerns not dissimilar to those introduced by Hirst, that is, that radical political projects can, despite the best of intentions, reproduce that which they originally set out to challenge. In an effort to conceptualise a form of radical subjectivity which might take account of such dynamics, I mobilise a joint reading of Freidrich Nietzsche and the anarchist-feminist Emma Goldman. In reading both of these thinkers as productive of a particular revolutionary archetype, The Dancer, I suggest that they can inspire ways of be(com)ing radical which champion perpetual insurrection, which focus attention on the ways in which totalising discourses of morality and strategy can serve to render radical projects authoritarian, and which begin from spaces of creativity.

Finally, Erika Cudworth and Stephen Hobden engage in an important and substantive defence of their previous moves to articulate a 'posthuman' approach to international relations. In response to criticism that a new-materialist and posthuman approach to international politics holds few prospects for an emancipatory politics, they argue that an approach which begins by recognising human beings' embeddedness within complex and material systems offers important resources for thinking critically about both the dynamics of political change and about ethical responsibility.

The articles contain no prescriptions, no clear or firm instructions for how radical subjects should be, or what they should do. Instead, they offer a rich series of provocations towards new ways of conceptualising, evaluating and imagining radical political praxis. In a world where millions of people are struggling to articulate fresh demands and build new forms of political community, the explorations here are of the most urgent and poignant necessity.

Reference

Foucault, M. (1997). On the genealogy of ethics: An overview of work in progress. In P. Rabinow (Ed.), *The essential works of Michel Foucault, vol. 1: Ethics: Subjectivity and truth* (pp. 253–280). New York, NY: The New Press.

Derrida and Political Resistance: The Radical Potential of Deconstruction

AGGIE HIRST

City University London, London, UK

ABSTRACT *This paper begins from the claim that the currently dominant approaches to the study of political resistance in global politics, namely the (Neo-)Gramscian and Foucauldian traditions, suffer from a common problem in that the forms of resistance they conceptualise are highly susceptible to appropriation by, or reinscription within, prevailing forms of global ordering. In an attempt to respond to this shortcoming, or, more properly, to explore how this reinscription of resistance might itself be resisted, the paper offers an account of political resistance developed using the thought of Jacques Derrida. Having established the parallel between the way in which prevailing relations of sovereign power and governmental ordering all too quickly co-opt and engulf resistance, and the way in which metaphysics calls thought back to order and tends towards onto-political totalisation, it is argued that by means of a deconstructive approach, acts of resistance may be further radicalised by adding to them second- and third-order onto-political critiques—namely of the resistance-act itself and the agent or actor of resistance herself. The core claim made is that inasmuch as deconstruction attempts to interrupt forms of thinking and knowing right up to and including processes of conscious and unconscious subjectification, it can provide valuable means by which the micro-gestures of onto-politics can be resisted at the (fundamentally interrelated) levels of political thought and concrete praxis.*

Introduction

The study of political resistance in the field of global politics has expanded and diversified over the last decade; the escalation of global dissent and protest activities, from the Arab uprisings to the Occupy movements, to ongoing struggles against the neo-liberalisation of higher education and the privatisation of public sector institutions, has injected renewed energy into academic research on the topic. In the Anglophone literature, the emergent scholarship has fallen broadly into two main traditions, namely a (Neo-)Gramscian approach and a Foucault-inspired orientation. These divergent approaches suffer, however, from a common problem in that the forms of resistance they conceptualise are highly susceptible to appropriation by, or reinscription within, prevailing forms of global ordering. In particular, existing accounts of the subject or agent of resistance, whether framed in terms of Gramscian counter-hegemonic social movements or the Foucauldian practitioner of counter-conduct, frequently fall prey to enacting unwitting reproductions of precisely the forms of both macro and micro-disciplinary processes of ordering they seek to resist. As Lara Montesinos Coleman and Karen Tucker note, 'governmental power may be exercised and the status quo stabilised in and through even the most grassroots or subaltern practices of contestation' (2011, p. 401). More forcefully put, in Judith Butler's words, one may believe that one is resisting, for instance, Fascism, 'only to find that the identificatory source of one's own opposition is Fascism itself, and that Fascism depends essentially on the kind of resistance one offers' (2000, p. 173).[1]

In an attempt to respond to this problem of the reappropriation of resistance back into the folds of global ordering, or, more properly, how this reinscription might itself be resisted, this paper builds upon the existing critical literature by offering a conceptualisation of political resistance and its agents or subjects utilising the thought of Jacques Derrida. The argument made begins from Derrida's claim that politics and metaphysics are fundamentally interrelated; the paper shows that a parallel may be drawn between the way in which prevailing relations of sovereign power and governmental ordering all too quickly co-opt and engulf resistance, and the way in which metaphysics calls thought back to order and tends towards onto-political totalisation. Both political and metaphysical ordering, it is suggested, operate through a cumulative plethora of micro-disciplinary gestures, sometimes clearly, but often imperceptibly, closing down avenues of thought and steering potentially disruptive action back towards the status quo. Accordingly, resistance to such ordering processes must meet both these obvious and barely visible but endless series of cooptations as they occur, pulling, in a variety of different directions, away from the appropriation of thought and action back into the same. It is here that a deconstructive approach to resistance has purchase; insofar as the ceaseless movements of deconstruction seek to knock relentless processes of ontologisation off course, they endeavour to interrupt and thereby resist such intricate processes of conceptual consolidation.

Consequently, while not claiming that such a formulation can finally avoid or resolve this complex problem, it is suggested that Derrida's thought provides means by which acts of resistance may be further radicalised, as they are conceived of and enacted, by adding to them second- and third-order onto-political critiques—namely of the resistance-act itself and the agent or actor of resistance herself—intended to pull away from such ontologisation. The paper argues that such second- and third-order critiques can have at least three politically radical consequences: an insistence on the limitlessness of responsibility which takes seriously the urgency of the political; the politicisation of intervention precisely as a consequence of its ultimate indefensibility; and the self-conscious attempt of the subject to interrogate and thereby endeavour to (re)write herself in light of the aforementioned. It thus proposes a different kind of subject of resistance to Gramscian counter-hegemonic movements and the Foucauldian practitioner of counter-conduct, that is, an auto-deconstructionist actor committed to viewing her own subjecthood, as well as her concrete interventions,[2] as a site of political struggle.

The paper begins by providing a brief overview of the prevailing Gramscian and Foucauldian approaches to the study of resistance, specifically as regards their respective framings of the subject or agent of resistance. Having provided this contextualisation, the discussion then turns to developing an account of the ways in which deconstruction provides salient means by which a form of resistance more resistant to its cooptation into forms of global ordering might function, drawing directly from Derrida's texts as well as from the work of scholars who utilise his thought. The paper finally turns to the crucial question of the concrete consequences of such a deconstructive mode of political resistance; countering the well-rehearsed charges that deconstruction is of significance only at the level of the philosophical or metaphysical (a claim which vastly underestimates the degree to which theory and practice—thought and action—are profoundly intertwined), a discussion of some of the substantive praxiological implications of deconstruction at the level of concrete intervention is provided via a brief engagement with feminist, queer, and post-colonial political sites. The core claim made in the paper is that inasmuch as deconstruction attempts to interrupt forms of thinking and knowing right up to and including processes of conscious and unconscious subjectification, it can provide valuable means by which the micro-gestures of onto-politics can be resisted at the (fundamentally inter-related) levels of both thought and concrete praxis. Challenging the limitations of both a Gramscian and Foucauldian reading of the subject or agent of resistance, it is argued that deconstruction can help one conceptualise modes of subject-becoming and political intervention which both take seriously their own indefensibility and violence in the context of a post-foundational political landscape *and* insist upon active and interventionary, if ultimately indefensible and therefore explicitly politicised, forms of radical praxis.

Conceptualising Deconstruction as a form of Political Resistance

Amongst other differences, what divides the prevailing Gramscian and Foucauldian approaches to the study of resistance in global politics is their respective accounts of the subject of resistance, the persons or groups conceptualised as the agents of dissent. The former, Catherine Eschle and Bice Maiguashca suggest, has proceeded by '[d]eploying the concept of "social movements" or "forces" and situating them in the realm of "civil society"'. These actors, they continue, are characterised as

> 'counter-hegemonic' to the extent that they reflect a collective will and seek to overturn class forms of oppression. We suggest that, for Gramscians, such movements embody alliances of diverse forces which transcend different ways of being and understanding, unite distinct realms of subjectivity around the interests of subordinated classes and reflect shared truths and goals. (2007, p. 292)

In Gramscian approaches, in other words, the subject of resistance is presented as more or less united collective social and political groupings, which intervene to pursue their interests in the political sphere.

This conceptualisation of the subject of dissent has been challenged by, amongst others, James C. Scott in his articulation of infrapolitical resistances 'which fall short of openly declared contestation' (Mittleman & Chin, 2005, p. 22), Roland Bleiker via his examination of 'networks of anti-discipline' and 'everyday forms of resistance' (2000, p. 200) and anarchist-inspired engagements with a range of contemporary resistance movements (Day, 2004; Rossdale, 2010). Similarly, scholars drawing explicitly on Foucault, Eschle and Maiguashca suggest, have voiced suspicion of the 'erasures entailed in narratives of identity and unity', emphasising instead 'the transitory and contingent nature of activist politics', and 'eschew[ing] the term 'social movement' in favour of concepts seen as less homogenising'. Importantly, they note, from such a Foucauldian vantage point, 'there is no unified subject performing acts of resistance; rather resistance acts are constitutive of an always incomplete subject' (2007, p. 292). At stake in this debate is the question of the complexities and complicities of the subject or agent of resistance; the Gramscian framing of an oppositional relation of hegemonic and counter-hegemonic forces both homogenises actors within resistance movements and underestimates the implications of their embeddedness within power relations. While it concurs with this Foucauldian critique, this paper suggests that a turn to Derrida's thought can provide avenues which help resist the reinscription of resistance back into forms of global ordering which the former cannot.

Derrida's thought enjoys considerable influence in the critical literature within the discipline of Global Politics. The many ways in which it is of significance for the study of the political have been elucidated at length by, amongst others, Arfi (2012), Bulley (2009, 2007, pp. 128–142), Campbell (1998a, 1998b), Dillon (2007, pp. 80–96, 2010, pp. 191–207, 2013), Edkins (1999, pp. 65–86, 2007, pp. 172–192), Fagan (2013), Hirst (2013a, pp. 120–197, 2013b), O'Callaghan (2012), Pinkerton (2012), Vaughan-Williams (2007), and Zehfuss (2002, pp. 196–249, 2007, pp. 97–111, 2009). It is not, accordingly, the intention of this paper to set out an extensive overview of the fundamentals of deconstruction or Derrida's oeuvre more broadly. Instead, the aim here is to respond to the specific problem of the reappropriation of resistance back into the folds of global ordering, or, more properly, to demonstrate how this reinscription of resistance might itself be resisted, utilising elements of Derrida's thought.

The question of such reinscription has played a central role in the ongoing debates which ensued following the events of 1968 between leftist movements of various denominations, both within and beyond the academy. Deconstruction has been widely criticised in these exchanges, not least for its apparent failure to provide a concrete platform from which an actor or agent may enact political interventions; the charge levelled has been that in undermining the political, ethical, and ontological foundations assumed to be necessary for radical intervention, deconstruction leads to immobilisation, acquiescence to the status quo, and/or relativism and nihilism. Pragmatists like Richard Rorty, for instance, have argued that deconstruction has

> done little for leftist politics. On the contrary, by diverting attention from real politics, it has helped create a self-satisfied and insular academic left which—like the left of the 1960s—prides itself on not being co-opted by the system and thereby renders itself less able to improve the system. (1996, p.15)

Similarly, many associated with the Marxian tradition, such as Terry Eagleton, have accused practitioners of deconstruction of indulging in a form of bourgeois *jouissance* in which 'political quietism and compromise are preserved' as a consequence of 'a dispersal of the subject so radical as to render it impotent as any kind of agent at all, least of all a revolutionary one' (1981, pp. 137–138). In such readings, deconstruction quickly slips back into propping up the status quo by removing any defensible platform from which to enact resistance.

Eagleton's critique provides, however, a useful platform from which to begin to elucidate an alternative account of deconstruction in which it can be viewed as having purchase in the context of political resistance. On the one hand, deconstruction can, he argues, be read as an

> extraordinarily modest proposal: a sort of patient, probing reformism of the text, which is not, so to speak, to be confronted over the barricades but cunningly waylaid in the corridors and suavely chivvied into revealing its ideological hand. Stoically convinced of the unbreakable grip of metaphysical closure, the deconstructionist, like any responsible trade union bureaucrat confronting management, must settle for that and negotiate what he or she can within the left-overs and stray contingencies casually unabsorbed by the textual power system. (1981, p. 134)

In this reading, deconstruction's interventionary potential is limited in advance because the metaphysical structures and strictures characteristic of Western political thought and praxis leave only the possibility of surface-level reform. Deriving from and reproducing the 'blend of euphoria and disillusionment, liberation and dissipation, carnival and catastrophe, which was 1968', post-structuralism in general, according to Eagleton, found itself unable to 'break the structures of state power', and turned instead to the task of 'subverting the structures of language' (1996, p. 123). What ensues in the case of deconstruction in particular, he claims, is that 'the Maoist "cultural revolution" is naively transplanted to the arena of language, so that political revolution becomes implicitly equated with some ceaseless disruption and over-turning' (1991, p. 197). The ultimate consequence of this is a process of emptying out of both the subject and object of political thought; Anglo-American deconstruction amounts, for Eagleton, to 'a power game, a mirror-image of orthodox academic competition. It is just that now ... victory is achieved by *kenosis* or self-emptying: the winner is the one who has managed to get rid of all his cards and sit with empty hands' (1996, p. 127). The implication of this is that deconstruction 'practices a mode of self-destruction that leaves it as invulnerable as an empty page. As such, it merely rehearses in different terms a gesture common to all ideology: it attempts to vanquish its antagonist while leaving itself unscathed' (1981, p. 136). Such a process offers little by way of politicised intervention.

On the other hand, however, Eagleton suggests that to frame it as such

> ignores the other fact of deconstruction which is its hair-raising *radicalism* – the nerve and daring with which it knocks the stuffing out of every smug concept and leaves the well-groomed text sha-mefully dishevelled. It ignores, in short, the *madness* and violence of deconstruction, its scandalous urge to think the unthinkable, the flamboyance with which it poses itself on the very brink of meaning and dances there, pounding away at the crumbling cliff-edge beneath its feet and prepared to fall with it into the sea of unlimited semiosis or schizophrenia. (1981, p. 134, emphases in original)

Such an intervention is, for Eagleton, 'ultra-leftist'; because 'texts', understood as both written artefacts and concrete socio-political configurations, are 'power systems', the deconstructionist 'must track a cat-and-mouse game within and across them without ever settling for either signifier or signified' (1981, p. 134). In this reading, deconstruction's radicalism consists in its capacity to substantively and tirelessly interrupt prevailing conceptual and praxiological modes of operating. In Derrida's words, the effect of this is to instigate 'the subversion of every kingdom. Which makes it obviously threatening and infallibly dreaded by everything within us that desires a kingdom' (cited in Bowman, 2010, p. 39). Amongst other things, what such a response poses is the question of what it is in 'us' that seeks such a stable or defensible platform from which to enact political intervention.

What is interesting about this dual framing is that it points to the possibility, on the one hand, that deconstruction, read as the continuous reflection upon, and evaluation of, norms, assumptions, and principles, is not really a big ask; any critical position worthy of the name should be engaging in reflexive auto-critique as a matter of course in order to respond to its inevitable shortcomings, exclusions, and oversights. On the other hand, the radicalism of deconstruction, Eagleton shows, consists in the scope, depth, and endurance of such auto-critique. Far from simply an isolated instance or contained process, deconstruction is interminable, never ceasing, and insists that no claim, assumption, or principle is to be viewed as given or unproblematic, no matter how apparently praiseworthy. Even as political interventions are conceptualised and performed, a deconstructive engagement insists upon reflecting again, challenging again the grounds upon which an action was taken, and making any certitude of one's correctness ultimately impossible. As will be shown below, however, the absence of such 'correctness' is in many ways a salutary, as opposed to debilitating, political moment.

This raises a second important question, namely that of the animating drive or momentum of deconstruction; if the grounds upon which one can base a political intervention have been fundamentally shaken, it is legitimate to ask what is it that animates deconstruction's ceaseless movements. On the one hand, both Derrida and many utilising his thought suggest that deconstruction can be described as always already in motion due to its relation to an undeconstructable otherness to which one is always already responsible: 'Once you relate to the other as the other, then something incalculable comes on the scene... That is what gives deconstruction its movement' (2006, pp. 17–18). Derrida frames this as springing from a relation to justice: 'Justice is what gives us the impulse, the drive, or the movement to improve the law, that is, to deconstruct the law' (2006, p. 16). In other words, deconstruction finds 'its "force, its movement or its motivation" in the "always unsatisfied appeal" to justice' (Bowman, 2010, pp. 43–44, citing Protevi). Such momentum is similarly framed by John Caputo in terms of a faith (2006, p. 165), or a 'nameless love' (2006, p. 173). The imperative that emanates from this relation to otherness is, Derrida suggests elsewhere, so significant that no other authoring force of deconstruction is necessary: 'the insistence on unbinding..., on the irreducibility of difference is so massive as to need no further insistence' (1998, p. 27). The aporia underpinning deconstruction, he argues, 'is just what impels deconstruction, what rouses it out of bed in the morning, what drives it on and calls it into action' (2006, p. 32).

Whether framed as emanating from an always unsatisfied appeal to justice, faith, love, or aporia, what these accounts share is the sense that deconstruction 'happens' as a consequence of the relation to otherness, that the authorising force 'is' this relation. This is, perhaps, the deconstruction of the 'to come', the deconstruction associated with the messianic promise made most explicit in Derrida's later work; in Caputo's framing, the 'import and the impulse, the drive and desire of deconstruction is not cognitive or constative but performative; deconstruction is not matter of knowing or seeing, but of believing...[,] driven by a faith in the impossible and undeconstructible' (2006, p. 166).

In contrast to this, on the other hand, Derrida and numerous scholars employing his ideas frame deconstruction as requiring a more explicit and deliberate intervention on the part of an actor or subject. In Bowman's framing, deconstruction 'has no power of its own' (2010, p. 38). Derrida similarly states that far from simply 'happening', deconstruction must be enacted: 'deconstruction is "yes", is linked to the "yes", is an affirmation' (cited in Caputo, 2006, p. 27).[3] As such, an active effort on the part of an agent is assumed; rather than springing solely from a relation to otherness, deconstruction is an interventionary process requiring constant work. Far from it occurring spontaneously as a consequence of the relation to otherness, one must *try* to find, for instance, the heterogeneity in texts (Derrida, 2006, p. 9). This necessitates an 'incessant vigilance about the doors that are constantly being shut by the "possible"' (Caputo, 2006, p. 134); as such it relies on an endless series of interventions on the part of an actor, a ceaseless resistance to the ever-present appropriations of the onto-political.

This is crucial in the context of resistance because it is precisely the commitment made on the part of the subject which makes possible the resistances deconstruction pertains to. To rely on the assumption that deconstruction simply 'happens' within the text, occurs spontaneously as a consequence of a relation to otherness, profoundly underestimates the struggle required to attempt to ceaselessly resist the micro-disciplinary ensnarements of the onto-political at intertwined levels of thought and the concrete political sphere. It further underemphasises the degree to which deconstruction is itself a violent and even fraught enterprise: in Derrida's words, deconstruction involves a 'sufferance': 'what makes it suffer and what makes those it torments suffer is perhaps the absence of rules, of norms, of definitive criteria that would allow one to distinguish unequi-vocally between *droit* and justice' (1992, p. 4).

I would argue that this latter reading of deconstruction as interwoven with struggle, experi-enced through the violence of the indefensible, is of much greater value in the context of con-ceptualising resistance than is the former messianic vision; as I and others have argued elsewhere (Hirst, 2013b; Houseman, 2013), insofar as the 'death of God'[4] precludes the possibility of an authoring 'Alter', and the horrors of Auschwitz and countless past and contemporary political violences situate the beatific hopefulness of the messianic promise beyond the bounds even of irony, such a promise is problematic at best. It may be that such a messianic framing of decon-struction informs Eagleton's important challenge that, 'in a world groaning in agony, where the very future of humankind hangs by a hair, there is something objectionably luxurious about deconstruction' (1981, p. 140). Simply put, one cannot wait for deconstruction to simply unfold before one's eyes; the urgency of the political demands an active, even fraught mode of engagement, in which the subject or agent proceeds with her own irredeemable violence in the forefront of her account of herself in a bid to write and rewrite herself anew in light of the political landscape encountered. Accordingly, the paper now turns to Derrida's thought in order to develop an account of how such a deconstructive mode of resistance might function.

Derrida and Political Resistance

While Derrida's oeuvre is vast, explicit references to the concept of resistance are few. The account of a deconstructive mode of resistance provided here, accordingly, focuses primarily on the works in which the issue is most directly addressed. In *Resistances of Psychoanalysis*, Derrida begins his account of the concept of resistance by marking his love of the signifier: 'Ever since I can remember, I have always loved this word'. He continues:

> This word... resonated in my desire and my imagination as the most beautiful word in the politics and history of this country, this word loaded with all the pathos of my nostalgia, as if, at any cost, I would like not to have missed blowing up trains, tanks, and headquarters between 1940 and 1945... Why have I always dreamed of resistance? (Derrida, 1998, p. 2)[5]

Paul Bowman takes up this question of why one might dream of resistance, noting a number of potential dangers associated with the concept. He identifies, first, a Žižekian reading in which '"politics" and "resistance" might be regarded as *alibis* covering a drive to repeat certain ges-tures (such as "politicizing" or "seeking resistance") rather than anything like an "authentic" desire to make a change' (2010, p. 47. Emphasis in original). Such a drive has more to do with the generation of particular forms of *jouissance* than it does substantive political intervention.

Bowman similarly notes the pessimism of Baudrillard and Adorno, both of whom might take 'the possibility of an intimate intertwining or wedlock between power and resistance to mean that oppositional resistance per se is "always already negated by the structure of the entity which it wishes to oppose"' (2010, p. 48, citing Docherty, 1993, p. 322). It is easy, he continues, to move from this position to the conclusion of Bourdieu and Wacquant that '*the very idea* of resistance... is simply a *fetish concept* which demonstrates a profound misrecognition and delu-sion of the part of those who "buy into it"'; in this reading, 'dreams of resistance are really only resistant dreams. Those involved in cultural theory may (claim to) dream of resistance, but that doesn't mean that anything is actually being resisted. Claiming to resist is not necessarily to resist' (2010, p. 49, emphases in original). Derrida is, of course, mindful of this: in

Bowman's terms, Derrida shows that 'even resistance organised by explicit appeal to the idea of (its own) freedom may not be free or self-determining and may instead be entirely overdetermined, symptomatic—possibly even more an *expression* of the power that is ostensibly being resisted than something independently resistant or *alter*-native' (2010, p. 48. Emphasis in original). Nevertheless, Derrida risks elucidating his self-identified 'idiomatic', even 'idiosyncratic', interest in the concept of resistance in the context of psychoanalytic theory.

Psychoanalysis, Derrida suggests, can be understood as 'analysis of resistance' insofar as the manifestations of resistance enacted both consciously and unconsciously by the analysand to the treatment offered by the analyst lay bare the limitations of, and violences immanent to, the latter. In his exploration of Freud's commentary on the problem of resistance to psychoanalysis, he is concerned, in his words, 'with something other than analysis, a certain analysis, something that, in another sense, perhaps, resists analysis, a certain analysis' (1998, p. 5). Derrida traces this 'something other' through a series of different forms of resistance to psychoanalysis; he shows that Freud identified five distinct registers at which resistance operates, which emanate variously from the ego, the id, and the superego, but suggests that the most enduring and resilient resistances are associated with the repetition compulsion and function at the level of the unconscious (1998, p. 23). This 'something other' which prompts such resistances is read by Derrida as interrupting psychoanalysis's claim to internal coherence, self-sameness, and reasonableness. This is because it transpires that the only means by which resistances can be finally overcome are non-rational, affective, and emotive; in Andrea Hurst's framing, Freud

> acknowledges that resistances can be nonrational, which means that struggles against them have to mobilize forces other than those of rational enlightenment... In other words, to persuade analysands to accept interpretations, analysts are required to capitalize on the emotional dynamics of a '*poleros*', that is, the polemics and erotics of resistance, power, and authority ... (2008, p. 172)

It is this 'something other' that connects the notion of resistance to the movements of deconstruction. Just as this force sabotages the imposition of order and stability of narrative on the part of the analyst in the context of psychoanalysis, so too does the deconstructive imperative resist the instantiation of totality in the sphere of the onto-political. Oliver Marchart describes something similar in his framing of the distinction between 'politics', understood as a particular set of instantiated socio-political arrangements, and 'the political', understood as something other which inexorably exceeds and disrupts these forms of ordering as a consequence of the exclusions and violences of any configuration of 'politics' (2007).

The nature of this sabotaging 'something other' at work in both resistance to psychoanalysis and a deconstructive political ethos can be discerned through an elucidation of the relationship between Foucault's and Derrida's respective approaches to resistance. For Foucault, as Jenny Edkins and Veronique Pin-Fat show, 'relations of power entail resistance: they would not count as relations of power were resistance not present' (2004, p. 5). As such, resistance is immanent to the structures of global order for Foucault in a manner not dissimilar to Derrida's identification of a resistant 'something other' always already at work within psychoanalysis; in both accounts, resistance is contained within and always already part of the relational ordering processes at work.

Similarly, Foucault and Derrida share in certain respects a commitment to genealogy as a mode of resistance. According to Roland Bleiker, genealogies 'trace the processes by which we have come to accept our world as natural or meaningful'; they are

> historical investigations into the ideas and events that have shaped our thinking, speaking and acting... [They] focus on the process by which we have constructed origins and given meaning to

particular representations of the past, representations that continuously guide our daily lives and set clear limits to political and social options.

Genealogies thus enact resistance because 'questions of agency are above all questions of power relations. And power relations are best understood, Michel Foucault argues convincingly, by examining specific attempts that are made to uproot them' (2000, pp. 25–26). Differently put, what is suggested here is that by conducting a genealogical exploration into specific configurations of power relations via an examination of forms of dissent, the political fault lines inherent to such relations are exposed and thereby (potentially or actually) challenged. Such forms of counter-writing can provide alternative accounts of particular power relations which expose and address the hierarchies, silences, and exclusions of prevailing historical and contemporary socio-political arrangements, and these can be used to conceptualise interventions intended to resist them.

Deconstruction shares with Foucauldian genealogy a commitment to such conceptual and concrete disturbances: in Derrida's words, deconstruction is 'always a matter of *undoing, desedimenting, decomposing, deconstituting* sediments, *artefacta*, presuppositions, institutions'. To this degree, he explains, deconstruction may be read as a 'critico-genealogical return' (1998, p. 27. Emphases in original). Deconstruction, he claims, follows the logic of the dual meaning of the word 'analysis': it 'undeniably obeys an *analytical* exigency, at once critical and analytic'. What emerges, he continues, is both an '*archeological* or *anagogical* motif... and the *philolytic* motif of the dissociative—always very close to the saying dis-social—unbinding' (1998, p. 27. Emphases in original). In other words, what Derrida identifies here is the dimension of deconstruction which shares a good deal with genealogy's commitment to an excavation and reinterpretation of the past and/or present in a manner which intervenes so as to denaturalise dominant social understandings and forces.

At this stage, however, Derrida appends a footnote which stipulates that 'the necessity of this genealogy must always be complicated by a 'counter-genealogy'. Simple genealogy always risks privileging the archeo-genetic motif, or even the at least symbolic schema of filiation, family, or national origin' (1998, n. 8, p. 120). While I would not use the word 'simple' in the context of Foucault's genealogical interventions, Derrida's comment highlights a crucial issue at stake in processes of counter-writing and counter-conduct. In his words, deconstruction 'radicalizes *at the same time* its axiomatics and the critique of its axiomatics'. What this entails is 'a movement of deconstruction that is not only counter-archeological but counter-genealogical'. This is because 'the deconstructive necessity drives one to put into question even this principle of self-presence in the unity of consciousness', (1998, pp. 27–28. Emphasis in original) upon which the construction of a genealogy depends. In other words, through deconstruction, critique extends not only to the object or issue prompting the initial genealogical re-writing but also, at the same time, to both any alternative story told and, indeed, the author or subject of any such alternative narrative.

The extension of critique to such second- and third-order sites is necessary because however apparently politically laudable the intervention, one cannot engage in a project of genealogical counter-writing or counter-conduct without enacting a privileging of a particular subject position and, consequently, a necessarily violent rendering of the objects in question. As such, as Paul Patton notes, genealogy may thus be read as a 'first step' in deconstruction (2007, p. 768), but beyond this first-order engagement, both the alternative account provided and the agent herself must also be put into question. This is because any alternative history or conceptual apparatus *as such* risks becoming its own totalising gesture, one as problematic as the last;

the intention is to resist the possibility that the critico-genealogical intervention itself becomes consolidated into a new prevailing account, as blind as was the last to its own exclusions, hierarchies, and violences. This gesture adds, I would submit, a further radical intervention which genealogy alone cannot provide. Michael Dillon suggests something similar in his statement that an interrogation of the politics of security

> requires something in addition to genealogy as well; because genealogy, however politicising it might be – Foucault arguing, powerfully, that this politicising takes place for, or rather around, the battle over truth as 'the ensemble of rules according to which the true and the false are separated and specific effects of power attached to the true' – does not directly pose and seek to think the question of the political as such. (1996, p. 22)

Without an accompanying series of counter-genealogical interruptions, any genealogy proffered, in other words, is implicated in precisely the politics of ontological totalisation and closure which underpin the historical or political phenomena genealogical counter-writing seeks to challenge. In attending to these second- and third-level critiques—of the alternative narrative and the narrator, respectively—deconstruction thus enacts a further form of onto-political resistance. This neither serves to undermine or destroy such interventions, nor does it entail the immobilisation of the subject; rather, it insists upon critique and reflexivity at the same moment as political interventions are being constructed and enacted.

In insisting on these second- and third-order critiques in addition to the original act of counter-writing, deconstruction can be framed as a 'principle of interminable analysis: an axiom of interminability, perhaps' (Derrida, 1998, p. 33). Simply put, the deconstructive imperative amounts to a commitment to disrupting processes of conceptual or ontological unification wherever they occur, whether within institutions of global ordering or within one's own discourse; for Derrida, if there were a sole thesis of deconstruction 'it would pose divisibility: difference as divisibility'; because 'there is no indivisible element or simple origin ... analysis is interminable' (1998, pp. 33–34). In its commitment to ceaselessly unpicking the apparent internal coherence of prevailing forces of material and conceptual ordering, which are at work within one's own attempts to enact resistance as much as within concrete processes of global politics, deconstruction performs a 'hyperanalyticism': it amounts to 'a hyperbolicism of analysis that takes sometimes, in certain people's eyes, the form of hyperdiabolicism' (1998, p. 29).

Such a hyperanalytic mode of engagement is both paradoxical and crucial because,

> in order to prevent the critique of originarism in its transcendental or ontological, analytic or dialectical form from yielding, according to the law that we well know, to empiricism or positivism, it was necessary to accede, in a still more radical, more analytical fashion, to the traditional demand, to the very law which had just been deconstructed. (1998, p. 29)

In other words, deconstruction paradoxically mobilises the very analytical and conceptual tools which it itself has already identified as divisible and deconstructible in order to challenge both these tools and resist the traditions of thought and praxis they derive from. For Bowman, deconstruction thus amounts to a process of 'literalisation'; it simply looks for 'that which is claimed or assumed to be real, present, actual or true (such as the notions of *presence, justice, responsibility, univocal truth*, etc). In looking, it reveals that these are both undecidable and yet forcefully imposed, in contingent constitutional forms' (Bowman, 2010, p. 39). But it insists that such looking be constantly undertaken both at the level of processes of global ordering and within one's own attempts to enact resistance to such ordering. The radicalism of such an extensive critical imperative is suggested by Adorno: such thought as such, before all particular contents, is an act of negation, of resistance to that which is forced upon it; this is what thought has inherited from its archetype, the relation between labor and material... The effort implied in the concept of thought itself, as a counterpart to passive contemplation, is negative already – a revolt against being importuned to bow to every immediate thing. (2004, p. 19)

As this suggests, the reason such second- and third-order resistances are necessary relates to the question of violence.

Deconstruction attempts to render explicit and address the violence which is immanent to political thought and praxis as such. In Adorno's terms,

[w]hile doing violence to the object of its synthesis, our thinking heeds a potential that waits in the object, and it unconsciously obeys the idea of making amends to the pieces for what it has done... [T]he resistance of thought to mere things in being, the commanding freedom of the subject, intends in the object even that of which the object was deprived by its objectification. (2004, p. 19)[6]

What this means is that a form of resistance which comprises second- and third-order critiques, as opposed to a single gesture of supposedly correct intervention, can better attend to, expose, and attempt to ameliorate the violent exclusions that necessarily accompany it.

A prevailing response to such a deconstructive imperative has been to insist that radical politics requires 'constructive', positive interventions and activities, not an endless picking apart of these; as Noys relays, it is claimed that 'the micro-politics of deconstruction can never pass to a constructive stage of building or creating radical alternatives...' (2012, p. 29). It is assumed in this reading, in other words, that deconstruction amounts to fruitless process of undermining intervention and a cyclical pattern of disruption which ultimately leads nowhere. On the contrary, however, these movements are precisely productive and generative of substantive political interventions; much as when an issue or concept is discussed in a classroom without ultimate resolution, or a text read which challenges one's views without offering an immediate ready solution, the consequence of a deconstructive engagement is not stasis and silence, but rather a sparking of fresh reflections, a rethinking and reimagining which itself amounts and makes possible further generative and productive acts, even if the ground upon which one bases such interventions has become decidedly shakier. Consequently, far from ineffectual, deconstruction is 'the act of taking a position, in the very work it does with regard to the political-institutional structures that constitute and govern our practices, our competences, and our performances' (Derrida, cited in Elam, 1994, p. 90). It remains to provide some specific examples of such deconstructive political praxis.

Deconstruction as Political Praxis

There are many manifestations of the practical consequences of deconstructive resistance across a range of academic disciplines and activist sites. Drawing on the work of scholars and activists who have explicitly linked their radical political projects to deconstruction, whether through endorsing or critiquing it, this section provides two accounts of deconstruction read as a form of activism, followed by a brief snapshot of three examples of its praxiological utility in the contexts of feminist, queer, and post-colonial political interventions. Crucially, I am not trying to claim for deconstruction the successes of these latter movements, nor am I suggesting that the actors involved by any means do or should self-identify as proponents of deconstruction. To do so would be a crude and colonising appropriation. Rather, the point made is that the movements and interventions discussed share with deconstruction a commitment to disrupting prevailing norms and assumptions reflective of the second- and third-order critiques outlined above, specifically as regards problematising essentialised or naturalised agents of resistance.

One pertinent account of the concrete consequences of deconstruction is provided by Martin McQuillan. He suggests it can be conceptualised as a form of 'textual activism': in deconstruction's movements, he argues, 'an intervention takes place (a textual activism) which produces the movement, history and becoming of a necessary political analysis which links the political to critical thought today' (2008, p. 6). This is because

> deconstruction (unlike philosophy) reads. Such reading qua reading does not generalise from the exemplary but accepts the challenge of the exemplary to thought as an articulation of the troubling otherness which presents itself as an arrival in reading. Reading in this sense has very little to do with the quiet spaces of university libraries... Rather, this reading is an interminable, unconditional critical liveliness to the world around us, its histories and its futures. (2008, p. 6–7)

In elucidating this notion of textual activism, McQuillan makes the point that deconstruction intervenes not simply at the level of thought or philosophy but rather in ways which have substantive material effects. Simply put, this is because the ways we think have a direct bearing on the ways we act; in the post-9/11 world,

> the stupefaction and mystification of domestic thought is inseparable from the military violence which is only one aspect of this world-wide struggle. Thus, critical reason and deconstruction are more important now than ever and this textual activism will be affiliated in unpredictable ways... to the material processes of the political. (2008, p. 9)

McQuillan emphasises here the extent to which 'textual' readings and interventions are by no means dissociable from the concrete sphere of global politics. While certainly not their sole origin or source, socio-political framings and discourses of war and militarism in the post-9/11 world clearly functioned to provide the conceptual foundations and parameters without which the justifications proffered by statespersons in the USA and elsewhere for the invasions of Iraq and Afghanistan could not have been convincing or indeed intelligible. Many scholars of global politics using Derrida's thought have made similar points in a range of empirical contexts (Arfi, 2012; Bulley, 2009; Edkins, 1999; Fagan, Glorieux, Hašimbegović, & Suetsugu, 2007; Zehfuss, 2002).

Concurrently, Paul Bowman frames deconstruction as a form of 'martial art'. He suggests that 'although Derrida mainly read and wrote (monstrously faithfully) about "mere" philosophical texts, these texts are to be understood as "indices of real history", produced by and productive of particular biases: effects that have effects' (2010, p. 38). This analogy emerges in part from the embeddedness of deconstruction in relations of violence: it is 'construed as responding to challenges, intimately attentive, listening, sticking, yielding, inverting and displacing, always patient, calm and adaptive' (2010, p. 40) in a manner reflective of martial arts, particularly t'ai chi. Bowman elaborates on parallel misreadings of deconstruction and t'ai chi as 'philosophical, isolated, inward-looking, navel-gazing: as not *really real*'; both are framed as 'digressions away from reality, truth, and direct, practical engagement' (2010, p. 41). However, like t'ai chi, deconstruction has, he demonstrates, a series of concrete praxiological implications. For instance, deconstruction makes possible a form of engagement with political antagonists which emphasises 'listening': in contrast to simply denouncing and dismissing interlocutors, deconstruction 'listens by *sticking* to the other... Derrida listened, stuck and yielded to the texts and institutions of philosophy, in order to invert and displace conceptual orders and foci' (2010, p. 44). Bowman suggests that in academic contexts, this might mean, for instance, seeking to publish in journals other than those reflecting one's own disciplinary and ethico-political commitments, dealing with difference in terms and contexts other than the familiar.

The practical consequences of such deconstructive resistance can be seen in a host of political sites. To take the example, first, of feminist political struggles, Diane Elam, for instance, suggests that feminism and deconstruction can usefully be read alongside each another because,

> [o]n the one hand, feminism shifts the ground of the political, interrogating the opposition between the public and the private spheres. On the other hand, deconstruction displaces our understanding of how theory relates to practice by rethinking the opposition of philosophical reflection to political action. (1994, p. 1)

Elam connects the rise of deconstruction to the rise of third-wave feminism, posing the question: 'must feminism always seek to erase difference by giving birth to a family of identical daughters who all fight for the same causes, who all pretend to share the same feminist goals? (1994, p. 73). In third-wave feminism's de-essentialisation of the category 'woman', forms of intervention which insist upon the inclusion of race, class, age, ethnicity, and sexuality in the forms of intervention they proffer have emerged, something which, as Elam shows, has hugely important consequences for issues such as the representation of women in institutions of government, abortion, past configurations of conjugal rights, gay marriage, and the gendered and Westerncentric writing of history, psychoanalysis, and philosophy.

To the anxieties espoused by those worried that problematising the category 'woman' spells disaster for the feminist project, Elam replies:

> this is not the same thing as being condemned to the land of relativistic nihilism, where political action—or any action for that matter—becomes impossible. Uncertainty... is neither an absolute obstacle to action nor a theoretical bar to political praxis. (1994, p. 31)

Such interventionism is reflected in Elam's formulation of the notion of 'groundless solidarity', a form of solidarity 'which is not based on identity' but relies rather upon 'a coalition built around suspicion of identity as the essential grounding for meaningful political action' (1994, p. 69). She suggests, in short, that 'the gains of feminism have produced a situation in which the meta-narrative of the affirmation of female identity has foundered precisely because its realization can only be imperialist'. Consequently, she continues, feminism and deconstruction work similarly towards challenging such essentialism: such an endeavour entails 'endless work, an abyssal politics...' (1994, p. 120). This example shows how the problematisation of foundational claims about sex and gender has lead not to the death of feminism but rather to a form of feminism committed to interrogating its own past and present exclusions and violences such that it can better resist (although by no means entirely avoid) reperforming conventional forms of onto-political ordering in its theoretical and concrete interventions.

Concurrently, in the context of queer activism and queer theory, Joshua Gamson explores the controversies which ensued following the announcement made in San Francisco that the 1993 pride celebrations were to be named the 'Year of the Queer'. For many, the signifier 'queer', Gamson shows, 'shakes the ground on which gay and lesbian politics has been built[,]... haphazardly attempting to build a politics from the rubble of deconstructed collective categories' (1995, p. 390). From this, Gamson notes, a series of dilemmas emerge regarding 'for whom, when, and how are stable collective identities necessary for social action and social change?... When and how might deconstructive strategies take aim at institutional forms [of oppression]'. What occurred in the shift towards embracing the signifier 'queer', he suggests, was a process of de-essentialisation, the very fracturing nature of which was politically salutary:

OCCUPYING SUBJECTIVITY

> Queer movements pose the challenge of a form of organizing in which, far from inhibiting accomplishments, the *destabilization of collective identity is itself a goal and accomplishment of collective action*. When this dynamic is taken into account, new questions arise. (Gamson, 1995, p. 403, emphasis in original)

As Gamson shows, the integration of transgender and bisexual issues into the sphere of debate represents a concrete effect of such a process of de-essentialisation. Thus, in challenging the contours and parameters of subject of resistance, the queer movement displays an imperative similar to the generative effects of a deconstructive mode of resistance.

To turn, finally, to post-colonial politics, Michael Syrotinski has explored what he frames as the 'uneasy encounter between deconstruction and the postcolonial' (2007, p. 2). He argues that for some, such as Robert Young, 'Derrida's work has always, even if somewhat indirectly, challenged the ethico-political tensions at the heart of colonialist ideology' (2007, p. 11). For Alberto Moreiras, the two traditions, Syrotinski notes, share the view that 'in order to wrest the possibility of a political affirmation from its continual foreclosure, we require a double articulation, akin to Spivak's "strategic essentialism" and Derrida's "double inscription"' (2007, p. 36). For others, however, he continues, Derrida 'is ultimately a representative of the Western philosophical tradition he is deconstructing, and... deconstruction is therefore at best a-political and a-historical, and at worst complicitous with a certain theoretical imperialism' (2007, p. 12). This raises the question of the Eurocentric and colonising dimensions of deconstructive thought itself. In particular, as Mustapha Pasha, amongst others, has shown, there is a danger in many prevailing critical-theoretical traditions that the insistence of putting into relief all forms of individual and collective identity in a similar manner assumes a general condition of post-foundational subjectivity and its consequences, a move which effaces other onto-political configurations (2011; 2013). As a form of engagement based on problematising its own as well as others' interventions, deconstruction can and must respond to its own violences, exclusions, and reinscriptions of hierarchy, and view such critique as a matter of urgency. In insisting on second- and third-order critiques, deconstruction impels its agent to pursue forms of auto-critique which problematise such potential colonialisms to the fullest extent possible, which is to say interminably, and without final resolution.

To restate, I am emphatically not suggesting that the radical political changes associated with third-wave feminism, queer movements, or post-colonial politics can or should be subsumed within, or be conceived of as derivative of or synonymous with, Derrida's thought or deconstruction as a philosophical tradition. Rather, the claim made is that the sites of political intervention mentioned here share with deconstruction, as I have framed it in this paper, a commitment to attempting to resist the hierarchies and exclusions associated with of prevailing forms of ordering by disrupting apparently stable categories and assumptions, in particular as regards problematising the subject or agent of resistance herself.

Conclusion

This paper has argued that there are a series of ways in which deconstruction contains the potential to resist resistance's cooptation back into interrelated processes of conceptual and global ordering. Such a form of resistance can be framed as occurring at three interconnected registers. First, as Eagleton's account of its pursuit of 'every smug concept' suggests, deconstruction's radicalism consists in its resistance to the possibility, or rather its highlighting of the violence of any claim to the possibility, of asserting defensibly that a particular issue or problem is not of concern or falls 'outside' the bounds of one's responsibility. Inasmuch as deconstruction highlights violence, its imperative is to identify and disrupt processes of totalisation *wherever* they occur. That one cannot attend to even a fraction of such processes adequately does not absolve one of this responsibility; this state of affairs comprises only a further layer of violence for which one cannot atone. Any claims to legitimate borders which demarcate the limits of responsibility are themselves subject to deconstructive reflection, and their necessarily forceful imposition demonstrated thereby. Such an intervention proceeds on the basis that responsibility is limitless, following the logic of both Emmanuel Levinas and Derrida. The all-too-common refusal of such limitless responsibility is thereby called into question, and all possible justifications exposed as indefensible. As such, the urgency of political intervention is reemphasised.

As this suggests, second, a deconstructive engagement is radically, if paradoxically, politicising. When the possibility of being finally 'correct' or 'just' is removed in the context of the subject's political deliberations, that is, when it is acknowledged that one's political interventions are inexorably violent, that one can only choose between violence and violence, the subject is obliged to consider the very difficult question of what s/he would intervene for or against, whether in concrete political practice or more conceptually, *in spite of* its ultimate indefensibility. Far from resulting in immobilisation or fatalistic resignation, this encounter with the indefensible can serve to allow the subject to encounter the violence of his/her position and commit to it nevertheless. That no position can be ultimately unproblematically correct does not mean that 'anything goes' or that 'nothing matters'; rather, this aporetic condition means that the course of action one chooses (because one always chooses, even, and especially, if one attempts to evade the taking of a position) must be argued for, defended, and reflected upon constantly in light of new ideas and encounters. Furthermore, this condition entails that the responsibility for the subject's position rests with her alone, rather than being legitimated in advance by some external principle. This has a denaturalising and politicising effect on positions taken, making possible a radical shaking up of notions once assumed to be essential or universal. It is to this that Derrida points when he notes that deconstruction 'is too political for some people, can seem paralyzing to those who only recognize politics with the help of pre-war slogans' (cited in Elam, 1994, p. 90).

Consequently, the radical potential of deconstruction consists, third, in the extent to which it intervenes at the level of conscious and unconscious processes of subject-production and reproduction. The question of the subject of resistance is explored by Eagleton, who suggests that deconstruction ultimately precludes the possibility of a functional and effective revolutionary subjectivity: it preserves 'some of the dominant themes of traditional bourgeois liberalism by a desperate, last-ditch strategy: by sacrificing the subject itself, at least in any of its customary modes'. The subject is consequently rendered 'impotent as any kind of agent at all, least of all a revolutionary one' (1981, p. 138). In contrast to this reading, Derrida suggests that 'a deconstructionist approach to the boundaries that institute human subjectivity... [can] lead to reinterpretation of the whole apparatus of boundaries within which a history and culture have been able to confine their criteriology' (1992, p. 19); as such, it is precisely the 'customary modes' of subjecthood identified by Eagleton that Derrida seeks to problematise.

At the heart of Derrida's intervention is the suggestion that prevailing Western modes of subjectification themselves are not innocent as regards contemporary concrete ethico-political problems, and that resistances to onto-political totalisations can emanate from challenging such processes at the level of one's subjecthood. The question that arises here is whether such a challenge to conventional forms of subjectivity amounts to a 'sacrifice', as Eagleton argues, or rather a politically salient attempt to reflect upon and intervene in the process of subjectification and identity-production and reproduction, as Derrida suggests. For Eagleton, insofar as the subject itself become implicated in and destabilised as a consequence of deconstruction, the price one pays 'is the highest of all: death' (1981, p. 136). He explains:

> Deconstruction is the death drive at the level of theory: in dismembering a text, it turns its violence masochistically upon itself and goes down with it, locked with its object in a lethal complicity that permits it the final inviolability of pure negation. The deconstructionist nothing lieth because he nothing affirmeth. (1981, p. 136–7)

Yet, he continues, such death is not final because metaphysics will live on; similarly deconstruction,

> as a 'living' death, will regroup its forces to assault anew. Each agonist is ever-slain and ever-resurrected; the compulsion to repeat, to refight a battle in which antagonist can never be destroyed because he is always everywhere and nowhere, to struggle towards a (self)-killing that will never quite come, is the dynamic of deconstruction... [D]econstruction is kept alive by what contaminates it, and can therefore reap the pleasures of a possible self-dissolution which, as one form of invulnerability, is mirrored by another, the fact that it can never die because the enemy is within and unkillable. (1981, p. 137)

In short, in this reading deconstruction is self-defeating; it comprises a form of intervention which renders it, and its subject, highly vulnerable to its own violent gestures whilst ensuring it, and its subject, live on to continue this masochistic process *ad infinitum*. Key here is the notion that a certain pleasure is derived from such self-annihilation; Eagleton concludes that 'the moment in which all of this occurs is of course the moment of *jouissance* or *petite mort*' (1981, p. 137).

The crucial question thus emerges of whether such a radical 'emptying out' effects anything politically salient, or whether it simply results in catatonic self-torturing/pleasuring at the precipice of a self-styled abyss. In contrast to Eagleton's reading, in the spirit of a more Derridean (and, on a different day, Nietzschean) tone, I would suggest that such a death only follows if the subject is construed in a particular Cartesian manner. To the degree that it insists upon second- and third-order critiques—of alternative narratives proffered and of the author of such re-writings herself—in addition to initial challenges to processes of conceptual and political ordering, deconstruction aims to 'put consciousness into question in its assured certainty of itself' (Derrida, 1982, p. 17), and in so doing, following gestures made by, amongst others, Nietzsche, Freud, Heidegger and Lacan, to begin to think the possibility of post-foundational forms of subjectivity. Eagleton objects to this on the basis that Derrida's thought

> ignores the extent to which a certain provisional stability of identity is essential not only for psychical well-being but for revolutionary political agency. It contains no adequate theory of such agency, since the subject would now seem no more than the decentered effect of the semiotic process; and its valuable attention to the split, precarious, pluralistic nature of all identity slides at worst into an irresponsible hymning of the virtues of schizophrenia. Political revolution becomes, in effect, equivalent to carnivalesque delirium... (1991, p. 197–8)

In this reading, such self-referentiality and fracturing precisely serves the interests of forces of global ordering insofar as a subject possessing particular, if provisional, certitudes about itself and socio-political orientation is necessary for radical political intervention and resistance. I would suggest, in contrast, that to the extent that the micro-workings of ordering occur simultaneously at the level of the material and within the subject, learning to explore the ways in which one is formed and reformed in light of processes of global and inter-personal ordering can comprise a crucial site of political resistance. This is, of course, not to suggest that one can finally identify and thereby renounce such processes, but rather that within the confines of these one can attempt to unpick parts of oneself such that elements of such micro-gestures of ordering and subject-(re)production become at least partially identifiable and interpretable. This reflects closely, for instance, ongoing feminist and post-colonial calls for the interrogation of patriarchal and colonial logics at work at the level of thought, consciousness, and language, the invisible micro-violences which undergird concrete political violences. For Hoy, such an intervention amounts to 'proposing a different moral psychology' (2004, p.180). Such a process entails that the subject take itself as well as its political locale as the object to be resisted; attempting to elucidate the ways which one is always constructed as part of, and therefore complicit in, that which one seeks to resist can be, somewhat paradoxically, a gesture of both defiance and agency.

Part of the radicalism of such a deconstructive mode of engagement is its defiance of the licence so central to prevailing forms of subjecthood cultivated with contemporary Western societies of the right to 'look away', to read lives, or tacitly accept scripting of lives, as being of differing value, of tolerating and sanctioning hierarchies of grievability and mournability (Butler, 2004). In a cultural context which accepts and encourages ignorance of and indifference to one's embeddedness in relations of violence, deconstruction can enact a form of resistance by insisting on looking, thinking, and feeling in sites of acute discomfort from which it would be easier to turn away. In this sense, deconstruction takes seriously Nietzsche's call for political subjects who are 'inquisitive to a fault, investigators to the point of cruelty, with unhesitating fingers for the intangible, with teeth and stomachs for the most indigestible' (1997, p. 32), subjects endeavouring to resist the violences of onto-political consolidation in the spheres of the material, the philosophical, and the recesses of their own subjecthood.

Notes

1   Concrete examples of this are too numerous to mention any but a few: one would be the prevalence of highly problematic gender politics as seen in many activist sites for instance, in the recent scandals surrounding the occurrence and handling of sexual assault and rapes within the Socialist Workers Party in the UK; another, the transphobia and colonialisms rife in many feminist organisations in Europe and the USA; a third, the widespread use of militarised imagery, clothing, and vocabularies utilised in many anti-militarist organisations. Specific examples of these will be discussed below. While I am not intending to draw a clear line between acts of resistance and acts which are re-entangled into propping up prevailing forms of global ordering—to do so would be neither possible nor desirable—what I am suggesting is that there is a widespread problem within radical sites, both within and beyond the academy, in that the reproduction of certain violences is ignored. This, in my view, amounts to at least a partial reinscription of the forms of resistance proffered in these spaces back into normalised forms exclusion and hierarchy characteristic of current of global ordering.

2   In invoking the notion of 'concrete' here, I am anticipating the criticism that such an auto-deconstructionist mode of resistance remains abstracted and removed from 'real world' or 'material' intervention. As will be demonstrated below, the realms of thought and action, or theory and practice, are by no means distinct, the one having a direct bearing on the other.

3   The question of 'affirmationism' in contemporary radical thought has been skilfully interrogated by Noys (2012). Further discussion of this important critique is, unfortunately, beyond the scope of this paper.

4   This is to be understood figuratively as a shorthand for indicating the (post)Enlightenment exposure of a certain abyss in which stable onto-political foundations and grounds were fundamentally undermined, rather than as a claim that religion has ceased to play a crucial role in contemporary political life. For discussion of this see the Forum entitled 'International Politics and the "Death of God"', in *Millennium: Journal of International Studies*, 42 (1).

5   The problems of the romanticism of this are important for what follows; such a framing is ripe for a deconstructive analysis itself.

OCCUPYING SUBJECTIVITY

6   There is much more to be said regarding the intersections and parallels between Derrida's deconstruction and Adorno's 'negative dialectics', in particular their different framings of the relationship between the subject and object of thought. This is, however, unfortunately beyond the scope of this paper.

References

Adorno, T. W. (2004). *Negative dialectics*. London: Routledge.

Arfi, B. (2012). *Re-thinking international relations theory via deconstruction*. London: Routledge.

Bleiker, R. (2000). *Popular dissent, human agency and global politics*. Cambridge: Cambridge University Press.

Bowman, P. (2010). Deconstruction is a martial art. In S. Houppermans, R. Sneller, P. van Zilfhout, (Eds.), Enduring resistance: Cultural theory after Derrida/La résistance persevere: la théorie de la culture (d')après Derrida (pp. 37–56). Amsterdam: Rodopi.

Bulley, D. (2007). Ethical assassination? Negotiating the (Ir)responsible decision. In M., Fagan, L., Glorieux, I. Hašimbegović & M. Suetsugu (Eds.), *Derrida: Negotiating the legacy* (pp. 128–142). Edinburgh: Edinburgh University Press.

Bulley, D. (2009). *Ethics as foreign policy: Britain, the EU and the other*. Abingdon: Routledge.

Butler, J. (2004). *Precarious life: The powers of mourning and violence*. London: Verso.

Campbell, D. (1998a). *National deconstruction: Violence, identity and justice in Bosnia*. Minneapolis: University of Minnesota Press.

Campbell, D. (1998b). *Writing security: United States foreign policy and the politics of identity*. Minneapolis: University of Minnesota Press.

Caputo, J. D. (Ed.). (2006). *Deconstruction in a nutshell: A conversation with Jacques Derrida*. New York, NY: Fordham.

Coleman, L. M. & Tucker, K. (2011). Between discipline and dissent: Situated resistance and global order. *Globalizations*, 8, 397–410. dio:10.1080/14747731.2011.585823

Day, R. J. F. (2004). From hegemony to affinity: The political logic of the newest social movements. *Cultural Studies*, 18, 716–748. doi:10.1080/0950238042000260360

Derrida, J. (1982). *Margins of philosophy*. Brighton: Harvester.

Derrida, J. (1992). Force of law: The 'Mystical Foundation of Authority'. In D. Cornell, M. Rosenfeld, & D. G. Carlson (Eds.), *Deconstruction and the possibility of justice* (pp. 3–67). New York: Routledge.

Derrida, J. (1998). *Resistances of psychoanalysis*. Stanford: Stanford University Press.

Derrida, J. (2006). The Villanova roundtable: A conversation with Jacques Derrida. In J. D. Caputo (Ed.), *Deconstruction in a nutshell: A conversation with Jacques Derrida* (pp. 1–27). New York: Fordham.

Dillon, M. (1996). *Politics of security: Towards a political philosophy of continental thought*. London: Routledge.

Dillon, M. (2007). Force of transformation. In M. Fagan, L. Glorieux, I. Hašimbegović, & M. Suetsugu (Eds.), *Derrida: Negotiating the legacy* (pp. 80–93). Edinburgh: Edinburgh University Press.

Dillon, M. (2010). Violences of the messianic. In A. Bradley & P. Fletcher (Eds.), *The politics to come: Power, modernity and the messianic* (pp. 191–207). London: Continuum.

Dillon, M. (2013). *Deconstructing international politics*. Abingdon: Routledge.

Docherty, P. (Ed.). (1993). *Postmodernism: A reader*. New York: Harvester Wheatsheaf.

Eagleton, T. (1981). *Walter Benjamin or towards a revolutionary criticism*. London: Verso.

Eagleton, T. (1991). *Ideology: An introduction*. London: Verso.

Eagleton, T. (1996). *Literary theory: An introduction*. New York: University of Minnesota Press.

Edkins, J. (1999). *Poststucturalism and international relations: Bringing the political back in*. Boulder: Lynne Rienner.

Edkins, J. (2007). What it is to be many: Subjecthood, responsibility and sacrifice in Derrida and Nancy. In M. Fagan, L. Glorieux, I. Hašimbegović & M. Suetsugu (Eds.), *Derrida: Negotiating the legacy* (pp. 172–192). Edinburgh: Edinburgh University Press.

Edkins, J., & Pin-Fat, V. (2004). Introduction: Life, power, resistance. In J. Edkins, V. Pin-Fat, & M. J. Shapiro (Eds.), *Sovereign lives: Power in global politics* (pp. 1–22). New York: Routledge.

Elam, D. (1994). *Feminism and deconstruction: Ms. En Abyme*. London: Routledge.

Eschle, C., & Maiguashca, B. (2007). Rethinking globalised resistance: Feminist activism and critical theorising in international relations. *British Journal of International Relations*, 9, 284–301. doi:10.1111/j.1467–856x.2007.00284.x

Fagan, M. (2013). *Ethics and politics after poststructuralism: Levinas, Derrida and Nancy*. Edinburgh: Edinburgh University Press.

Fagan, M., Glorieux, L., Hašimbegović, I., & Suetsugu, M. (Eds.). (2007). *Derrida: Negotiating the legacy*. Edinburgh: Edinburgh University Press.

Gamson, J. (1995). Must identity movements self-destruct? A queer dilemma. *Social Problems, 42*(3), 390–407.

Hirst, A. (2013a). *Leo Strauss and the invasion of Iraq: Encountering the Abyss*. Abingdon: Routledge.

Hirst, A. (2013b). Violence, self-authorship and the 'Death of God': The 'Traps' of the messianic and the tragic. *Millennium: Journal of International Studies, 42*, 135–154.

Houseman, T. (2013). Auschwitz as Eschaton: Adorno's negative rewriting of the messianic in critical theory. *Millennium: Journal of International Studies, 42*. doi:10.1177/0305829813492579

Hoy, D. C. (2004). *Critical resistance: From poststructuralism to post-critique*. Cambridge, MA: MIT Press.

Hurst, A. (2008). *Derrida Vis-à-vis Lacan: Interweaving deconstruction and psychoanalysis*. New York, NY: Fordham University Press.

Marchart, O. (2007). *Post-foundational political thought: Political difference in Nancy, Lefort, Badiou and Laclau*. Edinburgh: Edinburgh University Press.

McQuillian, M. (2008). *Textual activism: Deconstruction and the global political*. Unpublished manuscript.

Mittleman, J. H., & Chin, C. B. N. (2005). Conceptualising resistance to globalization. In L. Amoore (Ed.), *The global resistance reader* (pp. 17–27). London: Routledge.

Nietzsche, F. (1997). *Beyond good and evil: Prelude to a philosophy of the future*. Mineola: Dover.

Noys, B. (2012). *The persistence of the negative: A critique of contemporary continental theory*. Edinburgh: Edinburgh University Press.

O'Callaghan, R. (2012). Secular theology and noble sacrifice: The ethics of Michael Walzer's just war theory. *Review of International Studies, 39*, 361–383. doi:10.1017/ S0260210512000125

Pasha, M. (2011). Western Nihilism and dialogue: Prelude to an uncanny encounter in international relations. *Millennium: Journal of International Studies, 39*, 683–699.

Pasha, M. (2013). Nihilism and the otherness of Islam. *Millennium: Journal of International Studies, 42*. doi:10.1177/ 0305829813498806

Patton, P. (2007). Derrida, politics and democracy to come. *Philosophy Compass, 2/6*, 766–780. doi:10.1111/j.1747-9991.2007.00098.x

Pinkerton, P. (2012). Resisting memory: The politics of memorialisation in post-conflict Northern Ireland. *The British Journal of Politics and International Relations, 14*, 131–152. doi:10.1111/j.1467-856X.2011.00458.x

Rorty, R. (1996). Remarks on deconstruction and pragmatism. In C. Mouffe (Ed.), *Deconstruction and pragmatism* (pp. 13–18). London: Routledge.

Rossdale, C. (2010). Anarchy is what Anarchist make of it: Reclaming the concept of agency in IR and security studies. *Millennium: Journal of International Studies, 39*, 483–501. doi:10.1177/0305829810384006

Syrotinski, M. (2007). *Deconstruction and the postcolonial: At the limits of theory*. Liverpool: Liverpool University Press.

Vaughan-Williams, N. (2007). Beyond a cosmopolitan ideal: the politics of singularity. *International Politics, 44*, 107–124.

Zehfuss, M. (2002). *Constructivism in international relations: The politics of reality*. Cambridge: Cambridge University Press.

Zehfuss, M. (2007). Derrida's memory, war and the politics of ethics. In M. Fagan, L. Glorieux, I. Hašimbegović, & M. Suetsugu (Eds.), *Derrida: negotiating the legacy* (pp. 97–111). Edinburgh: Edinburgh University Press.

Zehfuss, M. (2009). Jacques Derrida. In J. Edkins & N. Vaughan-Williams (Eds.), *Critical theorists and international relations* (pp. 137–149). Abingdon: Routledge.

Paradoxical Peace: A Scholar-activist's Auto-ethnography on Religious Pacifism and Anti-capitalism

RUTH HALAJ REITAN

Motion Pictures, M.F.A., University of Miami's School of Communication, Coral Gables, FL, USA

ABSTRACT   *How can one subscribe to forms of ethico-religious pacifism and revolutionary communism or anarchism simultaneously, let alone conceive of their adherents as comprising the same transnational social movement? The author explores this conundrum via a playful probing of her own paradoxes related to violence and peace, dualism and non-dualistic thinking, and activist engagement along with more contemplative and quiet reflection. It experiments with expressive auto-ethnography in order to convey what living in and through these paradoxes feels like, and to access and convey other kinds of insights, (self) knowledge, and wisdom, unavailable or inadmissible by more orthodox forms of social science inquiry and writing. It embraces the postmodern relationship among authors, audiences, and texts and valorizes storytelling as deeply pedagogical, constitutive, meaningful, and meaning-making phenomena. The essay weaves together newspaper headlines, apocryphal diary entries, and dream poems into a methodological bricolage drawing from postmodern, poststructural and postcolonial scholars Deleuze and Guattari, Michael Shapiro, Anna Agathangelou, and Ruth Behar among others.*

The starting-point of critical elaboration is the consciousness of what one really is, and is 'knowing thyself' as a product of the historical process to date, which has deposited in you an infinity of traces, without leaving an inventory. Therefore it is imperative at the outset to compile such an inventory.

Antonio Gramsci, trans. by Edward Said (1979, p. 25)

Here we have made use of everything [that] came within range, what was closest as well as farthest away.... To reach, not the point where one no longer says I, but the point where it is no longer of any importance whether one says I. We are no longer ourselves. Each will know his own. We have been aided, inspired, multiplied.

Gilles Deleuze and Félix Guattari (1987, p. 3)

Preface

'Be the change you seek in the world', advised Gandhi. 'No war but the class war', admonished Marx. Both have inspired opposition to war, militarism, and imperialism across the world over the last century, including my own itinerant involvement. Yet their philosophies seem incongruent, even antagonistic: in a word, *paradoxical*.

How can one subscribe to forms of ethico-religious pacifism *and* revolutionary communism simultaneously, let alone conceive of their adherents as comprising the same transnational social movement? The Jungian psychologist Carol Pearson (1991, p. 49) offers a clue: 'The essence of the Self is paradox; ... [the] journey is a spiral, not linear.' Similarly, Deleuze and Guattari (1987, p. 3) in their introduction to the notion of the rhizome reflected, 'The two of us wrote *Anti-Oedipus* together. Since each of us was several, there was already quite a crowd.' If this holds true for individuals, so much more for social collectivities: there is no coherent, let alone static, collective actor called the Peace Movement. Further, any (hi)story of such is not a teleological progression, but a spiraling dance among innumerable paradoxes. As scholar-activists, we are fraught with our own contradictions and caught up in the larger whirl of movement in which we act and thus help make. And in the process, we forge some semblance of self and society, ethics, and strategy. These ensembles are tendentious and tenuous, in that the individual, social, ethical, and strategic that we are creating (or coming into being; becoming) are both anti-essentialist and anti-hegemonic.

In this essay I experiment with a particular kind of method—expressive auto-ethnography[1]— for three reasons: it provides a way of excavating and compiling this historical self-inventory that both Gramsci in *Prison Notebooks* and Said in *Orientalism* deemed necessary before embarking on critical and reflective scholarship. It further is a method that helps convey what living in and through paradox *feels like*. And it allows me to access and express other kinds of insights, (self) knowledge, and maybe even wisdom, derived from reflecting on paradox. All of these are largely unavailable or inadmissible via more orthodox forms of social science inquiry and writing.

Here, I will simply say what this piece is not (and will refer readers desiring a methodological elaboration along with a 'guide' to how to read this piece to endnote 6): it is not an eponymous history of the anti-war and anti-nuclear movements.[2] Nor is it a chronicle of the often heroic actors and practices of principled or strategic nonviolence.[3] It is not a detailed account of radical left Christianity.[4] Neither is it a study of the complex relationship between Marxian anti-imperialism and pacifism.[5]

It is something other.[6]

***

Circa 1980: The newspapers read:

AFGHANISTAN: Soviet troops invade, causing the Non-Aligned Movement to fracture and the US Senate to halt ratification of the second Strategic Arms Limitations Treaty (SALT II).

OCCUPYING SUBJECTIVITY

IRAN: Supporters of the Ayatollah Khomeini overthrow Shah Mohammad Reza Pahlavi; Militants seize 66 hostages at the American embassy.

IRAQ: Ongoing border disputes and heightened fears of a Shia insurrection fomented by Iran prompt Iraq's Saddam Hussein to invade his neighbor, with covert support from the US.

WASHINGTON, DC: Secret negotiations by President Jimmy Carter culminate in the Camp David Accords signed between Israel's Menachem Begin and Egypt's Anwar Sadat. Carter and his friend Doug Coe, head of The Family and the National Prayer Breakfast, launch a worldwide call to prayer with Sadat and Begin (Sharlet, 2009, p. 24); the latter two are awarded the Nobel Peace Prize.

The Iranian revolution sparks the decade's second petroleum crisis. Carter goes on national TV to put on a sweater and tell Americans to turn down their thermostats; he's trounced by Ronald Reagan in the polls.

The US House of Representatives' Permanent Select Committee on Intelligence launches an investigation into anti-war and anti-nuclear groups, domestic and foreign, for suspected links to the Soviet-funded World Peace Council.

CAIRO: Egypt is suspended from the Arab League; Sadat is assassinated.

NEW YORK CITY: Dorothy Day, the Christian pacifist, anarcho-communist, and founder of the Catholic Worker movement, dies at 83.

MIDDLETOWN, Penn.: Three Mile Island Nuclear Station's core melts down, causing widespread fear and protests including some 200,000 in New York, and over 100,000 in the West German capital Bonn; ignites the 'second wave' of anti-nuclear protests across the world.

WHITE EARTH, Minn.: American Indian Movement (AIM) activists found Anishinabe Akeeng to take back stolen and tax-forfeited reservation lands.

Dear Diary:

I don't read newspapers. I'm 10.
I read whatever teachers make me, plus the Bible.
Especially Revelation, but really we jump around in Sunday school
to try and cover the whole thing; and the *National Enquirer*,
which keeps me up-to-date on where the arisen Elvis is and what he's wearing.
I'm pretty sure I'm going to hell for a pile of sins, especially for not being mindful:
I just learned that if you pray 'on automatic' it don't count;
So I spend my nights sweaty, re-running lost years of 'Our Fathers'.
When my thoughts drift off, I start over.

We drive to Fargo for the Billy Graham Crusade.
(I've repressed most memories from that time, but recall):
Streaming-red heat like seedy lounge lighting in later Indian casinos and
sweat-shined faces beaming from stage. One of them's Johnny Cash
(I've no memory of this but my mother raises it in defense of those days).
And the 'come down to Jesus, sinner!' angst-inducing finale:
Do I damn myself in the falseness of going,

or take my damnation quiet and dignified by sincerely staying put?
A glance at my brother yields no help, as usual: Asleep.
(Maybe I faked another salvation—I was getting good at those—or maybe not. Cut to):
'troubled teens' movie after-show 'party' with Eric Estrada as Mexican gangbanger
who gets stabbed with a (clearly rubber) knife and
HALLELUJAH Jesus bends it!
Enrico's layin' down the leather and takin' up the cross!
I try to jive this humble cinematic start with
the disco-dancing casanova cop I covet weekly on CHiPs,
and conjure a faint hope that there's place for me yet in Hollywood/Heaven.

On the lonesome, star-filled, long drive home I'm awoken by flashlights, voices,
the car slowing down. A chain stretched across the road.
It's Minnesota-tense so as only dogs (and us) can hear it.
Few, maybe no, words spoken; we're allowed to move on.

My folks start talking about our house being *clouded*
so we couldn't sell and leave the reservation
if we wanted (I wanted).

The dream of the car-full of Indians bounding down the driveway
making us flee (fuite[7]) into the lake
(where I swim hidden through the dark weeds and water) starts around then.

***

Circa 1986:

GENEVA: The International Peace Bureau, the oldest anti-war federation founded in 1891, broadens to the left by merging with the International Confederation for Disarmament and Peace.

The Women's International League for Peace and Freedom (WILPF), the first international women's peace organization founded in 1915, launches a worldwide campaign supporting the Comprehensive Test Ban Treaty.

REYKJAVIK: Reagan and Mikhail Gorbachev meet for talks on intermediate missile reduction in Europe; they stall.

[WASHINGTON: The papers don't report that US Joint Chiefs of Staff General John W. Vessey, with his friend Doug Coe, invite Central American ambassadors to Prayer Breakfasts in order to arrange private talks among their generals, US Senators, and the Reagan administration (Sharlet, 2009, p. 25).]

LEBANON: News of the 'Iran contra scandal' breaks, alleging US government sales of weapons to Iran to free US hostages in Lebanon and fund 'contra' guerrillas based in Honduras attempting to depose Nicaragua's Sandinista government.

ISRAEL: The government implements an 'iron fist' campaign of military retaliation against Shi'ite guerrillas in southern Lebanon and civil disturbances in the West Bank and Gaza Strip and steps up land annexation for settlements; The First Intifada, involving massive nonviolent civil disobedience, is sparked in the Jabalian refugee camp and spreads through the Occupied Territories.

UK: The Campaign for Nuclear Disarmament (CND) membership surges to 100,000 in opposition to the US deploying Pershing missiles in Western Europe.
Prime Minister Margaret Thatcher defeats the striking coal miners.

CHERNOBYL: Nuclear power plant explodes, spewing radioactive fallout across Europe and causing thousands of cancer cases. Over 150,000 march in Rome, thousands of West Germans clash with police, and the Great Peace March for Global Nuclear Disarmament departs from Los Angeles to Washington, DC.

PARIS: UNESCO declares the International Year of Peace.

FARGO: Governor Sinner's brother Father Sinner—a veteran civil rights and anti-nuclear activist and Catholic priest—is again charged with freeing Central American war refugees from US internment camps and trying to smuggle them to Canada.

I still don't read newspapers.
I read *Seventeen*, *Rolling Stone*, sometimes the *Enquirer*
(Elvis sightings have died down considerably),
and what my teachers make me—and the Bible.

We're made to give a speech about our hero: I do Margaret Thatcher.
Mostly cuz she's the only tough famous woman I know of
and she's friends with the President.

Fired up from my speech, I write a letter to Reagan to alert him
to the injustice of what they call 'reverse discrimination' on my reservation.

I'm confirmed in the Lutheran church, wearing a string of tiny medal bars
for near-perfect Sunday School attendance (damn them chicken pox).

I get drunk on Thanksgiving. My funnest holiday ever.

Someone tells me Reagan's birthday is June 6th, 1906.
Shave his head and you'll find the mark of the beast.

At the twins' birthday party,
we sit around a circle on their trailer's bedroom floor
drinking beer and talking about Jesus. ZIP! up my spine-her spine-our spines:
shaking and crying, filling with the Holy Ghost
(it's impossible to recollect this feeling now).
Next morning we thunder into class
high on Christ, giddy witnesses to the Good News.
Nervous laughter and eye-rolls force our literal retort 'go to hell then.'
It wears off in about two days.

OCCUPYING SUBJECTIVITY

I'm nearly raped by an Indian boy in a car at a dance who I liked.
A miraculous appeal to reason saves my butt:
promised higher returns for delayed gratification
(Adam Smith's angel guards girls in lonely parking lots—who knew).
I hate him now and I'm sad because I can't be exactly like Jesus—not anymore:
Try me again, someone's gonna die and it might not be me.

A letter from the White House! . . . thanking me for my 'concern'.
A flash of anger, foolishness follows. The signature doesn't look real.

I teach Sunday school with Mom.
It keeps my Saturday night partying under control
and looks good on my college apps (and those kids are so darn cute!)

One of the girls I was born-again with gives a speech that her mom is her hero:
She refused to abort even when the doctor said her life was at risk.
I don't say so but that ain't heroic—it's reckless.

I don't think I'm Republican anymore.
***

A Docent's Dream

A child's hands (mine) before me, sun pours through a beveled-glass kitchen door at left. These
little hands a hundred years old—maybe many more.
Grandma (who was my grandma) is dead. We're preparing our home for the burial.

Mother (who is my mother)—an eternally busy bee—bakes, cleans, and clears away 'clutter'
of unadorned bottles from Grandmother's cupboards.
(no crystal-rock carved flasks these, yet objects of mystery and desire nathless,
echo-chambers of earth-caught prayers, locked in the heart of our reliquary; but nevermind):
'Out with the old and in with the new!' was and is still Mother's motto.

We are Christian, wealthy, well-respected. But Change hung its lead Crucifix
round the neck of our house.

The funeral cakes are Crusaders' crosses in deep rich brown and glistening. So
I as a child (perhaps only five) saw *cookie* and bit and tried and spat it out from bitterness:
'This Cross is not sweet but rancid!' tasting of church pews, sourdough, chicken bones. Blood.

Then Grandmother speaks (in part warning, part blessing):
'Don't let your mother throw out those bottles. We're Docents.
The flasks we tell people's stories into. Guard them, girl, from the gathering War.'
***

OCCUPYING SUBJECTIVITY

Circa 1992:

KUWAIT: The US leads a coalition of Saudi, UK, Egyptian and 30 other countries in Operation Desert Storm, an air and ground invasion that expels Iraqi troops.

USSR: Gorbachev promotes dramatic reforms. The Russian republic declares sovereignty. KGB and hardliners fail in their attempt to re-centralize control. Gorbachev resigns and the Supreme Soviet dissolves itself.

WASHINGTON: President George H. W. Bush (1991) declares victory in the Gulf War and heralds a 'new world order' of justice, protection of the weak, freedom, and respect for human rights. The UN will at last fulfill its historic mandate. For the US military, 'the hard work of freedom ... [and] enduring peace must be our mission ....'

I graduate summa cum laude and in the top five Business and Economics majors from a Lutheran
college in northwestern Minnesota. The major was a practical choice, aimed at landing a job.
An insurance company recruiter asks what my favorite classes are (Religion) and if I play golf
(nope). I don't get called back. I've become atheist, feminist, and socialist and of the opinion that
the only thing worth salvaging from the Bible is the social(ist) and pacifist doctrine of Christ—
whoever he was.

I volunteer at the Dorothy Day homeless shelter across the street from campus. The Catholic
Workers who run it join the Fellowship of Reconciliation (FOR) in their national 'No Blood for
Oil' campaign, and organize a local anti-war march: My first demo (if you don't count the 'pro
life' parade float I was thrust upon as a child around nine). Our small protest is heckled
(remarkable for the stoic Fargo-Moorhead) and we make the evening news. For 'alternative
Spring Break' I head to Coahoma, Mississippi, with Habitat for Humanity. On the bus down a
student introduces me to the Socialist Workers Party (SWP-US) paper *The Militant*. Some still
live in slave shacks in this town. At night, tired from work and full from supper, we watch TV,
quietly indignant, as coalition forces reign down bombs on Kuwait. Operation Desert Sabre
(sounds Biblical) is over before Spring Break is:
'We' 'won'.

I fall for the one Marxist in Fargo three weeks before I'm due to start a Master's in International
Relations at the University of Chicago. It's prestigious and I'm lucky to have gotten a half-
scholarship (I've turned down a full-ride at the University of Miami for these reasons),
but I still feel nervous and shackled by the debt I'll have to take on to go.
For my birthday he gives me Trotsky's *History of the Russian Revolution,*
and then leaves me for his ex.
I don't go.

Instead I travel to Cuba on a humanitarian caravan aimed at ending the US embargo, with the
Interreligious Foundation for Community Organization (IFCO)/Pastors for Peace. We're led by
Lucius Walker, a Baptist minister and seasoned civil rights activist, who was attacked by *contras*
in Nicaragua. Blaming Reagan, he created an organization to confront US imperialism in the
Americas via nonviolent direct action and fostering solidarity.

OCCUPYING SUBJECTIVITY

The multiple caravans stream across the continent visiting Peace Houses, Mennonite farms and church basements. We all converge in Laredo, Texas, and train for the border action. Our ragtag group is comprised of a couple hundred Christian and secular pacifists, communist anti-imperialists, and progressive youth.

The pacifists hail from the historic Peace Churches of Mennonites and Friends (Quakers) and a range of progressive Catholic orders, along with feminist peace activists like the radical-grandmotherly 'WILPFers' who track submarines on Lake Superior and the young San Francisco hippies with Global Exchange (This group's co-founder, Medea Benjamin, will go on to launch Code Pink in 2002, which is a prominent member of the main US anti-war umbrella United For Peace and Justice (UFPJ) and among the few US organizations active in the global anti-war assemblies and coordination meetings at the World Social Forums, involved in planning global days of action and campaigns.)

The communist anti-imperialists are a combustible mix of Worker's World and SWP comrades. Here I'm introduced to what these parties seem best at: purges. In a bewildering, mudslinging late night meeting, the SWP are nearly thrown off the caravan. (This drama makes sense with hindsight: While both are Trotskyist parties, Worker's World split off from the SWP in the late 1950s in defense of Maoism and the Soviet invasion of Hungary. Worker's World, along with IFCO/Pastors for Peace, are key members of ANSWER (Act Now to Stop War and End Racism)—the more radical umbrella group who first tenuously cooperated, but then conflicted and competed, with UFPJ to coordinate the post 9/11 US anti-war movement). An SWP member sells me a book of essays detailing Ernesto 'Che' Guevara's economic program, which is my introduction to this Cuban bureaucrat. I peruse the 16-page photo spread at the book's center and think, for an economist, this guy's pretty hot.

We successfully cross the Mexican border without visas to break the embargo, and wend our way to Tampico. At an anti-*yanqui* imperialist rally, we hear 'Zapatista!' cries. The mood is suddenly tense. Later that night I'm assigned to sleep with three nuns in an oval, king-sized bed in a pay-by-the-hour bordello with sticky floors and Spanish porn looping on television. I opt to spring for a room with my girlfriend. We're awoken hourly by bangs on the door from management to pay up, to which we shout, 'Pastores por la Paz!' so they leave us be for another hour.

We load the ships and fly to Cuba, where we're treated as heroes and celebrities to a very 'packaged' tour. It's the height of the Special Period, which means the nadir of Soviet patronage. The Party is taking no chances. The locals look pretty skinny. On our last evening in Havana, the *caravanistas* hanging around the hotel bar are herded onto a bus and whisked to the Palace of the Revolution for a midnight audience with Fidel. It begins giddy like an Elvis concert but drags on for a couple drowsy hours ... A more lasting impression is made in a quiet meeting arranged by Bay-area Baby Panthers with Assata Shakur, Black Panther fugitive turned Cuban Sociologist.

We return to the US to give report-backs in Minneapolis, San Francisco, and Miami at SWP bookstores. I join their new Young Socialists study group, but after a couple months pull back. Party forums and one-on-one conversations feel too much like the ecstatic evangelical encounters of my youth. I realize I'm deeply skeptical of Complete Programs and Confident Answers—religious *or* secular. Inspired by meeting Assata in Cuba, I decide to go to the University of Miami after all, assuming it'll be the ideal place to research the Cuban revolution's ties

OCCUPYING SUBJECTIVITY

to the US Black movement; It is a paradoxical and problematic vantage point I soon discover, but ultimately fruitful.[8]

***

One World: Possible?

I left Belém then returned to the real world and sleeping, dreamt a Forum that hadn't been.
I was searching for a meeting and walking, passed a long line of men laying down
prayer rugs and kneeling, bowing, chanting along a jagged patch of rocks facing the sea.
And to me it seemed the most natural thing to take my place beside them. Upon
empty mat at the far end I faced the wind, moist and cool, blowing off the grey-black sea.

And we were One: the men, Thee and me.

Then suddenly a loud hammering sound of workers coming down the line erecting barricades 'protecting' us from the elements; and thus severing us by plastic and wood from the sea and the wind and the howling of waves; and so I arose, ran and leapt the barricade telling myself, 'I will not worship here but if I flee across the barrier perhaps the others will rise up and tear it down.

And go searching again for the One pure relation.'

***

Circa 9/11/2001, and after:

WASHINGTON, DC: Following two years as an Americorps volunteer with Twin Cities Habitat for Humanity working as a community organizer, I marry a German Mennonite pacifist and co-volunteer. And I decide to pursue a Ph.D. in International Relations, and find an eclectically-good fit in the International Relations program at American University's School of International Service. I'm mentored by Gramscians, a Sufi mystic who reminds one of the Dalai Lama on a pinch of speed, a Palestinian-American mediator, a deep ecologist who's both Buddhist and Jewish, a feminist international lawyer and human rights activist, and the pioneer of 'exopolitics', or the study of extraterrestrial agents and structures on earth (He also leads yoga workshops, wherein I have the revelation that raising Kundalini shakra energy is the physiological equivalent to my youthful Christian 'born again' experience—the professor, who believes that President Bush is an ET reptile with scales beneath his skin, smiles at my insight like I'm the nuts one).

This program, coupled with additional courses at Eastern Mennonite University's Summer Peacebuilding Institute and a nascent interest in engaged Buddhism, helps me to discover and frame my core question of why suffering exists in the world. I begin to study the actors, social practices, and forms of power that exacerbate or lesson suffering at the interpersonal, community, national, and global levels.

Taking advantage of being in the capitol of the world's superpower—or the 'belly of the beast' as my old comrades would say—I interview key activists at progressive NGOs like the Institute for Policy Studies, 50 Years is Enough, American Friends Service Committee, Public Citizen and its Corp Watch, and the AFL-CIO. I also become involved in the main Washington, DC-based groups organizing demos and teach-ins against the World Bank and IMF, including the Mobilization for Global Justice and the Anti-Capitalist Convergence, along with an effort to launch a local social forum, modeled on the World Social Forum principles. I volunteer at the headquarters of the Green Party Presidential campaign to elect Ralph Nader and Winona LaDuke. LaDuke's from my reservation, which is how I'd normally say it; more accurately, my family occupies hers. After the election, the *Mahnomen Pioneer* publicizes the local voter tally. In our reservation township, the Green ticket got a single vote (my dad's).

My husband and I are staying in the guesthouse where I work part-time, waiting for an apartment to open up near the university. One morning I come down to breakfast—and to live images of the World Trade Center tower belching smoke from its belly. The other guests, mostly Europeans, are somber. A man from Ireland cautiously says that given America's foreign policy, it is no surprise that something like this has happened. No one contradicts him.

The second plane hits. And then one after the other the towers come down.

In that moment I feel horror for the people trapped and then crushed, and sadness for the ones who love them. I also feel what the Irishman said is true.

These two feelings can't be reconciled. Maybe it's the reservation in me, in a double sense. The gut-level insecurity bred from earliest times that this land is not our land, never mind the Woody Guthrie song we sang at choir and campfires. Americans were clumsy, girth-some occupiers, and ever-hungry drifters; interlopers, just passing through but taking their own sweet time doing it. I never wanted to be lumped in with them because it marked me as a target. I was schooled by death-stares from Indian boys on the bus and the hate-filled word 'honky'. It didn't hurt, exactly; it scared the shit out of me.

Meanwhile, this 'America the Beautiful/Home of the Brave' business they yammered on about felt meant for somewhere and somebody else, not for us: The blissful ignorance of far-away white suburbanites, or the willful blindness of the poor white farmers closer to 'home'.

I didn't buy it—How could I? Where was my purchase on that dream? The America I saw from the Reservation was one relentless project of attack, attrition, erasure; repeat. Of fucking and forgetting. Maybe others had the luxury or balls to forget, but I wanted to stop the fucking, to reverse it, heal it, somehow. I wanted things and people and the ground beneath to become unbroken. And I and everyone around me knew that was impossible. To be born on a reservation is to be born into confusion. We would mourn and rage against ghosts and play at battles that had already been lost. We would hurt each other but mostly ourselves. We would die together slowly and for awhile. And then those of us who could, moved on. Sort of.

Thus were we deprived of patriotism by our birthright: by our geography, intelligence, and conscience. Maybe that's why I married a German (and why Germans are so enamored by American Indians)—because they're the only people I know who've been forced to confront and carry their collective sins into the present. They are my teachers.

Back to DC: In that one fall day, Washington—spatially and discursively—is transformed, occupied, locked down and taken over by a hostile force: Not a terrorist group or foreign army, but George W. Bush's government and the alienating, calculated, authoritarian and bellicose apparatus of its Reaction. The progressive movement would become part of the massive collateral damage. Far from the post-Seattle euphoric slogan that 'we are winning', I get that old familiar feeling that suddenly we have lost—or that the other side is ratcheting up the ante but has yet to reveal the price.

The evening dinner my husband was to cook for Donald Rumsfeld, Colin Powell, and two hundred of their closest military contractor friends at a ritzy hotel four blocks from the White House is called off; but just as they and other Capitol Hill bureaucrats are fleeing the danger zone (or hiding in undisclosed locales), he and other service workers are ordered to come down and clock in as usual. Stranded guests must be fed.

Bomb threats cancel classes the week after. We receive a form letter from our landlord (or some Agency) urging us to report any 'suspicious' (read: young Arab male) renters who seem keen on living in basement units. WTF?

A few hardcore comrades will rise and even thrill to this game change, a quality I much admire but seem to lack. As a writer (which is what one *becomes,* like it or not, while dissertating) and a sensitive lass, I feel that I can't write or think freely in this psychological and physical terrain. It is like the city, and soon the whole country, has caught a nasty cold that will turn to a raging, hallucinogenic fever and will last for a very long time. I've experienced these bouts before in the Pentecostal religious fervor that sweeps the nation once a generation and explains the *habitus* of my youth.

I've got to get the hell out of here.

There's one graduate exchange program across the sea available to me, in an autonomous, German-speaking northern province of Italy that few Americans have heard of. We go there. Although Italian Prime Minister Silvio Berlusconi is a rare enthusiast of Bush's War on Terror, the country's majority—plus the Vatican—is strongly opposed.

Millions would take to the streets to demonstrate their dissent over the coming years. This magnificent sight I first witness on the closing day of the first European Social Forum in Florence, when over 700,000 flowed through the city streets: a sea of rainbow peace flags, red communist party and trade union banners interspersed with black, symbolizing the resurgent anarchism among European youth as well as the cross-fertilization and detente, of sorts, among pacifism, communism, and anarchism (though perhaps we have not yet been tested).

The day US soldiers begin bombing Iraqis, I sit in my little flat in Merano crying while *MTV Italia*, without comment or commercial break, has drawn the rainbow peace flag across its station logo and loops anti-war videos for hours.

In the years that follow, I engage as a researcher and activist in several more European and World Social Forums. I join a scholar-activist collective, the Network Institute for Global Democratization, and through it organize workshops at the WSF and attend International Council meetings. I follow the main coordinating meetings against the wars—the Global Anti-War Assemblies—and join activist listservs and attend workshops and seminars of the campaigns that grow out of it, namely the World Tribunal on Iraq, the International Network for the Abolition of Foreign Military Bases, the Israeli Boycott and Divestment Campaign, and the reinvigorated anti-nuclear movement in the wake of the Fukushima disaster.

Our efforts did not prevent nor end these wars. Yet our vocal, creative, and coordinated dissent visibly signaled and probably bolstered the broader opposition to the Bush-led wars in almost every nation on the planet. This widespread disapproval, both by an active minority and more quiescent majority, glaringly illustrated the so-called 'democratic deficit', especially in those countries that participated in the US's Coalition of the Willing.

I believe that *this* is an underappreciated legacy of September 11, 2001, the dynamics of which are yet to fully play out: the gaping chasm between the people's desires and demands for peace and the brazen way in which elected officials flouted our voices, votes, and protests exposed for a new generation the thin(ning) democratic veneer masking autocratic, technocratic, corrupt, and cartel-like, state-capital regimes.

More and more people now know: An elite class of cross-trained politicians, corporate heads, lawyers, bankers, and high-stakes gamblers (i.e. investors) have colluded to create an increasingly global legal system to suit their avaricious, hubristic, and destructive desires, and work to change or simply evade those few laws or norms that counter these base drives. In complicated ways, this paradox erupted in the 2011 Arab Spring and continues to incite protest across Europe, from general strikes called by trade unions and pitched street battles between precarious youth and 'robo-cops' to the *indignado* encampments in Spain and the Occupy movement across the US.

The Reservation is everywhere.

***

Knight of Regret

I dreamt I was a crusading knight 'tween the worlds. My death scroll was in hand, unfurled.
I read my name, place, date of birth, and band of Christian soldiers
bound for the Holy Land to whom I'd pledged hand, heart, life's work.

A most profound sense of sadness crept over me then
like a heavy stone of remorse hurled across ages, seas and tongues. And
I sighed aloud to angels—or demons—who might be beside and tried to get word
to my graveside companions:

Alas! A life wasted! In zeal did I fight to restore Jerusalem but was betrayed by my passions.
'Twas all for naught this blood-soaked path turn back oh friends turn back!

Then the shadows round I, the dead soldier, darkened.
The room in which I, the awakening, lightened.
The scroll in my hand disintegrating to dust
of memory—and mourning—in morning.

But remaining that day, and all the days since,
was the one pure thought, the heart-felt truth, the certain word: Regret.

***

Circa 2011: The newspapers read:

JAPAN: Following an earthquake and tsunami, the Fukushima Dai'ichi nuclear plant melts down, contaminating air, earth, sea, and mothers' milk. Authorities estimate it will take some forty years to decommission the plant. In response, German Chancellor Angela Merkel reverses her party's position and pledges to phase out all nuclear power in the coming decade.

AFGHANISTAN: The US continues to maintain around 90,000 troops, along with 30,000 more NATO allied soldiers, in 400 bases in its decade-long war against the Taliban and other insurgents. President Obama steps up the use of unmanned drone strikes here and in neighboring Pakistan, causing numerous civilian deaths and growing protests by civilians and local officials.

IRAN: The International Atomic Energy Agency expresses deep concern over the military dimensions of Iran's nuclear program. The US and Israel say 'no options are off the table' including air strikes. The EU, led by the UK, threaten harsher economic sanctions. Militants storm the British embassy in Tehran.

CAIRO: Following the popular revolution in Tunisia, the 'Arab Spring' protests sweep Egypt, toppling longtime ruler Hosni Mubarak with the army's acquiescence; but the interim military 'caretaker' government refuses to cede real authority or historic privileges, sparking a return of protests and increasingly bloody confrontations, threatening a civil war along the lines of Libya and Syria.

OCCUPYING SUBJECTIVITY

IRAQ: US-backed forces violently disperse Iraq's 'Arab Spring' of some 200,000 protestors in Baghdad. The last American troops are withdrawn from the warfront, marked by a flag-lowering ceremony in Baghdad that Iraqi journalists are barred from attending due to security concerns. They leave behind over 100,000 dead civilians (a conservative estimate) and millions of internally- and externally-displaced, the most fortified embassy in the world, thousands of private security contractors, a weak Shia government closely aligned with Iran presiding over an impoverished and largely illiterate younger generation in a country divided along sectarian lines. Foreign oil companies sign contracts with the breakaway region of Kurdistan, which the central government denounce as a violation of the country's sovereignty.

PALESTINE: *Exists* within its pre-1967 borders, according to some 130 countries. President Mahmoud Abbas, backed by the Arab League and an international campaign for 'State no. 194', submits a formal proposal to the UN for statehood. The US threatens a Security Council veto and withdrawal of Palestinian aid and UN funding to punish what it and Israel alone call this 'unilateral' move.

Dozens of right-wing Israeli settlers wage an ongoing 'price tag' campaign in the Occupied West Bank, storming an Israel Defense Forces base, accosting soldiers and setting fires. Israel's Defense Minister Ehud Barack denounces this 'homegrown terror' and Prime Minister Benjamin Netanyahu says they will be tried in military court, a procedure previously only reserved for Palestinians.

Fights break out in Bethlehem's Church of the Nativity over Christmas. No arrests are made, the authorities said, because all involved are 'men of God.'

OSLO: Self-described Christian knight Anders Behring Breivik, intent on defending Europe from cultural Marxists and Muslims and restoring the crusades of the Middle Ages, detonates a car bomb in the government quarter, killing eight. Hours later he murders 69 youth attending the Labour party's summer camp on the island of Utoya. 200,000 flock to a flower march in Oslo to peacefully commemorate their deaths and defend tolerance and openness in their society.

The Nobel Peace Prize is awarded to three women of color: two Liberians, Ellen Johnson Sirleaf and Leymah Gbowee, and a young, nonviolent and pro-democracy activist from Yemen, Tawakkol Karman.

NEW YORK CITY: Inspired by the Arab Spring and youth protests across Spain and Greece, activists launch Occupy Wall Street in Zucotti Park as a direct action against growing income inequality, corporate and bankers' greed, and impunity and corruption in US politics. Encampments and marches quickly spread across the country and beyond . . . .

I struggle with how to write about peace at a time and from a place like this:
I begin this essay in early summer in an idyllic Alpine nook in Europe,
where earthquakes, radiation leaks, wars and their refugees reach me only via newspapers and internet. I feel optimistic about next year's tenure process (though shouldn't)
and feel settled at home (though I'm not).
I also feel a restlessness I cannot name.

Then the Norwegian massacre: I let this one graze the heart's surface, afraid to take it in. Too many names sound like cousins and friends (and *were*, though distant and forgotten). Some I may have encountered at a social forum or protest march—those activist youth who touched me with their idealism and conviction that ethical, transparent, and pro-social governance is a basic

37

OCCUPYING SUBJECTIVITY

human right. This must be how Iraqis and Afghanis feel when a guy blows himself up in a market
or a mosque. Maybe more Westerners realize that anyone is capable of this,
and can now feel greater compassion for distant suffering as a consequence?

I light candles for these young comrades
at one of the innumerable shrines to the Goddess in this Italian city
(In the Age of Pisces out of which we're passing, She was known as Virgin and sacrificial
Mother, Mary. In the Aquarian age, I wonder which woman and virtues will she incarnate and we
celebrate?)

How come it seems so easy for one to destroy and cause great and lasting pain,
yet so difficult for a collective to make a comparable positive impact?
This is the ultimate conundrum: the metaphor of fire, or the seemingly tragic imbalance between
constructive and destructive labor, or labors of love and those of hate.
It sometimes seems our efforts as public intellectuals, citizens, and activists mirror this equation.
The emotional fires of anger, rage, violence, and hatred are not powers we easily counter,
much less harness or channel. Alone and together, better we muster and foster the quieter and
harder metaphorical labor of digging trenches, erecting fire walls, dumping cool water, and
cultivating forms of life that are strongly-rooted, hearty, and resistant, or
mobile, wily and resilient enough to withstand, contain and put out humanity's fires.

Rage is not working for us, or the planet. Our true work is otherwise.

Autumn brings my return to Miami, discovery of the Blue Ocean sangha,
start of a new school year, and Occupy to our city and campus.
Suddenly my 'utopian' social movement course is generating
such interest that I'll offer it again spring semester and it fills up.

It's December when this essay's completed,
in my childhood bedroom at my parent's house
on the lake, now made of glass, where I learned to skate.
The reservation this time of year has a stillness that says Christmas.
Though it's cold we feel held by the season. Few tidings of the world beyond reach us.

I try to stop struggling with how to write about peace
in a time and from places like these,
and simply breathe and be mindful of my many blessings.
They will pass but others will come.

The new pastor of my parent's church is the old tribal chief.
His voice's tenor and a subtle choice of metaphor turn Christmas Eve sermon
to an invocation for Mother Earth and Father Sky.
The Norwegian farmers don't seem to notice–
or maybe they do, and that's why they called him?

For the first time, this stick-build's placement
on a lake in a grove beyond White Earth seems about right.

OCCUPYING SUBJECTIVITY

I kill an afternoon wandering the web
nomad(or smith)-like for stories of Dorothy Day, the anarcho-pacifist.
With a click of the mouse I join the movement to make her a saint.[9]

***

Politics v. Poetry

Politics
when faced with apocalypse
grows desperate, venomous, accommodationist, collaborationist, resigned, cynical, despondent,
nihilistic. We are rendered
Speechless. Struck dumb and down in the space that surpasses
all reason and what we feel in our bones, *ovarios, coños* and soul
to be right–and wrong, so wrong.
Poetry
when facing this same certainty of our annihilation
and of all of the species known and imagined who will go to their graves along with us
grows flowery to honor the beauty that's lost; and
howling to wolves and wild creatures we've scorned;
enraged as the waves and the clamoring hordes
left on beaches and deserts upon sands of sorrow;
impassioned for lovers we must *take now* for tomorrow who knows?
and for children we must *bear now* though we know–and can't bear–
that they shan't walk out the length of their days upon this fair land. And yet
Wise
for we sense that whatever may come, and by our very hands
the Word was made flesh and the word will remain long after the lips, lungs
tongues and teeth and the trees and the flowers and seas
have breathed their last word to the world of Man:
Goodbye.

Acknowledgements

I wish to thank Chris Rossdale, Michael J. Shapiro, Florentina Andreescu, Marc Becker, Tadzio Müller, Andreas Neufeld, Teivo Teivainen, Naeem Inayatullah, Barry Gills, John Gery, and Mary de Rachewiltz, without whose inspiration and/or encouragement, this piece could not have been written nor published.

Notes

1   For examples of more analytic or journalistic auto-ethnographic works by scholar-activists in the most recent cycle of transnational contention, see Neale (2003) and Thomas (2000).

2   As is found for example in the works of Wittner (1993, 1997, 2003).

3   As theorized by Gene Sharp (see e.g. Sharp, Paulson, Miller, and Merriman, 2005) or documented by Ackerman and Duvall (2001).

4   See, for example, Gustavo Gutiérrez's *A Theology of Liberation* (1988) or Alexandre Christoyannopoulos' *Christian Anarchism* (2010).

OCCUPYING SUBJECTIVITY

5   In the US historical context, see Lieberman (2000). Transnationally in the post 9/11 era, see Cortright (2004), German and Murray (2005), Heaney and Rojas (2007), Maney, Woehrle, and Coy (2005), Reitan (2009, 2012), Sokmen (2008), Vasi (2006), Walgrave, Rucht, and Tarrow (2010), and Yeo (2009).

6   Methodological note and/or 'How to Read this Piece': this essay combines *bricolage* (Deleuze & Guattari, 1972; Lévi-Strauss, 1968)—that is, testing, experimenting, playing, and feeling resistances from and an urge to hide from the reader, but then submitting to the necessity, or logic, to reveal—with what Jones (2005, p. 767) calls 'purposeful and tension-filled "self-investigation"' of auto-ethnography. The latter strives for a kind of revelatory writing that is 'new and difficult', reflecting on and showing movement vis-à-vis our roles in and commitments to the social world.

To begin, my use of recurring news headlines aims to introduce the reader to prominent organizations and campaigns for peace and anti-militarism, as well as some key international developments these groups have mobilized against in recent decades. The repetition of geographical places in the first entry (circa 1979) and the last (2011) suggests a circularity or recurrence of issues and actors that peace activists must confront, and raises the specter that, despite our collective efforts, little if any progress toward a more peaceful world has been achieved. Furthermore, the juxtaposition on the page of these newspaper headlines with my apocryphal diary entries shows the spatial and social distance between myself as author/subject and the 'big events' of history. The page positioning of the first, second, and fourth diary entries as right-justified is meant to convey a greater spatial and social distance or marginalization: earlier, as a marginal(ized) youth in rural America and 'Indian country', and more recently as a relatively privileged and protected university professor and researcher in the USA and Europe. These two positions are contrasted to the third diary narrative detailing my role as a participatory action researcher and graduate student where, for a time, I felt *in* History (with a capital H) and thus a participant and promoter of another world in the making, as part of the anti-war and anti-neoliberal movements.

The auto-ethnographic method seeks to disrupt binaries and explore supposed paradoxes. One of these is the separation and elevation of science above art. Expressive auto-ethnographers embrace the postmodern relationship among authors, audiences, and texts (see Barthes, 1977; Derrida, 1978). They also welcome the postmodern revival of storytelling as deeply pedagogical, constitutive, meaningful, and meaning-*making* phenomena. Stories are said to convey ethics, modes of thinking, shades of feeling, and ways of understanding the self, the other(s), and society (Adams, 2008; Bochner, 2001; Ellis, Adams, & Bochner, 2011).

I adapt and draw inspiration from a number of postmodern anthropologists including Carolyn Ellis, Tony Adams, Arthur Bochner, Ruth Behar, and Norman Denzin, and the post-colonial and post-structural International Relations/Politics scholars Anna Agathangelou, Kyle Killian, and Michael J. Shapiro. I have taken from Ellis et al. (2011, p. 24) the technique of writing personal, evocative narratives treating academic, research, and personal life, and more fundamentally, viewing the author-self *as* the phenomenon under exploration. The qualitative measure for success is the degree and ways in which these revelations resonate with or expand readers' understanding. From Behar's (1997) method I take the lesson that deeper insights, or wisdom, may be gained by making oneself vulnerable within both the social movements themselves as a researcher-activist and within the *text* via self-revelation and exposure. Following Denzin (2006; see also Griffin, 1978/2000), I appreciate the emotional catharsis and self-understanding that expressive auto-ethnography enables, and adapt his *montage* and *poetics* methods (also shared by Agathangelou and Shapiro), and employ his switching among several writing styles and genres, including the political poet and novelist Dos Passos' (1937, in Denzin, 2006, p. 426) news of the day, or 'newsreel', which I adapt into the series of newspaper headlines.

Turning from ethnographic Anthropology to International Relations and Political Theory, and closer to the subject matter at hand, my work is akin to what Agathangelou and Killian (2006) term 'the poetics of peace epistemologies'. They follow Deleuze and Guattari (1987, p. 213) in the belief that politics occurs on both the macro- and micro-levels, and introduce the critical insight that poetic methods and strategies can be used by individuals or community groups to mitigate violence and promote peace at all layers of society, beginning with the 'self', and link the quest for more pacific social relations with an anti-capitalist ethic. Finally, my method shares considerable affinities with Shapiro's (2011) recent work, which takes inspiration from Benjamin (1990) and Rancière (2007). First, it is a montage juxtaposition of narrative devises—news headlines, diary accounts, and dream-poems—which together serve as encounters and clashes of heterogeneous or even paradoxical elements, between the sacred and secular, fear and playfulness, and fundamentalism and pragmatism. With this I hope to facilitate a break in the reader's perception, allowing for new associations among previously disparate ideas or sites. Furthermore, this strategy blurs the boundary, establishes equivalences, and reveals a deep connection between the more public spaces and practices of war and violence with those at the private, domestic, or biopolitical levels. As Shapiro notes, this connection is too often obfuscated by privileging the war front 'over there' manned by soldiers in uniform, while the myriad ways that both sacred and secular stories inscribe violence, hatred, and fear into our very selves, families, and communities are marginalized or erased completely. And in his 'self-writing as method', Shapiro analyzes stories and artistic creations of others; I take this a step further with expressive auto-ethnography, by weaving together my own stories and poems as paradoxical, cultural artifacts.

7 'FLIGHT/ESCAPE. Both words translate *fuite*, which has a different range of meanings than either of the English terms. *Fuite* covers not only the act of fleeing and eluding but also flowing, leaking, and disappearing into the distance.' Massumi (1987, p. xvi, on translating Deleuze and Guattari's concept as *lines of flight*).

8 Which resulted in Reitan (1999).

9 See http://dorothydayguild.org/hercause.htm.

References

Ackerman, P., & Duvall, J. (2001). *A force more powerful: A century of non-violent conflict*. Basingstoke: Palgrave Macmillan.

Adams, T. E. (2008). A review of narrative ethics. *Qualitative Inquiry, 14*(2), 175–194.

Agathangelou, A. M., & Killian, K. D. (2006). Epistemologies of peace: Poetics, globalization, and the social justice movement. *Globalizations, 3*(4), 459–483.

Barthes, R. (1977). *Image, music, text*. (S. Heath, Trans.). New York: Hill and Wang.

Behar, R. (1997). *The vulnerable observer: Anthropology that breaks your heart*. Boston, MA: Beacon Press.

Benjamin, W. (1990). N [Re the theory of knowledge, theory of progress]. (L. Hafrey & R. Seiburth, Trans). Ch. 4 In G. Smith (Ed.), *Benjamin: Philosophy, history, aesthetics* (pp. 43–83). Chicago, IL: University of Chicago Press.

Bochner, A. P. (2001). Narrative's virtues. *Qualitative Inquiry, 7*(2), 131–157.

Bush, G. H. W. (1991). *Address before a joint session of the congress on the cessation of the Persian Gulf conflict*. Retrieved from http://bushlibrary.tamu.edu/research/public_papers.php?id=2767&year=1991&month=3

Christoyannopoulos, A. (2010). *Christian anarchism: A political commentary on the gospel*. Exeter: Imprint Academic.

Cortright, D. (2004). *A peaceful superpower: The movement against war in Iraq*. Goshen: Fourth Freedom Forum.

Deleuze, G., & Guattari, F. (1972). *Anti-Oedipus: Capitalism and schizophrenia*. Minneapolis: University of Minnesota.

Deleuze, G., & Guattari, F. (1987). *A thousand plateaus: Capitalism and schizophrenia*. Minneapolis: University of Minnesota.

Denzin, N. K. (2006). Analytic autoethnography, or Déjà Vu all over again. *Journal of Contemporary Ethnography, 35*(4), 419–428.

Derrida, J. (1978). *Writing and difference* (A. Bass, Trans.). Chicago, IL: University of Chicago Press.

Dos Passos, J. (1937). *U.S.A.: I. The 42nd Parallel; II. Nineteen Nineteen; III. The big money*. New York: Modern Library.

Ellis, C., Adams, T. E., & Bochner, A. P. (2011). Autoethnography: An overview. *FQS Forum: Qualitative Social Research, 12*(1). Retrieved from http://www.qualitative-research.net/index.php/fqs/article/viewArticle/1589/3095

German, L., & Murray, A. (2005). *Stop the war: The story of Britain's biggest mass movement*. London: Bookmarks.

Gutiérrez, G. (1988). *A theology of liberation: History, politics, and salvation* (Revised ed.). Maryknoll, NY: Orbis Books.

Griffin, S. (1978/2000). *Woman and nature: The roaring inside her*. San Francisco: Sierra Club.

Heaney, M. T., & Rojas, F. (2007). Partisans, nonpartisans, and the antiwar movement in the United States. *American Politics Research, 35*(4), 431–464.

Jones, S. H. (2005). Autoethnography: Making the personal political. In N. K. Denzin & Y. S. Lincoln (Eds.), *Handbook of qualitative research* (3rd ed., pp. 763–792). Thousand Oaks, CA: Sage.

Lévi-Strauss, C. (1968). *The savage mind*. Chicago, IL: University Of Chicago Press.

Lieberman, R. (2000). *The strangest dream: Communism, anticommunism and the U.S. Peace Movement 1945–1963*. New York: Syracuse University Press.

Maney, G. M., Woehrle, L. M., & Coy, P. G. (2005). Harnessing and challenging hegemony: The U.S. Peace Movement after 9/11. *Sociological Perspectives, 48*(3), 357–381.

Massumi, B. (1987). Translator's foreword: Pleasures of philosophy. In G. Deleuze & F. Guattari (Eds.), *A thousand plateaus: Capitalism and schizophrenia* (pp. x–ixv). Minneapolis: University of Minnesota.

Neale, J. (2003). *You are G8, we are 6 Billion: The truth behind the Genoa Protests (Vision)*.

Oxford Dictionaries. (2011). *Paradox*. Retrieved from http://oxforddictionaries.com/definition/paradox

Pearson, C. S. (1991). *Awakening the heroes within: Twelve archetypes to help us find ourselves and transform our world*. New York: HarperOne.

Rancière, J. (2007). *The future of the image*. (G. Elliot, Trans.). New York: Verso.

Reitan, R. (1999). *The rise and decline of an alliance: Cuba and African American leaders in the 1960s*. East Lansing: Michigan State University Press.

Reitan, R. (2009). The global anti-war movement within and beyond the world social forum. *Globalizations, 6*(4), 509–523.

Reitan, R. (2012). Coalescence of the global peace and justice movements. *Globalizations, 9*(3), 337–350.

Said, E. W. (1979). *Orientalism*. New York: Vintage.

Shapiro, M. J. (2011). The presence of war: "Here and elsewhere". *International Political Sociology, 5*(2), 109–125.

Sharp, G., Paulson, J., Miller, C. A., & Merriman, H. (2005). *Waging nonviolent struggle: 20th century practice and 21st century potential*. Westford, MA: Porter Sargent.

Sharlet, J. (2009). *The family: The secret fundamentalism at the heart of American power*. New York: Harper Perennial.

Sokmen, M. G. (Ed.). (2008). *The world Tribunal on Iraq: Making the case against war*. Northampton, MA: Olive Branch Press.

Thomas, J. (2000). *The battle in Seattle: The story behind and beyond the WTO demonstrations*. Golden, CO: Fulcrum Publishing.

Vasi, I. B. (2006). The new anti-war protests and miscible mobilizations. *Social Movement Studies, 5*(2), 137–153.

Walgrave, S., Rucht, D., & Tarrow, S. (Eds.). (2010). *The world says no to war: Demonstrations against the war on Iraq*. Minneapolis: University of Minnesota Press.

Wittner, L. (1993). *One world or none: A history of the world nuclear disarmament movement through 1953. Vol. 1 of the struggle against the bomb*. Stanford, CA: Stanford University Press.

Wittner, L. (1997). *Resisting the bomb: A history of the world nuclear disarmament movement, 1954–1970. Vol. 2 of the struggle against the bomb*. Stanford, CA: Stanford University Press.

Wittner, L. (2003). *Toward nuclear abolition: A history of the world nuclear disarmament movement, 1971 to the present. Vol. 3 of the struggle against the bomb*. Stanford, CA: Stanford University Press.

Yeo, A. (2009). Not in anyone's backyard: The emergence and identity of a transnational anti-base network. *International Studies Quarterly, 53*, 571–594.

'A Direct Act of Resurgence, a Direct Act of Sovereignty': Reflections on Idle No More, Indigenous Activism, and Canadian Settler Colonialism

ADAM J. BARKER

Independent Researcher

ABSTRACT   *In the winter of 2012, the Canadian political scene was shaken by the emergence of 'Idle No More', a collection of protests directed by and largely comprised of Indigenous peoples. Originally, a response to a variety of legislation that was being passed through the Canadian government at the time, Idle No More spread across the country and around the world. In this paper, I argue that, drawing from Indigenous nationhood movements that extend back through five centuries, Idle No More represents a renewed assertion of Indigenous sovereignty in opposition to settler colonisation. Through transgressive actions, Idle No More has brought online activism into alignment with embodied defences of land and place, challenging Canadian sovereignty and Settler identity in multiple and creative ways. However, settler colonial tendencies in Canadian politics have sought to reinscribe Idle No More within established, generic political binaries. This paper positions Idle No More as a 'movement moment' that reveals significant insights about Indigenous activism, conservative politics, leftist resistance, and persistent settler colonialism in Canada.*

Introduction

In the freezing Canadian winter of 2012, as the holiday period loomed large in mainstream consciousness, a massive grassroots political protest movement emerged that challenged the very basis of Canadian sovereignty and political identity. Idle No More, an iteration of Indigenous resistance to settler colonisation that extends back through five centuries, began as social media rumblings, spread into community meetings and teach-ins, and then rapidly expanded into direct action flash mobs, significant protest rallies, and a media presence that was impossible to ignore. Indigenous people across Canada—and later in other countries around the world—

joined together to push back against both specific policies of the Canadian government, and the disempowering social discourses of Settler Canadians more generally.[1] The impact of Idle No More has been powerful, but also contested; this paper seeks to contribute to the debates around the meaning of this important protest movement by contextualizing it through the lens of contemporary Canadian settler colonialism and ongoing Indigenous resurgence.

Framed in the context of traditions of place-based resistance and resurgence of Indigenous nationhood, this paper combines geopolitical, scholarly analysis of Indigenous resistance movements in Canada with the voices of Idle No More activists to consider the role that Idle No More has and continues to play in shaping Indigenous-Canadian politics. By considering Kevin Bruyneel's 'thirdspace' of Indigenous sovereignty, I examine the ways that Idle No More has effectively deployed tactics of *transgression*, as well as the ways that Settler Canadian political discourses have attempted to counter these transgressions by re-inscribing Indigenous demands into mainstream political structures and identities. I position Idle No More as a 'movement moment', characterized by innovative uses of online and direct action tactics designed to disrupt settler colonial space. This is juxtaposed with trends in Settler Canadian leftist politics, and with specific reactions to the federal government under Prime Minister Stephen Harper and the Conservative Party, demonstrating how Settler Canadian 'support' for Idle No More may ultimately seek to define Indigenous politics through settler colonial political binaries. I conclude by offering thoughts on the place of Idle No More in the ongoing story of Indigenous resistance, including the importance of enduring relationships and lessons learned through contentious struggle.

Indigenous Resistance to Settler Colonialism: An Overview

I begin by acknowledging that Canada is a settler colonial state, whose sovereignty and political economy is premised on the dispossession of Indigenous peoples and exploitation of their land base. This point, while not uncontested, is gaining purchase, especially with the rise of settler colonial studies as a coherent field of research.[2] Moreover, the terms 'settler' and 'colonial' have been increasingly employed by activists and community members, especially in conjunction with Idle No More,[3] a trend that I assert speaks to the resonance these analyses have with peoples' lived experiences in Canada. As both state and imagined community, Canada stands as a settler colonial 'structure of invasion' (Wolfe, 1999), and in this state, Indigenous peoples face constant threats to their existence, as both formal powers invested in the state and informal socio-cultural discourses of the Canadian nation seek to erase Indigenous peoples' claims to the land in order to transfer legitimate possession to colonial authorities (Barker, 2013, pp. 224–246; Veracini, 2010a, pp. 33–52). However, the fact that settler colonisation is still ongoing in Canada is telling: despite centuries of concerted and evolving efforts, the settler colonial project has never succeeded, evidence of powerful, multifaceted, and enduring Indigenous resistances.

I believe that in order to understand the significance of Idle No More, one must first understand the tradition of Indigenous resistance that has constantly stood opposed to settler colonial processes. Generally, I follow the lead of Taiaiake Alfred (Mohawk) and Jeff Corntassel (Cherokee), employing 'Indigenous' as a situated identity. In their key 2005 article, Being Indigenous, they state:

> Indigenous peoples are just that: *Indigenous to the lands they inhabit*, in contrast to and in contention with the colonial societies and states that have spread out from Europe and other centres of empire. It

is this *oppositional, place-based existence*, along with the *consciousness of being in struggle* against the dispossessing and demeaning fact of colonization by foreign peoples, that fundamentally distinguishes Indigenous peoples from other peoples of the world. (Alfred & Corntassel, 2005, p. 597; emphasis added)

It is to a brief discussion of this oppositional, place-based existence in relation to Idle No More that I now turn.

During much of the twentieth century, Indigenous activists fought for their collective survival and recognition of their basic existence, often by (re-)claiming a particular place or site. As Kilibarda (2012) has pointed out, occupying contentious sites is one of the most powerful and long-standing tactics of Indigenous resistance in Canada and the USA. Though it is impossible to single out any particular occupation or standoff as exemplary, some are more well known than others. In the USA, the occupation of the town of Wounded Knee by members of the Oglala Sioux nation and the American Indian Movement from February to May of 1973 is likely the most widely discussed (Weyler, 1992, pp. 58–96). An analogous event in the Canadian context in terms of its impact on social discourses and general awareness is the 78-day standoff between Mohawk Warriors and Canadian police and military in 1990, known as the 'Oka Crisis' (York & Pindera, 1991). Many other examples could be found of Indigenous peoples occupying particular places; none of these incidents are isolated. Neither are Indigenous occupations limited to rural or wilderness areas; while the longest running Indigenous occupation site is that of Grassy Narrows, an Anishinaabe resistance action against logging in their traditional territory (Willow, 2011), other sites are common. The Ipperwash Standoff, which led to the death of Anishinaabe activist Dudley George at the hands of the Ontario Provincial Police in 1995, occurred in a public park (Edwards, 2003); the Musqueam have recently been protesting against the destruction of a burial site inside the bounds of greater Vancouver (Musqueam Indian Band, n.d.); the 2006 reclamation of land near Caledonia, Ontario, by activists from Six Nations Reserve, is the site of a suburban housing development (Keefer, 2007); and the Gitxsan and Wet'suwet'en people, who last year withdrew support from their treaty negotiators for cutting deals relating to the Enbridge pipeline project, occupied a space already nominally 'theirs' by physically blockading their treaty office (Stueck & Bailey, 2012). Similar dynamics are occurring across North America, including south of the 49th parallel. In the American southwest, Navajo communities are opposing the theft of water and destruction of their sacred spaces related to the construction of a ski resort (Chee, 2011), and in California the Winnemem Wintu have declared war on the American state as part of their reclamation of sacred river spaces (Fimrite, 2012).

It is crucial to understand the variety of sites that have been key to Indigenous occupations, in part to understand how protests and occupations of urban and suburban spaces relate to struggles over 'the land', often equated with rural—especially reserve—space. Anishinaabe scholar Leanne Simpson, in an interview with noted Canadian activist and journalist Naomi Klein, drew connections between Idle No More and the transfer of land through the metaphor of extraction as a key colonial process that affects both land and people:

Extraction and assimilation go together. Colonialism and capitalism are based on extracting and assimilating. My land is seen as a resource. My relatives in the plant and animal worlds are seen as resources. My culture and knowledge is a resource. My body is a resource and my children are a resource because they are the potential to grow, maintain, and uphold the extraction-assimilation system. The act of extraction removes all of the relationships that give whatever is being extracted meaning. (Simpson, 2013)

Against the extractive current of settler colonial transfer, I situate Indigenous peoples' traditions and strategies of resistance in Canada and the USA as a parallel *affective process*. Affective resistance is premised on the understanding that social relationships—the foundations of the spaces that people build and occupy (Massey, 2009, pp. 16–17)—are a crucial site of struggle. Larsen and Johnson (2012) have posited that phenomenological attachments to place can form the basis of affinity politics, as attachments to place can bring people together into spontaneous, creative action and contention, an argument clearly inspired by their own engagements with Indigenous geographies, activism, and place knowledge. The affective attachments to place need not be attachments to the place of protest, or to place as 'natural' or 'unreconstructed'; affinity-based movements can cohere around urban environments, as in the case of movements led by Indigenous women in the Vancouver Downtown Eastside (Culhane, 2003).

An Indigenous space can exist anywhere; it requires only Indigenous peoples, in place, enacting their indigeneity. As Corntassel and Cheryl Bryce (Coast Salish) assert:

> ... when approaches to indigenous cultural revitalisation and self-determination are discussed solely in terms of strategies, rights, and theories, they overlook the everyday practices of resurgence and decolonisation. Indigenous resurgence is about reconnecting with homelands, cultural practices, and communities, and is centered on reclaiming, restoring, and regenerating homeland relationships. Another dimension centers upon decolonization, which transforms indigenous struggles for freedom from performance to everyday local practice. This entails moving away from the performativity of a rights discourse geared toward state affirmation and approval toward a daily existence conditioned by place-based cultural practices. (2012, p. 153)

In this tradition of place-based reconnection and resurgence, indigeneity need not compete directly with American or Canadian sovereignty because it poses a more fundamental challenge to state territorialisation; Indigenous being on the land refuses to legitimate and recognise the absolutist, static boundaries of settler states (Alfred, 2005; Soguk, 2011). It is important to understand the radical challenge that the assertion of Indigenous political autonomy poses to settler colonial political structures, and also to Settler Canadian identity and culture. Canada, as state and nation, is built on the premise that Indigenous peoples are either absent or that Indigenous political challenges are 'settled' (Regan, 2010). While the colonial state—with the grudging support of some Canadians—can accommodate 'aboriginal' political claims as a demand for minority rights within the multicultural structure of Canadian law and policy (Alfred, 2005), Indigenous movements that reject the politics of recognition in favour of asserting Indigenous place-relationships and social spaces challenge the core of both Canadian political economy and Settler identity (Coulthard, 2014a). Just as settler colonialism is created by settler collectives spreading through places, building spatially stretched relationships, Indigenous resistance simultaneously disrupts settler colonial space while reasserting Indigenous spaces, altering the spatialities of both (Barker, 2013).

Bruyneel, writing about the relationship between the US and Indian tribes, asserts that Indigenous people exercise a 'thirdspace of sovereignty by both holding colonial systems to account ... and also challenging those systems as unjust in their basic imposition on independent Indigenous nationhood' (2007, p. xvii). Bruyneel locates the struggle between the American state and Indigenous nations as

> a battle between an American effort to solidify inherently contingent [spatial and temporal] boundaries and an indigenous effort to work on and across these boundaries, drawing on and exposing their contingency to gain the fullest possible expression of political identity, agency, and autonomy. (2007, p. 6)

I assert here that Bruyneel's analysis extends to the Canadian situation and is, in fact, typical of many settler colonial regimes. Settler colonial desires to naturalize on the land are predicated on a disavowal of Indigenous peoples and presence, and a re-reading of the relationship between Settlers and Indigenous peoples as a 'non-encounter' (Veracini, 2010a, 2010b, 2008). This generates what Bruyneel identifies as 'colonial ambivalence'—the assertion of a colonial state through the assertion of both spatial and temporal boundaries on Indigenous peoples, without the willingness to engage with Indigenous peoples after or beyond the assertion of those boundaries. However, colonial ambivalence 'is both a product of colonial rule and an opening for postcolonial resistance' (Bruyneel, 2007, p. 13).

Colonial ambivalence clearly marks average Settler Canadian ideas of indigeneity. While often happy to claim a relationship to 'aboriginal' peoples through a narrative of Canada as a peaceful, liberal, multicultural polity defined by 'peacemaking'—but dominated by whiteness, capitalist property ownership, and individual rights—Canadians have often reacted with hostility to assertions of Indigenous sovereignty that challenge this narrative (Regan, 2010). It is no surprise, then, that Idle No More—as one of the most visible, multi-vocal, and politically challenging Indigenous protest movements seen in Canada—should inspire passionate reactions from many quarters. I turn now to an overview of the events of Idle No More in order to more accurately interrogate how these protests relate to longer trends of settler colonisation and Indigenous resistance.

Winter of Discontent: The Events and Contexts of Idle No More

Idle No More is a contested label for a loosely organised but intense and powerful series of public and political engagements, community discourses, and direct action protests beginning in November 2012, increasing in size and frequency through January 2013, and decreasing in visible action and engagement thereafter, though retaining a powerful political presence in Canada.[4] This movement, primarily directed against the Canadian federal government (King, 2013 February), has been largely driven by Indigenous communities, especially as a largely grassroots, non-hierarchical effort. Although it is popularly regarded that there are 'four founders' of Idle No More, the movement's moniker developed organically as a signifier and began spreading through a number of teach-ins in Indigenous communities in the Canadian provinces of Saskatchewan and Alberta; the associated hashtag–#IdleNoMore[5]—grew out of its use in these contexts and was taken up as a rallying cry for mass political engagement.[6] The catalyst was a series of legislation bills pushed through Parliament in mid-to-late 2012, that directly threatened Indigenous peoples' interests, especially Bill C-45, an omnibus budget bill that contained changes to the Indian Act and to environmental protections, both of which drew the ire of Indigenous leaders and communities.

Even prior to the introduction of Bill C-45 into the House of Commons on 18 October 2012, community organisers in Indigenous communities—urban and reserve—were increasingly involved in community education and dialogue, raising awareness over the actions of the government and their implications for Indigenous communities. After C-45 was introduced, these community education sessions increased in frequency and intensity. On 10 November, an educational conference in Saskatoon, Saskatchewan, was organized by four women: Sylvia McAdam (Cree), Jessica Gordon (Cree/Anishinaabe), Nina Wilson (Nakota/Cree), and Sheelah McLean. This conference is often identified as the genesis point of the phrase 'Idle No More', and the organizers of the conference have become colloquially known as 'the four

OCCUPYING SUBJECTIVITY

founders' of the movement. The phrase spread quickly through the social media hastag #IdleNoMore, which gained widespread recognition and traction.

Alongside the growing use of #IdleNoMore as a rallying cry, a prominent Indigenous leader was preparing for her own form of protest, one that would ultimately prove to have a great deal of resonance with Idle No More. Chief Theresa Spence is the elected Chief of the Attawapiskat First Nation, an isolated reserve community in northern Ontario, which has been sparring with the Canadian government for years.[7] There has been a long-standing housing shortage on the reserve, a boil water advisory, pollution from nearby mining activity, and extreme economic depression. After several years of bureaucratic and legal frustration, on 11 December 2012, Chief Spence and a small group of supporters set up a tent and fire on an island behind the House of Commons in Ottawa, and began a hunger strike. Subsisting on only medicinal tea and fish broth, Spence demanded to speak directly with the Prime Minister, Stephen Harper, and the Governor General, David Johnston, the titular head of state and representative of the Crown in Canada. This protest immediately captured a great deal of media attention and polarised political commentary (Simpson, 2014).

Chief Spence's hunger strike, though not officially under the banner of Idle No More, was clearly coordinated to enhance the growing protest movement (Kino-nda-niimi Collective, 2014, p. 25). As Idle No More gained momentum, several days of action were called for. The first of these was on 10 December, and it was during the day-long set of protests, occupations, demonstrations and rallies that Spence's hunger strike was announced. Between the Day of Action and Spence's protest, Idle No More and Indigenous people's concerns began to capture the attention of many Canadians. However, the mainstream media was still slow to cover these events until 17 December, when a new form of protest rally took Canadians by surprise. On that day in Regina, Saskatchewan, a flash mob organized inside a shopping mall filled with Christmas traffic, and began performing a round dance. Round dances are a public dance involving as many or as few drummers and dancers as are available; the drummers play and sing a relatively simple social song, while the dancers move in a shuffling circle around the drummers. This tactic quickly spread—dubbed the 'Round Dance Revolution'—due to its ease of organizing and effect at generating attention and dialogue and was successfully deployed in shopping malls and busy public spaces such as urban intersections, an unexpected physical and conceptual transgression in spaces of capitalist consumption at a time when consumerism reached its yearly fever pitch.

On 21 December, a second Day of Action was called and a massive rally was held outside the House of Commons in Ottawa, the Canadian capital, with supporting protests being held around Canada and the world. Some—such as a one-person protest outside of the Canadian embassy in Cairo (APTN National News, 2012)—received more media attention than they may have warranted; others—including protests in remote places like Yellowknife in $-40°C$ temperatures (Allooloo, 2014, p. 197)—likely received far less. However, the most enduring image from these protests is likely the round dance held in the midst of the busiest intersection in Canada's largest city, Toronto, Ontario: just prior to the rally on Parliament Hill, Idle No More protesters turned Dundas Square, the intersection of Yonge St. and Dundas Streets East and West, into a massive protest space with a huge round dance.[8] Various Indigenous-led protests continued, some under the banner of Idle No More, others not, at irregular intervals through the rest of December and into January. On 30 December 2012, for example, the first of a series of blockades of rail lines between Montreal and Toronto was conducted; at the same time, round dances and other flash mob type actions were continuing across Canada and the USA, some involving violent encounters with Settler people,[9] or arrests.[10]

48

In January 2013, amidst the backdrops of ongoing flash mobs, blockades, and local rallies and teach-ins, Prime Minister Harper announced that he would meet with representatives of the Assembly of First Nations (AFN), the government-sanctioned and funded representative body for recognized First Nation bands made up of elected chiefs and council members. Chief Spence, a continuing lightning rod for criticism of the government, stated that although her fast would continue, she would attend the meeting. This changed when Harper made clear that the Governor General would not be participating, as Spence had demanded at the outset of her hunger strike; Spence immediately responded that she would boycott the meeting and that her hunger strike would continue. The day of the meeting between Harper and the AFN under Grand Chief Shawn A-in-chut Atleo (Nuu-chah-nulth), on 11 January, marked the single most concentrated day of protest and involvement in Idle No More, as rallies were held around the country organized under the hashtag #J11; the hashtag #idlenomore was used a record 55 334 times that day.[11] Despite this energy, with the outcome of the meeting between the AFN and Harper left ambiguous, and with legislation such as C-45 already passed, the discourse around Idle No More began to fragment. Further, a series of scandals not directly related to Indigenous issues rocked the federal government, distracting from the protests. After being hospitalized on 24 January and at the request of her family and community, Spence made the decision to end her hunger strike without having gained a hearing with either the Prime Minister or Governor General.

A number of important events happened after the end of January, perhaps most notably the public shaming of long-time Harper advisor and political scientist, Tom Flannigan. Idle No More members, protesting his speaking event at the University of Lethbridge, captured Flannigan on video making dubious statements regarding the legality of viewing child pornography (Bolen, 2013), which was later posted online and ultimately resulted in Flannigan losing both his political and academic positions. But the flash mobs and public protests flagged, as did the online use of #IdleNoMore. Some members of Idle No More also began publicly questioning the tactics of organizers and protestors in other locations, especially the use of blockades at Canada–US border crossings, which had a cooling effect on community activism. Anniversary rallies planned around the country in December 2013 drew limited numbers and were unable to replicate the energy and excitement of the initial outburst in December 2012 and January 2013. However, Idle No More's impact and relationship to broader currents of Indigenous activism and resistance continues to be both felt and debated.

Modes of Engagement: Continuity and Change in Indigenous Resistance

Idle No More has been critiqued as a moniker by some precisely because Indigenous peoples have never been 'idle' with respect to colonisation. As Simpson, a leading voice in Idle No More and Indigenous resurgence generally, states:

> Over the past 400 years, there has never been a time when indigenous peoples were not resisting colonialism. Idle No More is the latest—visible to the mainstream—resistance and it is part of an ongoing historical and contemporary push to protect our lands, our cultures, our nationhoods, and our languages. (2013)

In this vein, I argue Idle No More should not be dismissed as a name or as a movement but rather should be discussed as one particularly effective set of efforts to innovate and revitalize Indigenous traditions of resistance in Canada, while staying true to core precepts of place-based, third-space politics.

#IdleNoMore, Social Media, and Online Organising

Any analysis of Idle No More must begin with the relationship between the protest movement and the online hashtag. Recently, many social movements have developed in part through new and social media; the Arab Spring, for example, has been discussed as an example of how social media can aid and enhance social movements (see, e.g. Khondker, 2011). There is a resonance here with Idle No More: social media played a major role in both the development of Idle No More as a focal point for action, and of specific action tactics and strategies. The first tweet under the #idlenomore hashtag was made on 23 November 2012; two weeks later, on 7 December, there were 864 tweets with that hashtag. By 11 December, the first Day of Action, #idlenomore was tweeted 11,885 times, and the numbers continued to climb. Why did social media play such a large role in Idle No More?

First, it is important to recognize that mainstream media in Canada has traditionally been silent on issues of concern to Indigenous peoples, only engaging with Indigenous peoples and communities when they can be portrayed as threatening to the interests of corporations or framed as destablising Settler Canadian society (Johnson, 2011; Mickler, 2010; Palacios, 2014). As Idle No More coalesced, it became apparent that this scenario would be repeated, but with the difference that

> the movement often went around mainstream media, emerging in online and independent publications as articles, essays, and interviews. This was the first time we [Indigenous activists] had the capacity and technological tools to represent ourselves ... and broadcast those voices throughout Canada. (Kino-nda-niimi Collective, 2014, p. 25)

This prevented common media discourses of 'savagism' from taking root, while also generating new spaces for Indigenous activists and communities to speak to each other. While the ubiquity of the hashtag can overshadow the richness of the online engagement around Idle No More, longer-form articles on blogs[12] and online magazines, as well as video and audio interviews, and livestreamed teach-ins facilitated vibrant and thoughtful discourse. This is in addition to the massive use of electronic communication that was not publicly visible, including reaching out to 'coders, hackers, web developers ... sharing Google Docs and various ways of building out collaborative informating sharing' (Martineau, 2014, p. 116). So while #IdleNoMore and the associated Facebook groups are the most publicly visible aspect of Idle No More's online presence, they are in truth only a small part of a much larger marshalling of electronic communication to counter Canadian corporate media bias, much of which is still ongoing.

In addition to media bias, the colonial geography of Canada has often played a role in fragmenting Indigenous resistance. Against this, the speed and accessibility of social media helped to spread word through often spatially dispersed Indigenous communities, and it became common to read on Facebook or Twitter accounts of people driving through snowstorms or from isolated locations to attend community meetings that they had heard about online. The problems of distance were especially apparent in the north, where both dispersed population and the distance from major media and populations in southern Canada made the speed and accessibility of social media organizing a valuable tool. As Dene activist Siku Allooloo relates:

> Social media ... facilitated the movement, and it was hugely important in the North because it connected our actions with what was happening in the rest of the country and the world. Because of our distance, isolation and low population the North is often overlooked by Canadian society, even amongst Native populations in the South. But Northerners are very active and are sure to stay informed, so when Idle No More blew up on the scene we were quick to take action and represent

in our communities ... We connected ourselves with active Natives in other parts of the country and supported one another, as everyone else was doing as well. (2014, pp. 198–199)

The extended reach of Idle No More was not just limited to rural Canada. Personally, though I watched much of Idle No More unfold from the UK, I was able to stay up-to-date without relying on mainstream media coverage, as well as contributing in my own way through making and sharing two short 'talking head' style videos,[13] alongside 'signal boosting' information through social media.

Social media was also used for more than sharing information and engaging in dialogue; it was used as an effective organisational tool to coordinate protests and direct action on short timelines, in multiple locations, and with limited resources. The tactic of the Round Dance Revolution is certainly one of the prominent features of Idle No More that spread quickly online. On 17 December, the day of the first flash mob in Regina, there were only 8072 uses of #idlenomore; this rose drastically each day afterwards for several consecutive days, as the flash mob tactic spread: 11,445 uses on 18 December; 19,594 on 19 December; 19,777 on 20 December; and the highest single-day total until mid-January, 39,648 on 21 December, coinciding with the Day of Action rallies including the massive round dance at Dundas Square. Further, the Day of Action called for 11 January, which set the single-day record for uses of the #idlenomore hashtag, was itself organized under the #J11 hashtag; the proliferation of related hashtags became a common tactic for developing diverse actions under the broader banner of Idle No More. The teach-ins that were the first (and probably most enduring) feature of Idle No More also relied on social and new media to bring people into direct contact and conversation, and to continue dialogues on important issues after meetings had finished. Several of these, such as those organized at the University of Victoria by the Indigenous Governance Program, were broadcast and archived online (see, e.g. Martineau, 2013 January). This is significant because there is clear evidence that these forums were an important site of discussion and debate relating to movement tactics, including the efficacy of public critique of political leadership (King, 2013 March). However, while these online social movement dynamics remain an important feature of analysis in their own right, it is important to understand how these tactics of transgression—by eliding mainstream media and by creatively co-opting technological resources—correspond to the wider land-based movement in the tradition of centuries of Indigenous activism and resistance.

Transgressing Boundaries: From Cyberspace to Contending for Place

While social media activism may be dismissed by some as banal or problematic, it played a key role in the way that Idle No More's impact was felt simultaneously in cyberspace and in physical spaces. Activists and communities organized online, but danced and marched in public, crossing multiple boundaries in the process. One of the common threads through the effective actions taken under the Idle No More banner is that they are transgressive; they provoke a response from Settler society when they assert an Indigenous presence where and when it is least expected in the settler colonial geographical imaginary (Veracini, 2010b). This is, in fact, a long-standing feature of assertions of Indigenous sovereignty. Simpson has discussed how her attempts to live according to her Anishinaabe traditions and culture are perceived by Settler people as 'an aggressive act' (2012), underscoring the affective response of Settler people to Indigenous resistance and assertions of belonging on the land. Given the long history of Indigenous place-based resistance, the transgressive acts of Idle No More should not be considered apart from other forms of

Indigenous anti-colonial politics, but rather as complementary to them. Idle No More, in bringing indigeneity into electronic forums, as well as physically into shopping malls and urban intersections, disrupted the settler colonial relationships by which those spaces are integrated into settler colonial geographical imaginaries. This should be viewed in light of Culp's analyses of 'queering' public protest which 'revealed a disruptive power of bodies that lies outside their rhetorical suasion and thus the politics of identification', leading to a call for a 'politics of desire' that 'escapes easy identification' (2013, pp. 33–34). The publicly visible aspect of Idle No More protests asserted indigeneity into Settler social space, but articulated indigeneity in ways that defied easy categorization by settler colonial narratives.

Simpson further asserts that Idle No More has been conscious of the need to contend for place through relationship building and other affective process, with the explicit intent of decolonisation:

> People within the Idle No More movement who are talking about indigenous nationhood are talking about a massive transformation, a massive decolonization. A resurgence of indigenous political thought that is very, very much land-based and very, very much tied to that intimate and close relationship to the land, which to me means a revitalization of sustainable local indigenous economies that benefit local people. (2013)

This process is strongly in the tradition of Indigenous resistance that positions relationships to land beyond contestation for political power. Idle No More has been especially effective at transgressing Settler boundaries to empower assertions of Indigenous 'thirdspace' sovereignty.

Chief Spence's protest was especially confounding for Settler Canadians in this regard, in that her demand to speak with both the Prime Minister (the functional head of the federal government) and the Governor General (the ceremonial representative of the Crown) positioned the Canadian federal government as a necessary interlocutor in Attawapiskat, but not the ultimate (sovereign) authority. Chief Spence's demand inherently asserted that Canadian sovereignty could only be functionally practiced through a partnership between Chief and Crown, and that such a partnership would take precedence over the federal or provincial authorities in this territory. Canadian sovereignty was tacitly and subtly positioned a posteriori to a relationship between equals at the intergovernmental level.[14] This itself is a reflection of the demand for the recognition of the 'true intent' of various treaties, which are demands that long predate the existence of Idle No More.

This nation-to-nation and treaty-based understanding of Canadian sovereignty was perfectly demonstrated by an Idle No More re-reading of the Royal Commission on Aboriginal Peoples, or RCAP (Canada, 1996).[15] A pamphlet generated for the 21 December Day of Action by Alfred and Tobold Rollo (see Figures 1 and 2) explicitly referenced the recommendations of RCAP, including those that called for a revitalization of nation-to-nation relationships through the use of treaties:

> The Government of Canada must remove formal and informal restrictions placed on treaty negotiations with Indigenous governments over rights to land and culture. A refusal to negotiate in good faith amounts to a bare assertion of colonial sovereignty, which stands as an affront to international law and to the Constitution of Canada itself. (2012)

This and four other recommendations were condensed from those in the RCAP Final Report, but this one, in particular, is striking in part because of what it would mean if fully followed. It is important to consider what kind of treaty might be implied here, and as it was both a major symbol throughout the Idle No More protests, and is also the longest operational treaty in Canada, I look now to the Guswenta or Two-Row Treaty.

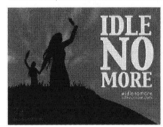

Figure 1. Exterior of pamphlet produced in support of Idle No More actions, December 2012, referencing the RCAP recommendations (Alfred & Rollo, 2012).

The Guswenta is a type of agreement made between the Haudenosaunee Confederacy and a number of nations—including other Indigenous nations—and has been recognized as an international treaty with clear and definite political and legal import. The Two-Row Treaty has been a major symbol at many sites of Indigenous–Settler conflict for many years—including those not in Haudenosaunee territory—because it is often considered the barest framework of mutual respect and non-interference that would be necessary for any just and decolonized relationship to function (Turner, 2006, p. 48). As Alfred and Rollo point out, by Canada's own Constitution and international law conventions, an international treaty is as fundamental to state lawmaking and policy as is a domestic constitution or Charter of Rights, and as such the Two-Row Treaty should have binding force upon the state. A state may not simply abrogate a Treaty without consequence. Among the primary (ignored) recommendations of the RCAP is that the Crown should honour its treaty obligations to Indigenous nations, that treaties should be interpreted broadly and towards the 'original intent', and that restitution should be made for historic and contemporary treaty violations.

While the appeal to this sort of treaty relationship may be made from within the system—referencing Canadian traditions of constitutional and international law, and the RCAP itself—it also challenges the state system as a whole, situating this as a definitive assertion of thirdspace sovereignty. The Two-Row Treaty, in that it is a true 'living document' immersed in oral history

1. Declaration of Responsibility.

To restore this relationship, the Government of Canada must acknowledge the systematic nature of Canada's colonial past and present. Recent governments have issued apologies for specific colonial programs, such as the Residential School System, but have yet to acknowledge responsibility for the full range of colonial institutions, including legislation currently enforced under the Indian Act.

2. Legislated Recognition of Political Authority.

The Government of Canada must enact legislation that recognizes the inherent rights of Indigenous Nations to designate political authority according to their own laws, governing principles, and customs. The law will provide guidance and give expression to the already existing recognition of the right of self-determination found in Section 35 of the Canadian Constitution and the nation-to-nation relationship established by previous treaties and agreements. In addition, it will allow systems of political authority and accountability to take root in Indigenous communities that will correct the democratically defective and dysfunctional Indian Act system.

3. Legislated Devolution of Governance.

The Government of Canada must devolve control over social, cultural, economic, housing, health, and educational services to Indigenous governments, in accordance with Section 35 of the Constitution of Canada. The current 'duty to consult' must be replaced with federally structured shared-jurisdiction over lands consider for urban and economic development. Indigenous jurisdiction will provide a stop-gap measure against the erosion of environmental protections under external pressures.

4. Legislation of Crown Fiduciary Duty.

The Government of Canada must provide funding, training, and resources sufficient to assist Indigenous nations while they re-establish their capacities and autonomy as Indigenous Nations. As these capacities are realized, the cost to Canada will diminish sharply until it is no longer needed.

5. Unrestricted Modern Treaty Process.

The Government of Canada must remove formal and informal restrictions placed on treaty negotiations with Indigenous governments over rights to land and culture. A refusal to negotiate in good faith amounts to a bare assertion of colonial sovereignty, which stands as an affront to international law and to the Constitution of Canada itself.

Figure 2. Interior of pamphlet, calling for an 'Unrestricted' approach to treaties (Alfred & Rollo, 2012).

and requiring continuous community participation, does not fit neatly into contemporary understandings of the role of the state and the extent of sovereignty over territory, thus transgressing the boundaries of Settler Canadian politics. To follow the RCAP recommendation and respect the principles of the Two-Row (or other treaties) as prior to the articulation and practice of Canadian state sovereignty would require a massive alteration to the political economy of the entire Canadian state. Obviously, this cannot be done simply by the fiat of the federal or provincial governments; it is in fact a social project of incredible scope. In this, the 'thirdspace' occupied by Indigenous resistance does not simply make a demand upon the Settler government—falling into the familiar trap of the politics of recognition (Coulthard, 2007, 2014a)—but rather declares a position with respect to the entirety of Settler society, and demands that Settlers dialogue and struggle among themselves in order to respond appropriately to this Indigenous positionality. While Idle No More remained a movement with a multiplicity of demands, the assertion of a nation-to-nation relationship and the demand to honour treaties underpinned many of these, drawing protests against particular bills and policies into far more complicated discourses about the nature of Canadian political sovereignty.

Settler Canadian Politics and Idle No More

Given the challenges that Idle No More posed to fundamental premises of the Canadian nation state, the responses by Settler people have been predictably complicated. In order to understand how Settler Canadians have interpreted and reacted to Idle No More, it is necessary both to clarify some of the specific contexts of Canadian political dynamics at that time, as well as more long-standing Canadian investments in settler colonial political systems.

Throughout the winter of 2012–2013, Idle No More, like many Indigenous movements, actively sought to engage with Settler communities to educate and seek their support. The response was, compared to some past conflicts, promising; as Alfred asserted, 'Idle No More has shown that there is support among Canadians for a movement that embodies principled opposition to the destruction of the land and the extension of social justice to Indigenous peoples' (2013). However, it must be remembered that transgressive acts like spatial occupations—whether in malls or at border crossings—are intended to provoke an affective response from Settler colonial ambivalence; this response may be revealing, but it is not necessarily (or even likely) positive, supportive or decolonizing. As Bruyneel presciently observes, Settler people do not think of Indigenous people in a rational or critical way, but rather as 'like the weather':

> Americans pose as experts on Indians, as they do on the weather, while simultaneously disavowing the capacity to create and maintain consistent, substantive policies to ameliorate the problems Indians face (just as they disavow their capacity to ameliorate the problems caused by the weather). In other words, Americans speak and act as if they have understood and are concerned for indigenous problems (just as they are concerned about the weather), and they may even complain about the fate of these problems, but ultimately they are unable to do anything about them. (2007, p. 137)

Further, as successful as Idle No More has been in rallying support from the Settler population, the majority of Canadians have continued to disagree with and oppose Idle No More and Indigenous sovereignty more generally. Sociologist Jeff Denis has detailed some of the more overt crimes—from violent assaults with vehicle to rapes—in which Settler perpetrators either explicitly targeted Idle No More protesters or referenced Idle No More as their motive, alongside opinion polls indicating that most Canadians did not support Idle No More or Theresa Spence, and in fact blame Indigenous peoples for the social injustices that they face (Denis, in press). How does this weigh out against the support received from Idle No More by groups such as the Canadian Nurses Association, Greenpeace, and the Council of Canadians, among others (Kino-nda-niimi Collective, 2014, p. 402)? Of course, Settler Canadians are not a homogenous group so variance is expected, but there are some important trends to consider in understanding how Idle No More's tactics and messaging have created affective responses in place of colonial ambivalence.

There must first be recognised a strong opportunistic current within Settler Canadian politics and activism. Settler people and collectives are very good at identifying diverse spaces of opportunity in the midst of Indigenous spaces (Barker, 2013, pp. 187–199), at times representing themselves as staunch allies while in fact embodying practices that further Indigenous transfer and displacement. Social movement scholars have increasingly engaged in criticism of activists, including various anarchist organisers or members of Occupy projects, who have demonstrated a tragic inability to take direction from or work respectfully with Indigenous communities, regardless of their stated intent (Barker, 2013, pp. 292–317; Barker 2012a; Barker & Pickerill, 2012; Kilibarda, 2012; Tuck & Yang, 2012). With that in mind, I turn here away from Settler opposition to Idle No More—a predictable, colonial response—towards an interrogation of some of the positions asserted by Settler Canadians seeking to act in solidarity with Idle No More, beginning with those at the intersection of Indigenous political assertions and Canadian political institutions.

The Anti-Harper Backlash

Settler people have a long history of appropriation and false affinity with respect to Indigenous peoples and symbols for the purpose of expressing anti-establishment discontent. From the Boston Tea Party, where nascent Americans dressed as Mohawk warriors, to the New Age and counterculture appropriation of Indigenous dress and symbols in fashion, indigeneity is held up as that which is outside and Other, and thus an object that can be extracted and appropriated, what Veracini calls 'transfer by performance' (2010a, pp. 43–48); indigeneity may be celebrated when a critique of privilege is required, but often as a caricature of authentic Indigenous life that reinforces colonialism as a whole. With that in mind, it must also be recognized that it is likely impossible to understand Settler Canadian responses to Idle No More without also understanding the parallel backlash against the unpopular federal government of the Conservative Party of Canada (CPC)[16] and Prime Minister Stephen Harper, which has generated the false appearance of affinity between a variety of political actors and activists.

Stephen Harper has been the Prime Minister of Canada since 2006, forming first a minority and later a majority government, in no small part because of his own personal reputation for economic leadership and that of his party for fiscal responsibility in the midst of the global financial crisis.[17] However, throughout 2012 and 2013, Harper's popularity plummeted along with confidence in the CPC government (EKOS, 2013). This may actually have been sparked off by the events that also catalysed Idle No More in the autumn and winter of 2012: the omnibus budget bills that undemocratically altered a number of key pieces of legislation. However, since then, Harper has seemingly been in a free-fall; a number of major scandals have dogged his government, most notably evidence of corruption and misappropriation of funds by a number of high-profile senators appointed by Harper (Weston, 2013). As a result, there is a growing body of the Canadian public who are galvanized against Harper specifically and the CPC more generally. Many Settler people and communities have gravitated towards Idle No More in no small part because of its vocal, pointed and long-standing opposition to Harper. Chief Spence, especially, had been legally and politically contending with the Harper government over funding and housing issues since it took power in 2006. Even relatively mainstream aboriginal organisations, like the AFN, have sparred with Harper dating back to his scrapping of the Kelowna Accord[18] upon taking office in 2006, and his subsequent speech that declared that Canada has 'No history of colonialism' (Hui, 2009).

A 'Paranoid Politics of Binarity'

Despite this, the extent to which the opposition to Harper and the CPC will translate into lasting solidarity with Indigenous struggles is questionable. Culp, in his analyses of the 2003 protests against the invasion of Iraq—which he calls 'an exercise in failure' (2013, p. 16)—notes how the over-focus on George W. Bush on the part of protestors served to become 'a mechanism for a restrictive, paranoid politics of binarity' (p. 22). This binary politics meant that Bush's persona became a stand-in for policies that he initiated, ultimately deflecting criticism away from the Iraq War and other imperialist, militant policies which remained in place throughout his tenure (and several of which continue under the Democratic presidency of Barak Obama). A similar dynamic is certainly observable around Harper, who has become a stand-in for the actual concerns articulated by Idle No More. By mid-2013, as the senate scandals spiralled, and protests under the banner of Idle No More tailed off, interest in Indigenous issues among mainstream Canadians plummeted. Actions in the trajectory of Idle No More continued—for example, the reclamation and renaming of PKOLS, a mountain in Coast Salish territory near Victoria, British Columbia, an event that I was fortunate enough to participate in directly—but these received comparatively little media attention.[19]

A further danger in sublimating Indigenous political concerns within critiques of the present government is that it reifies the established political system as *the* political authority of reference. Many movements and currents within what might be called the 'generic' Canadian political left[20] seek political engagements with Indigenous peoples through larger social justice or anti-racism movements, usually at the national or international level, and often demanding structural reform; for example, the left-nationalist Council of Canadians was very vocal and supportive of Idle No More. These political organizations, even when they press for changes in policy, law, or political leadership—as many currently do—often reinforce other (hidden or ignored) structures of colonial power. As Choudry observes:

> ... many supposedly progressive political organisations—while proclaiming that there are alternatives to free markets, free trade and transnational corporate power and that 'another world is possible'—reproduce dominant colonial worldviews and resist challenges by Indigenous peoples and activists to address colonial injustices. While some have asked whether the global justice and anti-globalisation movement is anti-capitalist, it is also important to ask whether it is anti-colonial. (2010, p. 99)

In this way, critiques of Harper and his government can excuse systemic settler colonialism. As Leitner et al. discuss with respect to the Immigrant Workers' Freedom Ride (2003), solidarities that are strong in one context may disintegrate when entering 'centres of corporate and political power' (Leitner, Sheppard, & Sziarto, 2008, p. 169). This indicates the degree to which 'any social movement ... has to negotiate power relations within the movement, and the power geometry of the socio-spatial relations it is embedded in' (p. 168). Voting against the conservative government and campaigning against Harper specifically becomes a 'move to innocence' (Tuck & Yang, 2012) by which Settler Canadians can excuse their own complicity in ongoing colonialism.

By contrast, Idle No More certainly frustrated and directly contested the political agenda of Stephen Harper, but as the movement progressed beyond a narrow focus on Bill C-45, this was articulated more and more in terms of Indigenous autonomy than political critique. For example, Simpson clearly framed Spence's hunger strike as 'not so much an act *against* Harper, but as a selfless act of bravery and sacrifice *for* our nations and our children' (2012). While it is worthwhile to investigate resonances between the backlash among Canadians against the Harper and CPC government, and Indigenous assertions of sovereignty through Idle No More, it is unlikely that lasting solidarity can be built on these grounds; the longer term goals of the generic left and of communities asserting Indigenous nationhood are not necessarily compatible.

Conclusions: Idle No More as a 'Movement Moment'

Rather than a self-contained political movement, Idle No More must be seen as a rallying cry within a long trajectory of Indigenous resistance and organising against colonisation and for the restoration of Indigenous nationhood and self-determination, a movement moment. In this, it has mobilised peoples in a number of different fields—some seen as antithetical, such as those pursuing systemic reform through the elected chief and council (AFN) system and those advocating direct action enactments of sovereignty—consistent with Indigenous political traditions and resistance generally. As a rallying call, it allowed for widespread and diverse challenges to settler colonial space, drawing inspiration and ideas from each other, and encouraging these actions to proliferate. This is the kind of 'cascade of contention' that social movement theorist Tarrow (1998) observes in successful social movements, and speaks to the ongoing power of embodied Indigenous resistance in spaces that Settlers take for granted as theirs (including online spaces). The most important of these cascades were clearly those between different Indigenous communities, both geographically and politically, as people came together electronically and at protests, rallies and round dances. Throughout the growth of Idle No More, it was clear that participants were building networks of solidarity, organizational and leadership capacity, and strategic and tactical plans to take advantage of the widespread support for and through Idle No More, while respecting local conditions and terrains of struggle. For example, when Idle No More protestors gathered in the Uptown Centre in Victoria, the capital of the province of British Columbia, they did not round dance the same way, in recognition that local dance traditions are different—the tactic was adapted to embody an authentic, local expression of sovereignty rather than a pan-indigenous practice assimilable by Settler society.

With this perspective in mind, it remains important to bring a critical frame of analysis to bear on Idle No More. Cree scholar Jarrett Martineau believes that a major shortcoming of Idle No More was the inability to capitalize on an excited and mobilized grassroots that had shown a willingness to pursue sustained and creative direct action (2013 March). For example, following initial rail line blockades, further proposed blockades of Canada–US border crossings were effectively shut down by the disapproval of leading figures associated with Idle No More in early January. The use of blockades and similar direct actions for economic disruption, while a common tactic in Indigenous protest movements, are very contentious. Many activists and community members disagreed with the use of blockades from the outset. Notably, Sylvia McAdams was quoted in an interview with *The National Post* as saying that blockades are 'irritating the public and that's not the purpose behind Idle No More', as well as distancing Idle No More from Chief Spence and criticizing the number of issues beyond Bill C-45 that Idle No More had begun addressing (Carlson, 2013 January). Several blockades planned for the near future were immediately called off.[21]

This had the simultaneous effect of 'capping' the escalation of Idle No More's spatial claims at the borders of Canada and the USA, and of disempowering grassroots organizers. This significance of this barrier to the effectiveness and transgressive politics of Idle No More was presciently foreshadowed by Dene political theorist Glen Coulthard in December 2012, when he wrote about conditions differentiating Idle No More from previous Indigenous protest movements. Among these was 'the absence . . . of widespread economic disruption unleashed by Indigenous direct action'. He went on to assert:

> If history has shown us anything, it is this: if you want those in power to respond swiftly to Indigenous peoples' political efforts, start by placing Native bodies (with a few logs and tires thrown in for good measure) between settlers and their money, which in colonial contexts is generated by the ongoing theft and exploitation of our land and resource base. If this is true, then the long-term efficacy of the #IdleNoMore movement would appear to hinge on its protest actions being distributed more evenly between the malls and front lawns of legislatures on the one hand, and the logging roads, thoroughfares, and railways that are central to the accumulation of colonial capital on the other. (Coulthard, 2014b, p. 36)

As much as round dances in public spaces are a creative and dynamic transgression of the social spaces of Settler society, the obvious and powerful boundaries of political structures must also be challenged or the movement becomes predictable, controllable and reconcilable with Settler politics of recognition (Coulthard, 2007).

Drawing from Coulthard and Martineau's assessments, it can also be surmised that assertions of transgressive thirdspace politics were foreclosed by perceptions of over-participation in systemic politics by various political figures, including the elected leaders of the AFN. Naomi Klein, while interviewing Simpson, asserted that some of the grassroots and potentially helpful Settler populations 'may have been lost a little when we start[ed] hearing some chiefs casting it all as a fight over resources sharing' (2013). Meanwhile, in Indigenous communities, the decision by Chief Atleo and the AFN to meet with government representatives on 11 January and ongoing-ambiguous relationship to Idle No More provoked a great deal of debate and dissent (Friesen, 2013 January 21), which in some instances served to fracture lines of solidarity that had been generated during the preceding months.[22] The combination of disapproval of economic disruption tactics and the monopolization of the political discourse by the AFN may have had a chilling effect on the growth of Idle No More, discouraging innovation that energized local and grassroots organizing and sapping vital energy from the movement. The result was a limitation on who could step into positions of leadership and how contention could be structured, discouraging the creative contention of the earlier phase of Idle No More and creating an over-reliance on a few core activists. As Mark Blevis discussed in his analysis of the #idlenomore Twitter and social media current, 'The rate of growth of the movement has stalled, there's no fresh blood' (Friesen, 2013 January 24).

Contrasted with the vibrant contention of Idle No More, it appears that the decision by Atleo and AFN leadership to work closely with the Harper government may have ultimately been more than Indigenous communities were willing to bear. As one of the primary outcomes of these negotiations, Atleo and Harper came together to announce the highly controversial and secretive First Nations Control of First Nations Education Act (FNCFNEA) on 7 February 2014, at Kainai Highschool on the Kainai Blood reserve. After a contentious press event backfired,[23] Atleo was eventually pressured to resign, the FNCFNEA was shelved, and the AFN chiefs adopted a much more militant stance in conjunction with a national Day of Action on 15 May 2014, even as some Indigenous scholars and activists openly questioned the relevance of the AFN itself (King, 2014). Would this sort of self-conscious and highly networked response to the FNCFNEA—which started online and spread to physical protests—have occurred were it not for the efforts and example set by Idle No More? While impossible to say, it seems doubtful; Idle No More may have been part of a long tradition of Indigenous resistance, but it has also left a very specific and powerful legacy with respect to strategy and tactics, and the activist relationships that empower them.

Further, creative contentions against settler colonial norms that were energised by Idle No More's trangressive actions have continued even if not under the same moniker. For example, the DJ trio 'A Tribe Called Red', which in some respects provided the soundtrack to Idle No More, have continued to use art as a means of transgressing temporal boundaries by combining traditional and contemporary musical techniques to create a distinctively Indigenous but undeniably modern musical form. Several of their songs feature prominently on YouTube videos created around Idle No More, and their most recent album carries the explicitly political title 'Nation II Nation'. They were recently awarded a Juno (prestigious Canadian music award) for Breakthrough Group of the Year for 2014. Woven throughout their music are messages of Indigenous nationhood and reassertions of Indigenous cultures; this becomes an act of creative contention against settler colonial cultural production, and one that clearly resonates with many Indigenous people (and Settler people as well).

OCCUPYING SUBJECTIVITY

While critiques are important, I must make clear: this paper does not seek to join the chorus of voices proclaiming Idle No More 'dead' or 'over'. Rather, as a moment in the movement towards Indigenous resurgence and nationhood, Idle No More has added a valuable version to stories of rebellion and liberation that fuel the long-term success of social movements (Selbin, 2010). The moment when Idle No More is the core of affective Indigenous resistance and place-based assertions of sovereignty may come around again. As Tanya Kappo asserted at the close of a presentation on the history of Indigenous resistance in Canada from the 1960s to the present, 'Nothing has changed' (2013), and that includes the refusal of Indigenous peoples to surrender to settler colonial power. If Idle No More has demonstrated anything, it is that Indigenous peoples will not cease pursuing decolonisation, nationhood, and social change because that is the condition and effect of their existence. Simpson's phrase explains best: 'For me, living as a Nishnaabekwe is a deliberate act—a direct act of resurgence, a direct act of sovereignty' (2012).

Acknowledgements

An early drafts of parts of this paper was presented at the Concurrences in Colonial and Postcolonial Studies symposium, 'Reconsidering the Politics of Decolonization: Indigenous Resurgences and Settler States', Linnaeus University, Sweden, March 2013. I would like to thank Chris Rossdale, Jarrett Martineau, Emma Battell Lowman, and Gurminder K. Bhambra for their comments on an earlier draft of this paper, as well as the critiques of two anonymous reviewers.

Notes

1   There is a great deal of debate over the terms 'Indigenous' and 'Settler', with some critics arguing that they set up 'Manichean' categories which deny the complexities the lived reality in contexts of colonial imposition and resistance (Faragher, 2014, p. 186; Byrd, 2011, xxix). Others, such as Wolfe, argue in favour of a strategic essentialism, acknowledging that such a binary is not perfectly accurate, but that it allows for a great deal of useful analysis (2013). Largely aligned with Wolfe, I deploy 'Settler' as a situated identity and positionality, which overlaps with both Indigenous identities and with the multiple and shifting identities of 'exogenous Others', migrants, refugees and other newcomers with ambiguous relationships to Settler society. This usage has been partially developed in my doctoral project (Barker, 2013), and is the subject of sustained analysis in *We, the settler people: Identity, colonialism and Canadian society* (Barker & Battell Lowman, in press). My usage of 'Indigenous' is in the tradition of Alfred and Corntassel (2005), and is articulated below. While I recognize that generalizations in this paper such as 'Settler Canadians' or 'Indigenous resistance' may not hold absolutely true, I use these terms to identify trends and tendencies that emerge through sustained analyses of settler colonisation and resistance.
2   I have previously argued this point extensively (Barker, 2013, 2009). Political theorists Veracini and Morgensen both consider Canada as a settler colonial state (Morgensen, 2011; Veracini, 2010a), as does Alfred (2005), among many others.
3   See, for example, the commonality of these terms throughout the anthology *The winter we danced: Voices from the past, the future, and the idle no more movement* (Kino-nda-niimi Collective, 2014).
4   The overview in this section is necessarily partial; for more detailed discussions of the events surrounding and comprising Idle No More, see generally *The Winter We Danced*, and specifically the Timeline of Major Events Spanning the Winter We Danced (Kino-nda-niimi Collective, 2014, pp. 389–409). For a timeline of Twitter usage related to #idlenomore, see the timeline generated through the website Makook, designed to track usage of that particular hashtag: "#IdleNoMore", *Makook*, online at: idlenomore.makook.ca/timeline.
5   The hashtag has become ubiquitous with the movement; it is discussed further below.
6   I am paraphrasing here from a presentation by Kappo (2013 May), Sturgeon Lake Cree, a long-time activist, writer and community leader who was involved in many of the earliest teach-ins and has remained a strong voice

OCCUPYING SUBJECTIVITY

throughout Idle No More's engagements. See also Hayden King's interview with Kappo in *The winter we danced* (2014, pp. 68–69).

7   For a thorough and stark view of the conditions in Attawapiskat relating to housing, water, employment, youth suicide, and other crucial issues, see Obomsawin's documentary, *The People of the Kattawapiskak River* (2012).

8   For a short visual of this protest, there are many videos posted on YouTube; the post by WorldTruthNow (2013) gives a good impression of the size and significance of the round dance.

9   See, for example, the incident on Queen Elizabeth II Highway near Edmonton on 16 January 2013, where one individual drove a truck through a group of protesters. At the same rally, another Settler identified only as 'Steve' attempted to provoke violence, with the man commenting, 'I'm tired of their movement … I was kinda hoping someone would take a swing at me' (Wingrove, 2013; see also: Denis, in press; O'Brien, 2012).

10   Among others, five people were arrested at Flatirons Mall in Colorado on 2 January 2013 following a round dance explicitly in support of Idle No More (Steele, 2013).

11   Figure from *Makook*, online at: idlenomore.makook.ca/timeline.

12   A number of blogs maintained excellent coverage of Idle No More events, but a few stood out for particularly clear and engaging analysis of the context of colonisation and resistance that remains crucial to understanding Indigenous activism in Canada. Several of these are referenced throughout this paper, but I would draw particular attention to the blogs of Hayden King (biidwewidam.com), Chelsea Vowel (apihtawikosisan.com), and the series of guest articles posted on *Decolonization: Indigeneity, Education & Society* (decolonization.wordpress.com), the blog page of the scholarly journal by the same name.

13   See, for example, 'An Open Letter to my Settler People', which was filmed and uploaded from the village of Sheepwash in rural Devonshire (Barker, 2012b).

14   The counter-assertion by the federal government, by comparison, was that Chief Spence should meet with the Minister of Aboriginal Affairs and Northern Development, which would position the Attawapiskat community as a sub-federal order of government that may only appeal to the Minister for redress.

15   The RCAP was a major governmental research project, completed in 1995, comprising an intensive study by the Canadian state into the relationships between the state, Canadian (Settler) society, and Indigenous peoples and communities, following the violent upheaval of the Oka Standoff. The RCAP recommendations, with the exception of a brief few, were never implemented.

16   The CPC is the most right-wing of the major federal political parties. Other relevant federal parties include the centre-right Liberal Party, the centre-left New Democratic Party (NDP), and the Bloc Quebecois, the separatist, Quebec nationalist party.

17   Harper's own reputation comes largely from his academic background and political experience; he holds a Masters in Economics from the University of Calgary, and has often campaigned on financial and economic platforms over social or cultural issues. The CPC, similar to the Republican Party in the USA, holds a reputation for economic responsibility based on austerity and corporate tax cuts to stimulate economic activity.

18   The Kelowna Accord was an agreement reached between the AFN and other Indigenous political leaders, and the Canadian federal government under Harper's predecessor, Liberal Prime Minister Paul Martin. It would have served as a new framework for the fiduciary responsibility between the Crown and First Nations, largely around issues of health care, education and economic development on reserves. It was completed just prior to the election that brought the CPC and Harper to power, and was never ratified.

19   For more on the PKOLS reclamation, see: nationsrising.org/campaigns/.

20   The term 'generic left' is Austin's (2010, p. 28); I use it in much the same spirit as he does, referring to the reformist, systemic, or otherwise non-radical tradition of leftist Canadian politics, often closely associated with the NDP and Green Party, and various mainstream NGOs.

21   McAdams later claimed that her words had been misconstrued, blaming media manipulation, and refusing further interviews with mainstream news outlets. Regardless, there were clearly deeply divided opinions over the efficacy of direct action for economic and political disruption throughout Idle No More.

22   King asserts that 'it is … important for us to acknowledge that there are significant political differences in Native politics (and within the Idle No More movement as well) with correspondingly divergent strategies for action' and that the implications of all of these—both within and outside of the Canadian legal and political system—need to be discussed by activists and academics (2013 March). I agree; my point here is not to argue for the 'hegemony of hegemony' (Day, 2005) in Indigenous politics, but rather to point out that some political differences were likely intentionally exploited to reduce the strength of the movement as a whole.

23   As community members entered the school, they were marked with yellow or blue stickers to indicate whether they were 'invited guests' allowed to enter the auditorium (yellow) where Harper, Atleo and other high-ranking guests were present, or 'uninvited guests' directed to the gymnasium (blue), where there was a video feed to the

OCCUPYING SUBJECTIVITY

proceedings. Several community members given blue stickers were later removed from the event by security. This sparked a 'blue dot' protest movement that began to galvanise opposition to the FNCFNEA, and by extension, to Atleo's participation with it (Sterritt, 2014).

References

Alfred, T. (2005). *Wasase: Indigenous pathways to action and freedom*. Peterborough, ON: Broadview Press.

Alfred, T. (2013, January 27). *Idle no more and Indigenous Nationhood* [blog post]. Taiaiake.net. Retrieved from http://taiaiake.net/2013/01/27/idle-no-more-indigenous-nationhood/

Alfred, T., & Corntassel, J. (2005). Being indigenous: Resurgences against contemporary colonialism. *Government and Opposition, 40*(4), 597–614.

Alfred, T., & Rollo, T. (2012, December 19). *Resetting and restoring the relationship between Indigenous peoples and Canada* [pamphlet]. Retrieved from http://nationsrising.org/resources/reset-restore/

Allooloo, S. (2014). "I have waited 40 years for this. Keep it going and don't stop!": An interview with Siku Allooloo. Interviewd by Leanne Betasamosake Simpson. In Kino-nda-niimi (Eds.), *The Winter we danced: Voices from the past, the future, and the idle No more movement* (pp.193–199). Winnipeg: ARP Books.

APTN National News. (2012, December 19). *Idle No more day of action Friday will begin in Egypt*. Retrieved from http://aptn.ca/news/2012/12/19/idle-no-more-day-of-action-friday-will-begin-in-egypt/

Austin, D. (2010). Narratives of power: Historical mythologies in contemporary Quebec and Canada. *Race & Class, 52*(1), 19–32.

Barker, A. J. (2009). The contemporary reality of Canadian imperialism: Settler colonialism and the hybrid colonial state. *American Indian Quarterly, 33*(3), 325–351.

Barker, A. J. (2012a). Already occupied: Indigenous peoples, settler colonialism and the occupy movements in North America. *Social Movement Studies, 11*(3–4), 327–334.

Barker, A. J. (2012b, December 21). *An open letter to my settler people* [video blog]. Retrieved from http://vimeo.com/56106760

Barker, A. J. (2013). *(Re-)Ordering the new world: Settler colonialism, space, and identity* (PhD Thesis). Retrieved from https://www.academia.edu/3789748/_Re-_Ordering_the_New_World_Settler_colonialism_space_and_identity

Barker, A. J., & Battell Lowman, E. (in press). *We, the settler people: Identity, colonialism and Canadian society*. Halifax: Fernwood Press.

Barker, A. J., & Pickerill, J. (2012). Radicalizing relationships to and through shared geographies: Why anarchists need to understand indigenous connections to land and place. *Antipode, 44*(5), 1705–1725.

Bolen, M. (2013, March 6). Tom Flanagan's 2009 child porn comments led to 2013 uproar. *The Huffington Post Canada*. Retrieved from http://www.huffingtonpost.ca/2013/03/06/tom-flanagan-2009-child-_n_2812103.html

Bruyneel, K. (2007). *The third space of sovereignty: The postcolonial politics of U.S.-indigenous relations*. Minneapolis: University of Minnesota Press.

Byrd, J. A. (2011). *The transit of empire: Indigenous critiques of colonialism*. Minneapolis: University of Minnesota Press.

Canada. (1996). *Report of the royal commission on aboriginal peoples*. Retrieved from http://www.collectionscanada.gc.ca/webarchives/20071115053257/http://www.ainc-inac.gc.ca/ch/rcap/sg/sgmm_e.html

Carlson, K. B. (2013, January 15). Idle no more co-founder distances movement from planned blockades, hunger-striking Chief Spence. *The National Post*. Retrieved from http://news.nationalpost.com/2013/01/15/idle-no-more-co-founder-distances-movement-from-planned-blockades-hunger-striking-chief-spence/

Chee, C. R. (2011, August 9). Protesters arrested after blocking road to Snowbowl. *Navajo Times*. Retrieved from http://www.navajotimes.com/

Choudry, A. (2010). What's left? Canada's 'global justice' movement and colonial amnesia. *Race and Class, 52*(1), 97–102.

Corntassel, J., & Bryce, C. (2012). Practicing sustainable self-determination: Indigenous approaches to cultural restoration and revitalization. *The Brown Journal of World Affairs, XVIII*(II), 151–162.

Coulthard, G. (2007). Subjects of empire: Indigenous peoples and The 'Politics of Recognition' in Canada. *Contemporary Political Theory, 6*(4), 437–460.

Coulthard, G. (2014a). *Red skin, white masks: Rejecting the colonial politics of recognition*. Minneapolis: University of Minnesota Press.

Coulthard, G. (2014b). #IdleNoMore in historical context. In Kino-nda-niimi (Eds.), *The winter we danced: Voices from the past, the future, and the idle No more movement* (pp. 32–36). Winnipeg: ARP Books.

Culhane, D. (2003). Their spirits live within us: Aboriginal women in downtown Eastside Vancouver emerging into visibility. *The American Indian Quarterly*, *27*(2), 593–606.

Culp, A. (2013). Dispute or disrupt? Desire and violence in protests against the Iraq War. *Affinities: A Journal of Radical Theory, Culture, and Action*, *6*(1), 16–47.

Day, R. J. F. (2005). *Gramsci is dead: Anarchist currents in the newest social movements*. Toronto: Between the Lines.

Denis, J. S. (in press). A four directions model: Understanding the rise and resonance of an indigenous self-determination movement. In Elaine Coburn (Ed.), *More will sing their way to freedom: Indigenous resistance and resurgence*. Halifax: Fernwood Press.

Edwards, P. (2003). *One dead Indian: The premier, the Police, and the Ipperwash crisis*. Toronto: McClelland & Stewart.

EKOS. (2013, October 29). *Stephen harper plumbing record lows on trust, direction and approval* [poll report]. *EKOS Politics*. Retrieved from http://www.ekospolitics.com/wp-content/uploads/full_report_october_29_2013.pdf

Faragher, J. M. (2014). Commentary: Settler colonial studies and the North American frontier. *Settler Colonial Studies*, *4*(2), 181–191.

Fimrite, P. (2012, May 26). Winnemem Wintu tribe stages war dance as protest. *San Francisco Chronicle*. Retrieved from http://www.sfgate.com/news/article/Winnemem-Wintu-tribe-stages-war-dance-as-protest-3588954.php

Friesen, J. (2013, January 21). Returning Atleo sidesteps Spence, idle no more. *The Globe and Mail*. Retrieved from http://www.theglobeandmail.com/news/politics/returning-atleo-sidesteps-spence-idle-no-more/article7593545/

Friesen, J. (2013, January 24). End of Spence's protest leaves idle no more at crossroads. *The Globe and Mail*. Retrieved from http://www.theglobeandmail.com/news/politics/end-of-spences-protest-leaves-idlenomore-at-a-crossroads/article7830673/

Hui, S. (2009, October 2). Shawn Atleo criticizes Stephen Harper over 'no history of colonialism' remark [blog post]. *The Straight*. Retrieved at http://www.straight.com/blogra/shawn-atleo-criticizes-stephen-harper-over-no-history-colonialism-remark

Johnson, D. M. (2011). From the Tomahawk Chop to the road block: Discourses of savagism in Whitestream Media. *American Indian Quarterly*, *35*(1), 104–134.

Kappo, T. (2013, May). *The continuation of the 'modern Indian Movement': From the red paper to idle no more*. Presentation at the indigenous leadership Forum 2013, University of Victoria, Victoria, BC.

Kappo, T. (2014). "Our people were glowing": An interview with Tanya Kappo. Interviewed by Hayden King. In Kino-nda-niimi (Eds.), *The winter we danced: Voices from the past, the future, and the idle no more movement* (pp. 67–70). Winnipeg: ARP Books.

Keefer, T. (2007). The politics of solidarity: Six nations, leadership, and the settler left. *Upping the Anti: A Journal of Theory and Action*, *4*, 107–123.

Khondker, H. H. (2011). Role of the new media in the Arab Spring. *Globalizations*, *8*(5), 675–679.

Kilibarda, K. (2012). Lessons from #Occupy in Canada: Contesting space, settler consciousness and erasures within the 99%. *Journal of Critical Globalization Studies*, *5*, 24–43.

King, H. (2013, February 8). *What's next for idle no more? Why provincial governments should matter to the movement* [blog post]. Retrieved from http://biidwewidam.com/2013/02/08/whats-next-for-idle-no-more-why-provincial-governments-should-matter-to-the-movement/

King, H. (2013, March 5). *The utility of debate to idle no more is beyond dispute* [blog post]. Retrieved from http://biidwewidam.com/2013/03/05/the-utility-of-debate-to-idle-no-more-is-beyond-dispute/

King, H. (2014, May 5). After Atleo, does the Assembly of First Nations serve any purpose? *The Globe and Mail*. Retrieved from http://www.theglobeandmail.com/globe-debate/after-atleo-does-the-assembly-of-first-nations-serve-any-purpose/article18459188/

Kino-nda-niimi Collective, eds. (2014). *The winter we danced: Voices from the past, the future, and the idle no more movement*. Winnipeg: ARP Books.

Larsen, S., & Johnson, J. T. (2012). Toward an open sense of place: Phenomenology, affinity, and the question of being. *Annals of the Association of American Geographers*, *102*(3), 632–646.

Leitner, H., Sheppard, E., & Sziarto, K. M. (2008). The spatialities of contentious politics. *Transactions of the Institute of British Geographers*, *33*(2), 157–172.

Martineau, J. (2013, January 15). *#J16Forum: Idle no more—where do we go from here?* [blog post]. Culturite blog. Retrieved from http://culturite.wordpress.com/2013/01/15/j16forum-idle-no-more-where-do-we-go-from-here/

Martineau, J. (2013, March). *#IdleNoMore: Mobilizing decolonial consciousness and indigenous resurgence*. Paper presented at Concurrences in Colonial and Postcolonial Studies symposium, 'Reconsidering the Politics of Decolonization: Indigenous Resurgences and Settler States', Linnaeus University, Vaxjo, Sweden.

Martineau, J. (2014). "Give people a hub": An interview with Jarrett Martineau. Interviewed by Stephen Hui. In Kino-nda-niimi (Eds.), *The winter we danced: Voices from the past, the future, and the idle no more movement* (pp. 115–117). Winnipeg: ARP Books.

Massey, D. (2009). Concepts of space and power in theory and in political practice. *Documents d'anàlisi geogràfica, 55*, 15–26.

Mickler, S. (2010). Illiberal and unmodern: Conservative columnists on Indigenous self-determination in Australia and Canada. *Borderlands, 9*(1), 1–26.

Morgensen, S. (2011). The biopolitics of settler colonialism: Right here, right now. *Settler Colonial Studies, 1*(1), 52–76.

Musqueam Indian Band. (n.d.) *c'əsnaʔəm* [information sheet]. *Musqueam: A living culture* [website]. Retrieved at http://www.musqueam.bc.ca/c%CC%93%C9%99sna%CA%94%C9%99m

Obomsawin, A. (2012). *People of the Kattawapiskak River* [documentary]. Ottawa: National Film Board of Canada. Retrieved from http://www.nfb.ca/film/people_of_kattawapiskak_river/

O'Brien, J. (2012, December 20). Woman caught on tape attacking native protest vehicle. *The Toronto Sun*. Retrieved from http://www.torontosun.com/2012/12/20/woman-caught-on-tape-attacking-native-protest-vehicle

Palacios, L. C. (2014). Racialized and gendered necropower in Canadian news and legal discourse. *Feminist Formations, 26*(1), 1–26.

Regan, P. (2010). *Unsettling the settler within: Indian residential schools, truth telling, and reconciliation in Canada*. Vancouver: UBC Press.

Selbin, E. (2010). *Revolution, rebellion, resistance: The power of story*. London: Zed Books.

Simpson, L. (2012, December 21). Aambe! Maajaadaa! [What #IdleNoMore Means to Me]. *Decolonization: Indigeneity, education & society* [blog post]. Retrieved from http://decolonization.wordpress.com/2012/12/21/aambe-maajaadaa-what-idlenomore-means-to-me/

Simpson, L. (2013, March 5). Dancing the world into being: A conversation with idle no more's Leanne Simpson. *Yes! Magazine*. Interviewed by Naomi Klein. Retrieved from http://www.yesmagazine.org/peace-justice/dancing-the-world-into-being-a-conversation-with-idle-no-more-leanne-simpson

Simpson, L. (2014). Fish broth and fasting. In Kino-nda-niimi (Eds.), *The winter we danced: Voices from the past, the future, and the idle no more movement* (pp. 154–157). Winnipeg: ARP Books.

Soguk, N. (2011). Indigenous transversality in global politics. *Affinities, 5*(1), 37–55.

Steele, C. T. (2013, January 3). Idle no more supporters arrested at Flatirons Mall. *The Denver Progressive Examiner*. Retrieved from http://www.examiner.com/article/idle-no-more-supporters-arrested-at-flatirons-mall

Sterritt, A. (2014, February 12). Blue dots becoming for First Nations Education Act resistance. *CBC News*. Retrieved from http://www.cbc.ca/news/aboriginal/blue-dots-becoming-symbol-for-first-nations-education-act-resistance-1.2534518

Stueck, W., & Bailey, I. (2012, June 10). Gitxsan blockade coming to an end as forensic audit begins. *The Globe and Mail*. Retrieved from http://www.theglobeandmail.com/news/british-columbia/gitxsan-blockade-coming-to-an-end-as-forensic-audit-begins/article4246337/

Tarrow, S. (1998). *Power in movement: Social movements and contentious politics*. Cambridge: Cambridge University Press.

Tuck, E., & Yang, K. W. (2012). Decolonization is not a Metaphor. *Decolonization: Indigeneity, Education & Society, 1*(1), 1–40.

Turner, D. (2006). *This is not a peace pipe: Towards a critical indigenous philosophy*. Toronto: University of Toronto Press.

Veracini, L. (2008). Settler collective, founding violence and disavowal: The settler colonial situation. *Journal of Intercultural Studies, 29*(4), 363–379.

Veracini, L. (2010a). *Settler colonialism: A theoretical overview*. Eastbourne: Palgrave Macmillan.

Veracini, L. (2010b). The imagined geographies of settler colonialism. In T. Banivanua Mar & P. Edmonds (Eds.), *Making settler colonial Space: Perspectives on race, place and identity* (pp. 179–197). Hampshire: Palgrave Macmillan.

Weston, G. (2013, January 2). Is 'a walk in the snow' in Stephen Harper's future? *CBC News*. Retrieved from http://www.cbc.ca/news/politics/is-a-walk-in-the-snow-in-stephen-harper-s-future-1.2480564

Weyler, R. (1992). *Blood of the land: The government and corporate war against first nations*. Philadelphia: New Society Publishers.

Willow, A. J. (2011). Conceiving Kakipitatapitmok: The political landscape of anishinaabe anticlearcutting activism. *American Anthropologist, 113*(2), 262–276.

Wingrove, J. (2013, January 16). Edmonton idle no more protest meets resistance as truck pushes crowd. *The Globe and Mail*. Retrieved from http://www.theglobeandmail.com/news/national/edmonton-idlenomore-protest-meets-resistance-as-truck-pushes-crowd/article7446747/

Wolfe, P. (1999). *Settler colonialism and the transformation of anthropology: The politics and poetics of an Ethnographic Event*. London: Cassell.

Wolfe, P. (2013). Recuperating binarism: A heretical introduction. *Settler Colonial Studies, 3*(3–4), 257–279.

WorldTruthNow. (2013). *IdleNoMore Toronto FlashMob Shuts Down Dundas Square* [YouTube video]. Retrieved from http://www.youtube.com/watch?v=mG4bBu234ko

York, G., & Pindera, L. (1991). *People of the pines: The WARRIORS and the legacy of Oka*. Toronto: Little Brown.

Real Politics in Occupy: Transcending the Rules of the Day

ANNA SZOLUCHA

Maynooth University, Maynooth, Ireland

ABSTRACT *This paper analyses the Occupy movement in order to explore the mode of its participants' engagement with radical change. It also sketches the framework of real politics within which they were acting. It is a politics that accepts the constitutive lack of the political sphere, irreducibility of social antagonisms and alterity. First, by utilising Lacan and Derrida's theoretical constructions, the article examines ways in which Occupy aimed to transcend the 'rules of the day'. It then describes the challenges of non-hierarchical organising and radical inclusion that the movement faced. Subsequently, I briefly analyse 2 aporias that were endured in Occupy: between the ideal and non-ideal as well as between unity and singularity. These aporias did not mark a stalemate that paralysed the movement but pointed to the limits that had to be negotiated by Occupy's participants. Occupy demonstrated that, in reality, direct democracy does not work like an ideal of a self-transparent and completely non-alienated form of decision-making; this is perhaps the most important lesson that has to be borne in mind when considering the question of whether it is inevitable that the lacks in the system and in subjects continually re-emerge, and when asking what this can mean for the potential of universalising direct democracy and the future of radical activism. This paper draws on 'militant ethnographic' and participatory action research within Occupy in Dublin and semi-structured interviews with participants from Ireland and the USA.*

Looking down at the empty Peace Park at the junction of Grand Parade and South Mall in Cork (Ireland) from behind a thin layer of window glass, it seems so unreal that this small area housed one of the longest running Occupy encampments in the world. Yet this unexpected occurrence was the reason why I was there, strolling carelessly around a warm flat as the town was waking up to a grim and wet morning. I have grown so used to Occupy's ethic of care that I did not even realise that there was breakfast being made for me in the kitchen. 'We've all learned how to make these amazing smoothies in Occupy'—said a young woman handing me a glass of mushy green liquid. We sat chatting about Occupy. She looked focused, tilting her shaved head backwards trying to remember what happened a year ago. She had her hair cut to raise funds for the Occupy camp. It was she who told me:

> I have such problems with Ireland being called democratic when we have a choice of six political parties and all of them are the same. I felt really disenfranchised for the last three to four years and actively worked to get involved in campaigns that would fight against this force that made me feel very alone in this world. Occupy really did provide that for me and that's why I found it so depressing when I was leaving. I found this base, these people to overcome that loss that was just created by the system that we are in right now. And I found it and then I foolishly broke away. (9 March 2013 interview A)

Since the 1970s, politics in the global North has gradually been turned into a depoliticised, professionalised form of governance, where divisions between dominant political parties have become heavily diluted (Stavrakakis, 2007). Paradoxically, what was celebrated as a victory of liberalism has for many actually meant an assault on democracy in the name of democracy (Derrida, 2005). Analysis to this effect has been made since the late 1990s. Various challenges to neoliberal politics have also been taking place elsewhere: in Latin America or recently in Tunisia and Egypt where anti-austerity protests turned into full-scale revolutions. A wave of anti-austerity dissent has also swept across Europe but until recently it had still been hard to imagine that there might emerge a mass-based challenge to post-politics in the North. From a historical perspective, when the Occupy movement formed in 2011, it was not the first or a uniquely significant challenge to neoliberal politics—there have been many movements in all parts of the world struggling to delegitimise the system in their own ways. From a subjective perspective, however, the movement is significant and unique because many of its participants experienced it as such. They experienced it as something new, their first or most important breach of post-politics. It is this embedded perspective of people's lived experience that this paper adopts.

Being post-political meant steering away from any reminders that the system in which one lives is not perfect, that certain problems persist beyond all reformist and charitable interventions. As the quote above demonstrates, the people who did not succumb to this attitude experienced post-politics primarily as a loss or a lack that they strove to remedy. This loss of 'real' democracy is also inextricably linked with subjects' feeling of 'being alone in this world'— their repeated failures to construct their full identity within the restrictions of the current socio-political system. There are, then, two lacks involved here: one has to do with the lacking dominant social systems, the post-political symbolic space that forecloses real democracy; and the other with the lacking subject.

Such an understanding grasps the socio-symbolic dependence of subjectivity without foreclosing the subject as an empty vessel of objectivist determinations or imbuing it with a positive essence (Glynos & Stavrakakis, 2008). This is where Lacanian psychoanalysis and Derrida's thought become relevant for consideration of the political domain. They help to explain the complexity of people's experiences in radical social movements better than celebratory or scathingly critical analyses that may tend to glance over the socio-subjective interdependence and universalise their own experience. The political appropriations of Lacan and Derrida are not only concerned with voids in the subject and a social system, but also with people's continuous attempts to fill these lacks. It is their contention that despite our very best efforts, these lacks do not stop re-emerging.

The introductory quote captures this dynamic in recalling an apparently inescapable cycle of finding a remedy for one's lack and then breaking away from it. This phenomenon raises interesting questions about the nature of political activism and social transformation that I want to examine here. This paper analyses the Occupy movement in order to explore the mode of its participants' engagement with radical change. First, I draw on Lacan's conception of an act and Derrida's notion of a decision in order to explain the characteristic features of this movement situation and to examine how Occupy was different from post-political reformist social activism. In what ways was it a practical exercise in participatory democracy and direct action that aimed to transcend the rules of the day?[1] Why did it feel 'like something has been opened up, a kind of space nobody knew existed' (Klein, 2012)?

Far from creating unilateral theoretical constructs, I then describe moments when the 'criteria' of an act and decision fail to account for what actually happened in the movement. Subsequently, I show that in the context of social change, it can only make sense to speak about aporias that were endured in Occupy. I understand an aporia to mean an impasse of undecidability usually between contradictory demands, premises, or solutions. An aporia also marks the point at which the system undermines its own—seemingly stable—foundations. I use the analysis of aporias that were endured in Occupy to argue that they did not paralyse the movement but pointed to the areas in which its participants had to engage in complex negotiations with the real limits of their situation. This allowed them to take real responsibility for their actions. Lastly, I raise the question of what this analysis can mean for the future of activism and direct democracy. I argue that the main contribution that it makes is to show that direct democracy as practised by Occupy was not an ideal of a self-transparent process. This is not a critical conclusion that rules out the possibility of universalising this form of organising, but rather it treats it as part of real politics and real democracy that are by definition fraught with inconsistencies and aporias.

This paper draws on more than 5 months of 'militant ethnographic' (Juris, 2008) and participatory action research (Fals-Borda, 1991; McIntyre, 2008) within Occupy Dame Street (ODS) in Dublin, Ireland, as well as semi-structured interviews with 40 participants from Dublin and Cork in Ireland, and Oakland, San Francisco, and Berkeley in the USA. I understand that Occupy had a different force in different countries but by drawing on research from two thoroughly different states (with different political and activist histories, radically different populations in terms of scale as well as diversity, and position in the global financial economy), and still finding striking similarities in participants' lived experiences, I may suspect that many of the arguments that I am making about particular Occupy camps may also apply to the movement more generally. In the broadest sense, participants' experience of Occupy has revealed the cyclical and paradox-ridden nature of political engagement. This article looks at it in more detail in search for insights for future radical activism and social change.

Occupy as a Political Act

Non-intentionality and Hyperpoliticisation as Depoliticisation

One of the most common themes in Occupy participants' stories is about how they had not expected it to be anything 'bigger' (Taylor et al., 2011), different, or more profound (19, 28 June 2012 interviews B, Bp2) than any other protest they have joined or heard about before. Some 'couldn't believe that this was going on' at all (20 June 2012 interview B). For many participants, Occupy encampments were unique because they lacked any parallel comparisons on a national scale within the horizon of at least two decades. As one ODS participant told me:

The five months that we spent in front of the Central Bank—if you told anyone else in Ireland in the last fifteen years that people would have done that, they wouldn't believe you. Certainly the last twenty years I've been here. (7 May 2012 interview)

The scale of Occupy was also unprecedented, as this other ODS participant recounted on his blog in November 2011:

consider how crazy the idea would have seemed this time last year that a bunch of people would have camped out for a month in front of the Central Bank on Dame Street and that they would be part of a global movement of people doing the same in 1600+ cities around the world. Or that one of those camps would have called a general strike in Oakland that shut the 4th largest port in the US or that another could have organised a day of action in New York that involved 35,000 people. (Flood, 2011c)

If nobody thought that Occupy was going to be this big, or even expected that it would happen at all, how come did it happen? Part of the answer may lie in post-politics itself. Since it claims that all ideological struggles are over and celebrates the expert management of populations as the highest incarnation of democracy, it intensifies social antagonisms. With no outlets in the form of representative political parties, there must occur a moment when these antagonisms come to the fore. In other words, one has to 'measure politicization in terms of the degree of depoliticization … What would the symptom of neutralization and depoliticization … reveal? In truth, an over- or hyperpoliticization' (Derrida, 2000, p. 129).

Why is action a political act when it is non-intentional? The act is decisive, revealing of social antagonisms, and deeply politicising—all characteristic of occurrences that are rare and seem improbable before they actually appear. There is then an inextricable link between non-intentional action and the broadest scope of political contention that aims to question the very basis of socio-political systems.

Political acts can also only be non-intentional because they are not carried out from a position that is beyond the current dominant systems, that is, from a position that 'knows' what different system can be introduced in the place of the old one. The overwhelming majority of the people who participated in Occupy were part of the capitalist and liberal democratic models of governance or—to use Lacan's terminology—they were part of this Symbolic framework (Žižek, 2007). Through Occupy, however, they became able to separate themselves from it.

Traversing the Fantasy and Questioning the Legitimacy of the Status Quo

This radical separation from the big Other of capitalism and representative democracy was possible because people identified the fantasy at the heart of these systems, and through radical and direct action questioned the legitimacy of the status quo.

A short detour to psychoanalysis may be useful here. Lacan claimed that fantasy is an imaginary construction that helps sustain the coherence of the big Other which is a set of social rules, norms, and laws that govern individuals' behaviour. Fantasy sustains our reality insofar as it fills the inconsistencies and lacks in the big Other—it provides an explanation of them and helps forget the (necessary contingent and indeterminate) origins of any established order (Hoedemaekers, 2008; Lacan, n.d.).

Fantasy serves a function of setting people's desire in motion. By attempting to fill the lack in the big Other, it aims to regain the big Other's fullness, which is posited as a precondition for an ideal state of happiness, *jouissance*, the absence of further wants. As people's constant attempts at perfecting their fantasies show, their desire is never satisfied and they are reminded that it can never be by constant cracks in this reality. What emerges through these cracks in the Symbolic is the Real—this part of our reality that escapes its schema and reveals the incoherence of our dominant constructions (Stavrakakis, 1999).

(Post-)politics can be understood as fantasmatic (based on the Lacanian understanding of fantasy) because its primary institutions and processes do very little to question fundamental assumptions that govern our everyday perception (Hoedemaekers, 2008). In a political act, on the other hand, one traverses the fantasy. He/she changes his/her position in relation to the big 'Other as language' (place where all signification, law-making comes from) as well as the 'Other as desire' (place where our desires originate) (Fink, 1995).

In Occupy, participants refused to continue believing that the current systems can come up with a solution that would respond to the needs of the 99%. The Occupy Wall Street (OWS) call to global action on 15 October 2011 read: 'Neoliberalism is your future stolen ... This has to stop! We must usher in an era of democratic and economic justice.' The participants also questioned the workings of liberal democracy: '[as] society in the West we think about our-selves as democracy, ... but I'm not sure if it really is. There's no active participation in that democracy from most of the society' (7 May 2012 interview). Many Occupiers clearly sought to detach themselves from the dominant economic and political system as a site of any guarantees for their future. As one participant from Occupy Atlanta wrote: 'Our only option left is to occupy public spaces in order to assert our right to freely assemble and to redress our grievances, rights guaranteed to us by the First Amendment' (Flank, 2011, pp. 122–123).

Through direct democratic practices and multiple acts of civil disobedience, Occupy partici-pants did not seek to be recognised by the powers that be. Their aim was not to produce a list of wishes that could be negotiated with the government. They were against the traditional, repre-sentative ways of doing politics. In the second issue of the *OWS Journal*, they spelled it out very clearly: 'We are not pleading with the Congress for electoral reform. We know electoral politics is a farce. We have found another way to be heard and exercise power' (Hedges, 2011). This other way of exercising power was the General Assembly (GA) process and participatory and direct democratic decision-making that were, as one ODS participant wrote, not 'a way of con-trolling the politicians but of replacing them' (Flood, 2011b). Through these bottom-up, leader-less processes, radical change was to be achieved (Van Gelder, 2011). Occupy's anti-state attitude also extended towards its relations with other state agencies, primarily the police. The 'Long live Oakland Commune and fuck the police' slogan was one of the clearest identifi-cations of Occupy's desire to self-govern and make a radical break from other forms of protest that may still be entangled in the state's mechanisms of power.

It was not the movement's explicit aim to ask anybody for support. 'Don't look at us, join us!' said one of the most popular cardboard signs and chants in the early days of ODS. ODS refused to co-organise actions and cooperate with political parties and trade unions. However, many par-ticipants were not against the *idea* of unions or parties per se. As a member of ODS explained:

> I didn't believe in political parties or trade union organisations [but] I support the idea of trade unions. I'd defend anyone's right to be either in a trade union or in a political party. And if they were attacked for their just being in their existence, I'd defend them with a whole heart. [Political parties have] become very populist ... They're waiting on polls to tell them about what people wanted to hear so that they could them put that on a manifesto and encourage people to vote for that reason as opposed to being of a conviction to politics. (7 May 2012 interview)

Why is this distancing oneself from the state and established political entities important in a pol-itical act? This indifference to the Symbolic social reality, a refusal to play by its rules, is already transgressive. However, in this negative rejection, a political act makes a leap of faith into the unknown as a precondition for taking radical ethical responsibility for one's actions.

At the subjective level, Occupy was creating something new precisely because it refused to accept any patronage of established political entities, and thus constituted a break with much of what participants had known about politics. Although there was a general agreement about the refusal of Occupies to cooperate with mainstream political parties for the reasons discussed above, different Occupy camps held different positions with respect to the question of working alongside other leftist groups and unions. Some of the most successful Occupy Oakland actions involved quite tight cooperation with unions. In ODS, on the other hand, there was a lot of tension around its refusal to cooperate with unions and non-mainstream leftist parties—most of which was played out during the GAs where the proposals for cooperation with the Trotskyist Socialist Workers Party (SWP) and the Dublin Council of Trade Unions were discussed. In the end, both of the proposals were blocked since the people who blocked it felt that there was a risk that ODS would be used as 'a power towards something else and a power for good but only if it was within [the party's] doctrine' (7 May 2012 interview). The fantasy that was behind the idea of cooperation is captured beautifully by this ODS participant:

> We were doing something new. There was no naivety about the philosophy behind it. There may be naivety about the practicalities of it. [People from political parties] weren't arguing on those points. They were arguing about—we need to be associated with the unions, we need to be associated with parties. We're all one big happy family. But myself and L and several other people were aware that in anti-war groups and other groups in the past, political parties tried to control them ... And we didn't agree with them. (7 May 2012 interview)

There was a danger that ODS would serve as a tool for applying the SWP's narratives about anti-capitalist resistance, and that the diversity that that movement was trying to cultivate and cherish would be subsumed under the party's strategies of increasing its own membership and influence, and its hierarchical ways of organising. Some have criticised ODS' refusal to cooperate with particular leftist groups such as the SWP.[2] Critics point out that by blocking proposals to work alongside leftist groups, ODS lost an opportunity to engage in 'inter-sectoral efforts'. Such a stance is often portrayed as being motivated by attempts to preserve the supposed 'purity' of the movement, usually by a small, camp-centric, closed-in group of Occupiers (Kiersey, 2014; Sheehan, 2012). This critique is limited, both because it is factually inaccurate with respect to claims about a small minority holding back cooperation with the SWP and because it substantially misinterprets the reasons for scepticism within the camps.

Reflection on the reasons for the refusal to cooperate with the SWP, for example, should not rest at the inferential level: 'ODS thought parties were bad. SWP is a party, therefore ODS must have thought the SWP was bad.' What is lost in such an analysis are the substantive debates and processes that were going on around that issue in ODS. It was not only important that the SWP was a political party; other considerations concerned who presented the proposal to cooperate with them at the GA, in what way that happened, what arguments were put forward in favour and against that cooperation, and so forth. Finally, throughout the occupation, Occupy's participants also developed a meaning of what the SWP represented or could be associated with. These processes of meaning-making were partially driven by Occupy's anti-hierarchical ethos, but also developed through live interactions with members of the SWP during GAs. Through these interactions, the SWP came to be associated with a confrontational debating style as well as with highly controlled and very specific forms of organising, where the imperative to increase party membership drove all strategising. This contrasted sharply with ODS' consensus-based deliberation processes and its autonomous tendencies which emphasised the space for a diversity of tactics. Instead of becoming associated with any political entity (or believing that Occupy was enough to effect real social change in Ireland, for that matter), ODS' participants often voiced their encouragement for all groups (including political parties) to independently organise and strive for social change in the way they themselves consider appropriate.

It is then not surprising that, for the Occupiers, there was not an easy compatibility between the SWP and ODS. By refusing to cooperate with the SWP,[3] however, ODS might have actually acted in defence of responsibility because it prevented 'unity from closing upon itself'. This is because 'separation, dissociation [should not be] an obstacle to society, to community, but the condition ... Dissociation, separation, is the condition of my relation to the other ... That is not an obstacle but the condition of love, of friendship, and of war, too' (Derrida in Caputo, 1997, p. 14). Far from poor strategising, then, this refusal to be associated with any established political entity meant that the movement took responsibility for what it was and recognised itself as only one way of struggling for social change.

This separation from the dominant structures of power, emphasis on new creations, and taking responsibility for one's position within a broader political and social context are part of a political act because they change one's place with respect to the Other as language. These processes go in parallel with a repositioning with respect to the Other as desire. First, after freeing oneself from a fixated dependence on the dominant Symbolic structures, people's desire is liberated and enters the movement of signifiers in which it becomes more fleeting. As Lacan puts it, a subject can enter the realm of his/her drive which is a pursuit of enjoyment that exists separately from the Symbolic reality and takes shape in the Real (Hoedemaekers, 2008; Lacan, 1998). I take him to mean that in the context of subjects' drive, we are encouraged to experiment, create, innovate, and constantly circle round the place of a remainder left behind by the imposition of any Symbolic structure. What is transgressive in the notion of *objet petit a* (object little-a)—the name that Lacan gives to this leftover—is that he posits this structural remainder as the cause of the subject's desire. In a political act, innovation and change are then directed towards that which is excluded from the dominant structures of power. Similarly in Occupy, its participants experimented with various forms of organisation in order to establish a new type of social relationship that would respond to the needs and desires of the 99%. The 99% in this case was the leftover of the current Western liberal democratic models that offer formal but not substantial inclusion and participation in the state's political processes for a vast majority of its citizens.

Decisions and the Violence of Law

Although the subject is always already thrown into the Symbolic order and its fantasy, in a political act, it has to 'presuppose [itself] as the one who *posited* it' (Žižek, 2006, pp. 243–244). It has to assume responsibility as if it created this order and set it in motion. This is an unlimited responsibility and an important dimension of a political act because it points to the 'beyond' of current political arrangements, deconstructing their 'originary violence' and establishing undecidability as the condition of all decisions that achieve the impossible. By taking responsibility for creating a system that one starts seeing as unfair, one is also prompted to deconstruct the reasons why 'things went wrong'. This helps uncover moments, decisions, or actions, the assumptions of which turned out to favour a particular view or group and exclude other views or groups. This is the moment when 'originary violence' was committed. At the same time, however, as striving to remedy that violence, a political act does recognise the fact that all meaningful decisions (that radically change the ways of social and political organising) are subject to such violence. This is because they are made under the conditions of undecidability—where there are no established directives as to what decision to make and the choice is riddled with contradictory demands. As Derrida says, awareness of undecidability ensures that we 'avoid good conscience at all costs' (1993, p. 19).

Political reality and politics are constituted at the level of the Symbolic. A political act, however, connects with the Real, that is 'the political' (see, e.g. Mouffe, 2005; Schmitt, 2008). The act taps into the necessary alterity of society when there is a disconnect between the social lives of its members and the dominant socio-political structures. This helps explain why Occupy participants often appealed to something that is more just than the law or more democratic than the democracy that they had. In Occupy discourse, many were framing this in terms of people waking up to something that was more real than the reality in which they had been living (see, e.g. Flank, 2011).

The police and municipalities' handling of Occupy in the USA revealed two important aspects of law and the authorities' relation to it. First, they were quite hypocritical in applying the existing regulations. Mayor Bloomberg's statement on clearing the Zuccotti Park in New York assumed the priority of public's right to 'passive recreation' in the park over protesters' right to free speech and assembly. He claimed to be protecting citizens' First Amendment rights by evicting the Occupy camp from the park and prohibiting protesters from exercising the First Amendment because, as the Mayor saw it, it was about 'liv[ing] outside the law' (Office of the Mayor, 2011). Mayor Quan in Oakland followed suit and evicted the encampment because of 'safety reasons'. Revealed documents show the cooperation against Occupy at the level of the FBI, Homeland Security Department, and local police. They also expose the role of the Domestic Security Alliance Council that is a curious fusion of the above with private-sector actors ('FBI Documents', 2012).

Another aspect of law to which Occupy pointed was that the existing regulations (or their particular interpretations by the authorities) turned out to be unjust and undemocratic because they did not serve the needs and interests of the 99%. Hence, protesters felt they had to break the law in order to be true to democracy and justice itself. The involvement of individual US marines and war veterans, such as Scott Olsen who was shot by the police in Occupy Oakland, was also important in fostering this sense of righteousness.

The state, then, appealed to law and employed its enforcement mechanisms in order to uphold the status quo. The protesters, on the other hand, often appealed to the same law (like the First Amendment) but in an attempt to open it up for an interpretation (or change) that would respond to the demands of a society and economy in crisis. The authorities also chose to close the space for protest even further by limiting the scope for action that would constitute a lawful protest. In the midst of Occupy Oakland, for example, the City Council proposed (and later passed) a law banning the use of 'tools of violence' during protests. These could mean such items as hammers and knives, but also water bottles or tripods for cameras. This legislative proposal proved that it was very easy for those in power to make any form of dissent legal or illegal. This also illustrates how there is an originary violence at the core of all power structures—a *coup de force* that haunts them. It 'implies that right will never quite be entirely right, but always opened up by this movement of violence at its foundation' (Bennington & Derrida, 1999, p. 204). This 'violence at its foundation' is at the same time regrettable and paradoxically is that which allows change because it supplies movements with real reasons for challenging dominant structures of power.

When the violent foundations of these dominant structures are deconstructed, the undecidability that conditions all political acts is exposed. Past undecidability is considered as violence while present undecidability constitutes a positive condition for a political act. It is also often experienced as a necessity, something that 'we can no longer wait for'. In the context of grand social change, decision that merits real responsibility cannot be made when it is dictated by knowledge about calculable consequences or deployed automatically following a pre-determined plan (Derrida, 2005). As Derrida puts it:

> Between knowledge and decision, a leap is required, even if it is necessary to know as much and as well as possible before deciding. But if [the] decision is not only under the authority of my knowledge but also *in my power* ... , if it is only the predicate of what I am and can be, I don't decide either. (Derrida & Roudinesco, 2004, p. 53)

Occupy and Its Challenges

Challenges of Non-hierarchical Organising

The Occupy movement came about unintentionally. This is not to say that it was simply a spontaneous outburst of repressed hyperpoliticisation. Occupy would not have happened, nor have taken on its particular form, if it had not been for the immense organisational effort of its participants. The movement put in place some very elaborate structures and processes in order to remain non-hierarchical. The two immediate concerns that were raised in this context were: first, do we as participants know how to organise to effect social change? And second, do we have to have an alternative plan for a world 'after Occupy'?

Regarding the former, the fact that informal hierarchies arose despite an explicit desire to avoid hierarchy was highlighted by all of my interviewees. These hierarchies were usually experience-based (Deseriis & Dean, 2011), which meant that the more work a person was able to commit to Occupy, or the longer they have been camping out, the more their voice was respected. As this member of Occupy Oakland told me:

> There were certainly prominent voices at the GA—folks who you could tell that when they spoke that it meant more. I think there is something really subtle about the way it worked cause it wasn't like there was some official recognition of these opinions ... [I]f somebody who nobody knew came in and was like: 'hey, I want to occupy a building tomorrow', everybody would be like: 'yeah, right'. Whereas if the more established folks came and said: 'all right, this is what we're doing tomorrow', everybody would be like: 'OK, I got it. I'll adjust my schedule to make sure to be there.' ... And part of it is that certain folks have a reputation for getting things done. (20 June 2012 interview B)

The issue with informal hierarchies, however, was paradoxical. On the one hand, the challenge was that there were hidden hierarchies between members. On the other—that there was a negative fetishisation of hierarchy. The Occupiers did not want hierarchies and at the same time, they did want them (13 October 2012 notes).

Certainly, part of this inconsistency can be explained by different political persuasions of the participants. Some seemed to be fully committed to anti-hierarchical ways of organising, while others regarded hierarchies as strategically necessary. However, it was overwhelmingly the people who were committed to the non-hierarchical ethos that also to some extent accepted certain power structures:

> [W]e're all about direct democracy but in fact, you quickly realise that there is like a hidden power structure. You know, I knew that there was a hidden power structure but I wasn't all that sore about it exactly cause I kinda understood that there is larger things. (19 June 2012 interview B)

This member of Occupy Oakland accepted certain hierarchies because he thought there were other things that the movement wanted to achieve, so Occupy would not be harmed by temporarily turning a blind eye to these power imbalances. However, not everybody wanted to agree with this logic. As one Occupier from Cork said: '[People would] be saying that we have this space outside of capitalism ... and yet this stuff is still happening. So people just ... assumed that because it was stated and ... [because] you wanted it to be different, that it was' (5 March 2013 interview). There was then a real gap between the ethos and explicit organisational structures of the movement on the one hand, and how things worked in reality on the other.

People responded differently to this gap. Some accepted it and recognised how difficult it was in practice to organise in non-hierarchical ways. They also became aware that they did not really know how to organise this unusual form of protest (5 March 2013 interview). Others, however, wanted to move past focusing on this non-ideal embodiment of direct democracy and work out a plan for a grand social change. One of the participants wrote after the 100th day of ODS:

> [ODS] needs to be able to articulate a clear and coherent vision of an alternative to our deeply unequal and unjust society, or risk being left behind in the wake of those who can ... #OccupyDameStreet has spent three months establishing its voice, now it needs to start using it. (Johnson, 2012)

Others were concerned that this refusal to lay out a plan for change would make Occupy irrelevant. Klein (2012) said, for example: 'to make things better, there has to be a positive demand ... My worry is that ... the movement risks defining itself by what it is not, rather than what it is or, more importantly, might become'. Another challenge of focusing on non-hierarchical organising was then that there was always pressure on affecting a temporal closure that would give a definite aim to our struggles.

Part of the reason why it was so difficult to agree on a positive programme was the movement's emphasis on collective, non-hierarchical decision-making, which made making grand and sweeping demands and programmes difficult to agree on. Some have suggested that the refusal to formulate demands was not a strategic choice but reflected Occupy's organisational deadlock (Deseriis & Dean, 2011). This is only partially true, as some of the Occupies such as in Dublin, Cork, and Chicago did agree on a set of demands. However, the issue of demands has to be distinguished from the calls for a plan for effecting change on a grand scale. ODS, for example, had four demands; so while it *was* possible for various Occupies to agree on demands, the movement was far from proposing a grand plan for how to get what they demanded.

In summary, the challenges of non-hierarchical organising brought to light the gap between Occupy's ethos and the workings of its organisational structures in reality. The issue with informal hierarchies, however, was complicated because participants' assessment of the impact of those hierarchies on the movement did not automatically reflect their political persuasions. The challenges with non-hierarchical organising also revealed tensions that Occupy members experienced between the movement's refusal to formulate a plan for a grand social change on the one hand, and pressures to be more specific on how to get what the movement demanded on the other.

The 99%—the Vicissitudes of Radical Inclusion

The 'we are the 99%' slogan that Occupy adopted originated as a statement of vast inequalities in the US society. Subsequently, the 99-1% division began to signify a call for democratic control over the political process by the overwhelming majority in societies that have witnessed the increasing influence of money on politics. It also expressed the movement's intention to be radically inclusive.

It soon became apparent, however, that it is very difficult to live up to this associational metaphor. Some of the challenges were anti-social behaviour, problems with alcohol, personality clashes, dominance of men, security, and the lack of analysis of what the 99% actually meant (13 October 2012 notes). If persuasion failed, one strategy was exclusion. In ODS, for example, one male member was asked to leave the camp after he was accused of harassment. Other cases that were discussed concerned persons who were under the age of 18, were repeatedly anti-social, or had a past in organisations displaying fascist ideals. When it started, Occupy did not have any rules for excluding any of its participants. Soon, however, safer space policies were drawn up in many Occupies. Safer space policies recognised different forms of oppression from which people suffer. In ODS, they also asked that people's emotional and physical boundaries be respected and underscored mutual responsibility for maintaining the camp as a 'platform for political discussion and organisation for everyone—everyone should feel they have a right to participate' (16 November 2011 notes).

Obviously, the policy was more like a statement of principles, but since it was adopted by consensus, it provided an explicit tool for flagging anti-social or discriminatory behaviour as unacceptable. Paradoxically then, it established limits to inclusion in order to keep Occupy as inclusive as possible, even if that meant excluding some of the 99%.

Disagreements about the imperial connotations of the word 'occupy' exemplify another dimension of the inclusion/exclusion conundrum. In November 2011, a proposal was put forward to change the name of Occupy to Decolonize Oakland in recognition of the rights of the indigenous people. Since the movement invited people who were experiencing all forms of oppression, adopting a name that was so insensitive to this particular type of domination seemed highly inappropriate. The proposal did not pass the supermajority vote in the GA but the results still show that there was huge support for the name change (Oakland had a 90% threshold and the proposal gained 68.5% of votes). Nevertheless after the Assembly many accusations of racism were thrown at the camp.

At the core of this dispute was the question of how much can a name be a barrier to participation. As one member of the security group in Occupy Oakland told me, the entire debate felt like the 'Who's The Most Oppressed?' Games. The ones who proposed the name change did that from the position of racial and indigenous oppression, whereas others felt that the proposal was made from a position of privilege and high cultural capital. There was a feeling that people became too invested in the semantics (18 June 2012 interview) and that the proposal did not resonate with rank and file people of colour (27 June 2012 interview Ap3). This demonstrated that the unity of the 99% cannot simply be assumed but might need to be deliberately fostered. This, however, was far from a straightforward task.

Many GA attendees, for example, soon realised that the injunction to engage with every voice was deeply problematic. Since the movement was radically inclusive, it meant that decision-making was a long and laborious process where political views and personalities clashed frequently. It could be a chaotic space as this member of the facilitation committee in Oakland describes:

> [we did not know] how to cope with a situation where there is somebody just acting out and ... our default is to allow people to have their voice be heard so how do we do that in a way that's not subjecting everybody else to a whole bunch of stuff that they don't want to hear or see? ... I experienced a GA when somebody else was facilitating once, and they tried to be a little too responsive to the needs of the crowd and then the whole thing became just complete chaos ... So then it was just every step of the way, we'd have to stop and vote on something and at times we didn't even know what it was that we were voting on ... (25 June 2012 interview A)

In order for the decision-making process to remain at least somewhat operative and productive, it became understood among experienced facilitators that they should silence the voices that were abusive, and respectfully 'get over' the voices that were off topic, conspiracy theory, or mainstream. This was to protect the democratic debate and allow it to go forward instead of going off on a tangent and discouraging everybody from participating, which could lead to a quick dissipation of the movement and be an impediment to democracy itself. Hence and again paradoxically, some voices were cut off in order to sustain the democratic debate and the movement itself.

Occupy and Its Aporias

Democracy Is To-Come

The Occupy phenomenon was unintentional in that there was not any grand plan for a global wave of protest against representative democracy and financial capitalism prior to the emergence of this wave of which movement was a part. Nonetheless it involved immense human effort to organise it. Occupy claimed to be non-hierarchical, refused to make demands on the state, and articulated the needs of the 99% through a direct democratic process. The everyday reality of the movement was, however, more complex. Informal hierarchies soon arose. Moreover, there were many participants who urged the movement to develop a positive plan for social change. These were calls for effecting a kind of closure to the fluid deliberation and strategising processes in Occupy for the sake of entering the political process. The aporia that was endured in this case is one between ideal and non-ideal, closure, and openness.

The experience of the Irish and US Occupies shows that the terms in each of these binaries are contaminated by their opposite. The structure of decision is aporetic when people find themselves caught up in a binary set-up and try to 'act with equal justice to both sides' (Hurst, 2008, p. 325). Organising in non-hierarchical ways and remaining open to the diverse needs of the 99% by rejecting any blueprint for grand social change were two of the main characteristics of direct democracy. At the same time, they were seen as obstacles to the further development of the movement. Throughout its existence, Occupy negotiated between its uncompromising commitment to direct democracy and an understanding that obsessive fixation on its ideals could be harmful to the movement and perhaps lead it to subside altogether.

The movement, then, had to make decisions in the absence of any clear directives, in the face of a choice between interdependent options, and this is what made its actions political. The political act is the lived experience of enduring an aporia, not overcoming it or stopping at it (Derrida, 1993), but acting in the face of it. Enduring the aporia was possible because Occupy did not want to take over state power. It did not portray itself as the only way to social salvation. Instead temporalisation and an understanding that the political and social contexts are highly malleable and revisable were recipes for enduring the aporia between the ideal and non-ideal. The experience of an aporia accepts neither conformism nor utopianism but draws one's attention to the living temporalities of the movement, all that is excluded from the dominant systems, and the radical alterity of the other. It is like Derrida's democracy-to-come that is not simply a regulative idea, but an urgent task that people inherit as a promise. It is worthwhile to quote Derrida at some length here:

> It would be too easy to show that, measured by the failure to establish liberal democracy, the gap between fact and ideal essence does not show up only in … so-called primitive forms of government, theocracy, and military dictatorship … But this failure … also characterize[s], *a priori*

and by definition, *all* democracies ... At stake here is the very concept of democracy as concept of a promise that can only arise in such a *diastema* (failure ..., being 'out of joint'). That is why we always propose to speak of a democracy *to come*, not of a *future* democracy in the future present ..., or of a utopia—at least to the extent that their inaccessibility would still retain the temporal form of a *future present* ... (2006, pp. 80–81)

It is only possible to know that there may be progressive political change (democracy-to-come) when the current system fails, revealing a disconnect between politics and social reality.

Democracy is to-come not because it is constantly failing to live up to a set ideal. It is to-come not because all it needs is a few adjustments that could easily be made through the channels that are either currently available or will be in a 'future present'—a little-perfected version of the current system in the future. Instead, democracy is to-come because it is open to a redefinition of the political system as a whole, to a political act that it cannot know of before it has happened. Hence, democracy's intrinsic relation to historicity that stems from its always aporetic structure that in the case of Occupy was exemplified in the paradoxes surrounding the questions of hierarchies and grand plans for social change. Democracy is a constant play between various sedimentations and a radical openness to the unforeseeable political acts. By making decisions in the face of this structure of play without settling for any of the two sides, Occupy acted in authentically political ways.

Real Democracy

Direct democratic processes and the realities of living in Occupy camps demonstrated that 'the 99%' is far from homogeneous. The injunction to include everyone soon became a challenge that was dealt with by careful exclusion or facilitation. This dimension of Occupy signifies the aporia between unity and singularity.

One of the biggest weaknesses of the movement's decision-making was that everyone could just show up and sway the vote (29 June 2012 interview). This was why ODS stuck to the 100% consensus rule so that other groups could not fundamentally change the nature of the movement (Flood, 2011a). Whatever the method: exclusion, skilful facilitation, etc., the participants were searching for ways in which Occupy would be democratic and yet radical and different. As this participant of Occupy Oakland put it: 'What do you really want—do you want everybody to agree or do you want this to be really interesting? If everybody participated, it might have been a lot more moderate' (20 June 2012 interview B). These kinds of dilemmas are characteristic of democracy. This is because it is impossible to speak of an 'authentic' democracy as its concept and practice are always contaminated by its opposite. As Derrida puts it: 'must a democracy leave free and in a position to exercise power those who risk mounting as assault on democratic freedoms and putting an end to democratic freedom in the name of democracy' (2005, p. 34). A society can either allow anti-democratic forces to seize power by democratic means or it may try to prevent it using undemocratic procedures (Patton, 2007). Similarly, direct democracy in Occupy could only be protected by ensuring that swaying the vote was virtually impossible. Even if the possibility of swaying the vote was only hypothetical, it points to the internal limit to all unity and symbolisation. In Lacanese, it points to the Real. The tensions between unity and singularity are central to democracy.

There is no democracy without respect for irreducible singularity or alterity, but there is no democracy ... without the calculation of majorities, without ... representable subjects, all equal. These two laws are irreducible one to the other ... political desire is forever borne by the disjunction of these two laws. (Derrida, 2000, p. 22)

It is important that Occupy faced the aporia between unity and singularity because it helped its participants dispel the fantasy that if it was not for the corrupted political system and greedy bankers, there would be some ideal union of all people. By practising direct democracy, the movement revealed the hidden underside of all concepts of democracy, highlighting and negotiating the essentially ambiguous nature of any and all judgements about what the content of democracy actually is.

All of those aspects of democracy were brought to light in a moment when there was a sudden crack in the dominant symbolic structures, when the movement was tapping into the disconnect between the system and its remainder. While occupying and trying to practise real democracy in the here and now, we cannot eliminate the possibility that it will be a messy and challenging endeavour with its own inconsistencies, deformations, and problems. This is exactly why I call it *real* democracy. Real democracy in this understanding does not merely signify 'substantive' as opposed to the void liberal representational form of democracy. Instead of idealistic or pragmatic content, real democracy in my usage affirms various inconsistencies and uncertainties that are revealed through people's lived experience. It also points to the messiness, temporality, and singularity where others would see or wish for unity.

Tomorrow, It's Back to the Streets—Again and Again?

As the Occupy experience demonstrates, the above aporias do not signify a stalemate that paralysed the movement. Rather, they mark a limit through which that part of reality that is excluded from the dominant symbolic construction announces itself in an affirmative fashion (Raffoul, 2010). This is also the mode of what I have come to call real politics. Real politics connects to the Real of the political sphere, that is, the political. It entails acceptance of its constitutive lack, antagonism, and alterity. There are two ways of conceiving of the lack that drives movement action. One is that it keeps disturbing the dominant socio-political structures because any finite system cannot master the infinite empirical richness of social relations. The other understanding of this lack, and one that Derrida and Lacan are more interested in, is that it re-emerges as a reminder that subjects are always already operating within a field that excludes totalisation (there is already an exclusion at the basis of the structures we are born into). The subjects are also always already alienated—by their immersion in the dominant discourses, power balances, and in the structure of language itself. Lack is not a derivative of the infinite richness of social life because there is no centre that would be outside of it to attest to this richness before the lack actually emerges (Derrida, 2001).

Lack re-emerges every time social structures are about to become destabilised and dislocated. Lack, then, facilitates social change. If this re-emergence is inevitable, what does it mean for people's future political engagement? Does it mean that taking to the streets to enforce radical change will remain not only a prevailing social phenomenon, but also the only way to enact real transformation? In other words, does that mean that tomorrow it is back to the streets again ... and again?

A logical conclusion would be to put the above sentence in the affirmative and assume the inevitable re-emergence of lack and subsequently, a new system of social relations that claims full representation and institutes a new order of subjection. However, the analysis of the aporias that is performed from a place of an embedded subject makes one appreciate the fact that social change does not happen automatically but requires immense human effort. This is why I would like to pose that sentence as a question. Does the experience of Occupy help to answer it?

Occupy in Ireland and the USA very clearly challenged the dominant economic and political system in its entirety. The system has lost its self-evidence to the extent that its critiques are now formulated by mainstream politicians such as Barroso or President Higgins in Ireland, and indeed even the Pope. What used to be the mantras of embittered ideologues whispered in meetings of radicals are now common understandings. Occupy also aimed to provide a palpable experience of an alternative as practised through participatory democratic processes. However, we still do not know whether direct democracy or a different form of institutionalising real politics can become an actual alternative to representative democracy. To what degree may it actually be universalised? Or is direct democracy only a mirage of self-transparent and non-alienated decision-making that cannot exist as such? As a way of answering and, at the same time, leaving the issue unresolved, I would only note that in reality, participatory democracy is not a non-alienated and self-transparent form of making decisions. Where does that leave one with respect to the opening that Occupy has imposed on its participants? Perhaps there are already answers to this question but we have not yet come up with appropriate realities and categories to make sense of them.

Acknowledgements

I would like to thank all Occupy participants who shared their stories with me. This work would have never been possible without your unending generosity and kindness. A special note of thanks to Dr Laurence Cox, Dr Eamonn Slater, and the Editor Chris Rossdale for their comments on the original draft of this paper. This work was supported by Maynooth University through the Doctoral Teaching Scholarship.

Notes

1　In this article, I use 'rules of the day' as a shorthand for the currently hegemonic set of social, legal, and cultural rules and norms that guide people's behaviour.
2　However, ODS did cooperate quite successfully with community groups, such as around the Spectacle of Defiance and Hope—an annual demonstration of the Community, Youth and Voluntary sector in Ireland.
3　ODS refused to cooperate with the SWP as a political entity but in principle, Occupy participants were not against cooperation with SWP members, provided that they left their political affiliation at the door.

References

Bennington, G., & Derrida, J. (1999). *Jacques Derrida.* Chicago, IL: University of Chicago Press.
Caputo, J. D. (Ed.). (1997). *Deconstruction in a nutshell: A conversation with Jacques Derrida.* New York, NY: Fordham University Press.
Derrida, J. (1993). *Aporias: Dying-awaiting (one another at) the 'limits of truth'* (T. Dutoit, Trans.). Stanford, CA: Stanford University Press.
Derrida, J. (2000). *The politics of friendship* (G. Collins, Trans.). London: Verso.
Derrida, J. (2001). *Writing and difference* (A. Bass, Trans.). London: Routledge Classics.
Derrida, J. (2005). *Rogues: Two essays on reason* (P.-A. Brault & M. Nass, Trans.). Stanford, CA: Stanford University Press.
Derrida, J. (2006). *Specters of Marx: The state of the debt, the work of mourning and the new international.* New York: Routledge.
Derrida, J., & Roudinesco, E. (2004). *For what tomorrow: A dialogue* (J. Fort, Trans.). Stanford, CA: Stanford University Press.
Deseriis, M., & Dean, J. (2011, December). Occupy Wall Street: Marco Deseriis in conversation with Jodi Dean. *Arena.* Retrieved January 31, 2012, from http://www.arena.org.au/2011/12/occupy-wall-street/

OCCUPYING SUBJECTIVITY

Fals-Borda, O. (1991). Some basic ingredients. In O. Fals-Borda & M. A. Rahman (Eds.), *Action and knowledge: Breaking the monopoly with participatory action research* (pp. 3–12). New York, NY: The Apex Press.

FBI Documents Reveal Secret Nationwide Occupy Monitoring. (2012, December 22). Partnership for civil justice fund. Retrieved February 7, 2013, from http://www.justiceonline.org/commentary/fbi-files-ows.html

Fink, B. (1995). *The Lacanian subject: Between language and jouissance.* Princeton, NJ: Princeton University Press.

Flank, L. (Ed.). (2011). *Voices from the 99 percent: An oral history of the Occupy Wall Street movement.* St Petersburg, FL: Red and Black.

Flood, A. (2011a, November 7). Occupy & democratic decision making—consensus v majority—SWP v ODS. *Anarchist Writers.* Retrieved November 17, 2013, from http://anarchism.pageabode.com/andrewnflood/democratic-decision-making-consensus-occupy

Flood, A. (2011b, November 10). *Occupy—the assembly process is the revolution.* Workers Solidarity Movement. Retrieved October 24, 2013, from http://www.wsm.ie/c/occupy-movement-assembly-process-revolution

Flood, A. (2011c, November 18). A fork in the road for Occupy Dame Street? *Anarchist Writers.* Retrieved October 24, 2013, from http://anarchism.pageabode.com/andrewnflood/fork-road-occupy-dame-street

Glynos, J., & Stavrakakis, Y. (2008). Lacan and political subjectivity: Fantasy and enjoyment in psychoanalysis and political theory. *Subjectivity: International Journal of Critical Psychology, 24*(1), 256–274. doi:10.1057/sub.2008.23

Hedges, C. (2011, October 8). This rebellion will not stop. *The Occupied Wall Street Journal,* p. 1.

Hoedemaekers, C. (2008, January 10). *Performance, pinned down: A Lacanian analysis of subjectivity at work.* Erasmus University Rotterdam. Retrieved from http://www.erim.eur.nl/doctoral-programme/phd-in-management/phd-projects/detail/181-performance_pinned_down_a_lacanian_analysis_of_subjectivity_at_work/

Hurst, A. (2008). *Derrida vis-à-vis Lacan: Interweaving deconstruction and psychoanalysis.* New York, NY: Fordham University Press.

Johnson, D. (2012, January 17). Occupy Dame Street: The first 100 days. *Politico.ie.* Retrieved April 5, 2012, from http://politico.ie/social-issues/8207-occupydamestreet-the-first-100-days.html

Juris, J. S. (2008). *Networking futures: The movements against corporate globalization.* Durham: Duke University Press Books.

Kiersey, N. (2014). Occupy Dame Street as slow-motion general strike? Justifying optimism in the wake of Ireland's failed multitudinal moment. *Global Discourse, 4*(2–3), 141–158. doi:10.1080/23269995.2014.898530

Klein, N. (2012, January 9). Why now? What's next? Naomi Klein and Yotam Marom in conversation about Occupy Wall Street. *The Nation.* Retrieved from http://www.thenation.com/article/165530/why-now-whats-next-naomi-klein-and-yotam-marom-conversation-about-occupy-wall-street

Lacan, J. (1998). *The four fundamental concepts of psychoanalysis* (A. Sheridan, Trans., J.-A. Miller, Ed.). New York, NY: W. W. Norton.

Lacan, J. (n.d.). *The seminar of Jacques Lacan: Logic of phantasy* (Book XIV) (C. Gallagher, Trans.). Jacques Lacan in Ireland. Retrieved November 21, 2013, from http://www.lacaninireland.com/web/wp-content/uploads/2010/06/14-Logic-of-Phantasy-Complete.pdf

McIntyre, A. (2008). *Participatory action research.* London: Sage.

Mouffe, C. (2005). *On the political.* London: Routledge.

Office of the Mayor. (2011, November 15). *Statement of Mayor Michael R. Bloomberg on clearing and re-opening of Zuccotti Park.* Office of the Mayor. Retrieved from http://www.nyc.gov/portal/site/nycgov/menuitem.c0935b9a57bb4ef3daf2f1c701c789a0/index.jsp?pageID=mayor_press_release&catID=1194&doc_name=http%3A%2F%2Fwww.nyc.gov%2Fhtml%2Fom%2Fhtml%2F2011b%2Fpr410–11.html&cc=unused1978&rc=1194&ndi=1

Patton, P. (2007). Derrida, politics and democracy to come. *Philosophy Compass, 2*(6), 766–780. doi:10.1111/j.1747–9991.2007.00098.x

Raffoul, F. (2010). *The origins of responsibility.* Bloomington: Indiana University Press.

Schmitt, C. (2008). *The concept of the political: Expanded edition.* Chicago, IL: University of Chicago Press.

Sheehan, H. (2012, January 19). Occupying Dublin: Considerations at the crossroads. *Irish Left Review.* Retrieved April 5, 2012, from http://www.irishleftreview.org/2012/01/19/occupying-dublin-considerations-crossroads/

Stavrakakis, Y. (1999). *Lacan and the political.* London: Routledge.

Stavrakakis, Y. (2007). *The Lacanian left: Psychoanalysis, theory, politics.* Edinburgh: Edinburgh University Press.

Taylor, A., Gessen, K., editors from n+1, Dissent, Triple Canopy, & The New Inquiry (Eds.). (2011). *Occupy! Scenes from occupied America.* London: Verso.

Van Gelder, S. (2011). *This changes everything: Occupy Wall Street and the 99% movement.* San Francisco, CA: Berrett-Koehler.

Žižek, S. (2006). *The parallax view.* Cambridge, MA: The MIT Press.

Žižek, S. (2007). *How to read Lacan.* New York, NY: W.W. Norton.

The Political Subject of Self-immolation

NICHOLAS MICHELSEN

King's College London, London, UK

ABSTRACT   *This article examines the political practice of protest by self-burning. Focussing on Mohammed Bouazizi's self-burning in the Tunisian town of Sidi Bouzid in 2010, I explore the intellectual background for, and implications of, conceptualising such acts as 'self-sacrifices' or 'self-immolations'. I argue that the use of the concept of sacrifice to define the politics of the act, given the difficulties in determining intentionality, is to focus only on its retrospective interpretation or semiotic capture. The result is that the self-annihilating subject is bypassed altogether, and his or her distinctively suicidal politicality is ignored. I argue that these subjects do not occupy political space due to a myth-making appeal to transcendence, heroic urge to sovereignty or assumed desire for community. Rather, drawing on Walter Benjamin, I argue that in such acts we bear witness to the shattering of sovereign order by a reminder to a politically constitutive excess.*

Introduction

The desire to inoculate politics from commitments that reach all the way to death is central to modern historicism. As Toscano (2010) has noted, naming a subject 'fanatic' constitutes the definitive act of distancing in this tradition. The 'refusal of compromise and seemingly boundless drive to the universal' implicit to the pursuit of a project up to the point of willing self-destruction is seen to personify the un-reasoning and un-enlightened subject (Toscano, 2010, pp. xii, 43). 'Fanatical' subjects are both 'anti and ultra' historical; embodying the threat of modernisation's interruption due to their adoption of sacralised criterion for political action, and 'a sign that cultural and political advance, under the banner of secularism . . . is not yet complete' (Toscano, 2010, p. 43).[1] Willing self-destruction exposes a political practice as tainted by pre-modern religiosity. What is successfully precluded under the idea of fanaticism is therefore any possibility that 'some unconditional and unyielding abstract passion . . . [is] intrinsic to a universalising rationality and emancipatory politics', and that excessive commitment to a project up to the point of violent self-destruction may emerge in the pursuit of 'expansive' as well as 'exclusionary' political projects (Toscano, 2010, p. 251).[2]

Benjamin, in his seminal *Critique of violence* (1986), argued that all sovereign juridico-political formations find their origin in such a moment of what he called 'divine' excess, which authorises itself as a precondition for subsequent sacralisation under a cycle of myth. Politics is thus not simply a matter of the narrative formation of affective communities, defending territories of identity or seeking ontological security under a sovereign semiosis, it constitutively includes a violence that marks the foundationlessness of all such projects. All sovereign political orders thus remain vulnerable to an originary anarchic violence that would expose the foundations of that order as literally mythical. Such a violence is originary, Benjamin (1986, p. 292) implied, only inasmuch as it eludes semiosis and refuses any instrumental justifications of ends or means. Its politicality *is* violence; it momentarily breaks with, and so negates, the cycle of myth that underpins any and all claims to sovereignty.

I argue in the following article that it is precisely this *non-sovereign politicality* that is in question in protest self-burnings and similar acts of self-destructive political violence. I develop a reading of Mohammed Bouazizi, who set himself alight in the Tunisian town of Sidi Bouzid in 2010, to excavate the analytic value of a Benjaminian concept of *political suicide* in this context. I illustrate the importance of recognising the *suicidal politicality* of such acts by exposing the analytical limits of recent characterisations of such events as 'political sacrifices'. The concept of 'a sacrifice' or 'immolation' is mobilised by a number of authors (see Andriolo, 2006; Craig, 2012; Giddens, 1971; Houen, 2010; Park, 2004; Sweeney, 1993; Uehling, 2000), but most recently, systematically and coherently by Fierke (2013), to critically interpret the subject of self-destructive political acts, risks providing support for a modernist distancing strategy akin to that described by Toscano (2010). Fierke (2013, pp. 2, 34, 52) argues that 'the suicide' has no place in political space, whereas 'the self-sacrifice' is suggestive of politics inasmuch as semiotic contestation around such acts allows for the restoration of the sovereignty of a repressed community. By ignoring the immanent politicality of the subject that self-annihilates and focussing only on their relationship to a transcendent (if liminal) semiosis, Fierke (2013) averts her eyes from these acts' disturbing rupture with any and all sovereign political projects.

The article begins by introducing the political practice of self-burning in protest, culminating in a detailed account of the self-burning of Bouazizi in 2010. The following section examines the claim that self-destructive subjects are political only inasmuch as they can be interpreted as making sacrificial offerings or immolations. I then critically examine the determinant focus on the *intentions* or *mythic consequences* of these acts in recent accounts. I argue that a focus on the mythic products of semiotic contestation surrounding the act of self-destruction risks occluding the self-annihilating political subject, as well as the contingency of his/her narrative and affective consequence, and thereby ignores the violent rupture with law and social order which opens the possibility space for a proliferation of signifiers and emotional identifications. Having challenged the sufficiency of a sacrificial definition along the lines of Fierke (2013), in the final section I develop a supplementary Benjaminian reading of the politicality of protest by self-burning. I conclude that to view individuals like Bouazizi as 'political subjects of self-immolation' occludes the politics of suicide that is the precondition for any retrospective sacralisation as a martyr.

Politics and Self-destruction

The historic and geographic range of self-destructive politics is striking testament to the enormity of the 'political problem of mortality' noted by Seery (1996). Where authors have grappled with contemporary acts of political self-destruction, focus has often been restricted to religious, and recently especially Islamic, genealogies (see Andriolo, 2002; Hoffman, 1995). Such theological frames reaffirm our 'modern' detachment from self-destructive subjects (Asad, 2007). Rapaport (1984, p. 660), for example, famously argued that self-destruction is peculiar to 'sacred' forms. Contrasting with the utilitarian character of political terrorism, the 'transcendent source of holy terror' ensures aims and means are set in advance, resulting in a far 'lower premium on the assailant's risk'. This clearly has not precluded the use of suicidal-like methods by secular groups.[3] The classical modernist response is that transcendent ideals also orientate these secular political ideologies (Berman, 2004; Eagleton, 2005; Laqueur, 2003). In this sense, an appeal to some framework of transcendent meaning is always necessary to make self-destruction possible. The totalitarian nationalist states of the twentieth century are generally taken as defining examples in this context. Munich's tomb of the martyrs, or the Yasukuni Shrine in Tokyo, architecturally embodied the transcendent glorification of heroic death for nation, blood, and fatherland.[4] Willingness to die for the nation-state is deemed self-evident proof of the atavistic character of such acts (see Berman, 2004), and any continuing currency today simply suggests that we are perhaps not so 'modern' after all (Asad, 2007; Barkawi, 2004).

That national politics has a structure in common with theology was most famously argued by Schmitt (1985, p. 36), but it was his contemporary, the political theologian Kantorowicz (1951, 1957), who developed most systematically the political genealogy of self-destruction in this context. Kantorowicz (1951, p. 473) charts the emergence of heroic death for one's country (*Pro Patria Mori*), 'within the political concepts of the medieval Christian world'. Kantorowicz maps the process by which, in the political discourse of Medieval Europe, death for the heavenly Jerusalem originally took precedence over earthly cities, whilst the *corpus mysticum* of Christianity came to be bound to the social body itself, and the idea of charity or *caritas* for which Christian martyrs died became identified with love of country or *amor patriae*. He argued that the secularisation of the sacrificial *corpus mysticum* allowed 'the state as an abstract notion or the state as a juristic person' to achieve 'a semi-religious or natural-religious exultation' (1951, p. 473). This suggests the fundamentally morbid roots of the sovereign nation-state as a sacred or ideal form constructed, at least in part, through acts of individual sacrifice.

As I have argued elsewhere, Kantorowicz's study does nothing to challenge the observation that, in an age of modern, Liberal or biopolitical rationality, the space for political self-destruction narrows to the point of disappearing, rendering such events the remnants of pre-modernity (Michelsen, 2013). Indeed, what Toscano (2012) refers to as Philosophy's 'Long Cold War' has rendered any subject willing to 'go to the edge', as the hunger striker Bobby Sands famously put it, *anti-modern* in precisely this sense (see Feldman, 1991). The willingness to take a project to its morbid limit has been symptomatic of movements seeking emancipation or radical social transformation, whether Communist, Fascist or Anarchist. The modern tradition views them all as expressions of a martyring political theology 'dealing out what God deals out, which is death' (Berman, 2004, p. 50).

Whether this modernist political–theological distancing provides us with sufficient tools for interpreting even explicitly religious murder–suicides today (like the Jihadi human-bomb) is highly debatable—with respect to the articulation of all self-destructive political practices it clearly lacks analytical sufficiency (see Michelsen, 2013). As Fierke (2013, p. 18) has cogently argued, it is always 'necessary to "look and see" how meaning is put to use, how different historical forms of argumentation and memory combine to constitute contextually specific forms of action and interaction'. Rendering all such events as the straightforward outputs of a ciphered theology is thus an exercise in the reduction of social and cultural complexity. Fierke's (2013) argument is that the politics of self-destructive acts reside in their (sacrificial) association with the affective construction of ideals of community, through interpretative contestation surrounding the act. This, I will argue below, retains ontological commitments that preclude a grasp of the political subject in question, despite the postpositivist approach, inasmuch as politics remains solely identified with the reach for a sovereign semiosis.

The political practice of self-burning in protest will be the central focus of this article, though the implications of the argument have bearing on related political practices like hunger-striking and suicide-bombing. There is broad agreement that the political practice of protest self-burning can be dated quite precisely from Thich Quang Duc's self-incineration in Vietnam in 1963. The majority of academic works dealing with protest by self-burning are in psychiatric journals, where a 'political' dimension is seen simply to distinguish it therapeutically from other suicides (Bhugra, 1991; Biggs, 2003; Crosby, Rhee, & Holland, 1976; Husni, Koye, Cernovsky, & Haggarty, 2002; Park, 2004). The printing of the image of Quang Duc's self-incineration in US broadsheets impacted powerfully upon US domestic support for the Diem regime, fostering imitators worldwide. Ten more Vietnamese monks followed Quang Duc's lead in the subsequent 2 years, alongside several Americans, including Norman Morrison—whose act McNamara credited in his autobiography as having transformed his and his family's opinions on the war (see King, 2000). The practice continued in Vietnam in 1966–1967, with a further 17 self-burnings, alongside 6 more Americans and a Russian (Biggs, 2003). 1969 witnessed the passage of the practice into Europe with Jan Palach's self-immolation, a largely impactless protest at the reversal of the Prague Spring reforms by the invasion of the Warsaw Pact (Suk, 2009; Treptow, 1992). Palach was followed by four self-burnings in Czechoslovakia, and sympathisers in Hungary and Scotland (Biggs, 2003). The 1970s saw its arrival in France, with six cases, and the decade witnessed its practice in the USA, Soviet Russia, and South Korea, where up to 100 leftists and Trade Union activists have self-burnt since the 1970s (Park, 2004). India has seen an even larger number of self-burnings in the last three decades, often in protest at political–economic conditions (Bhugra, 1991). Other notable groups of cases have been amongst Kurds outside and within Turkey, Romanians, Chinese, and Pakistanis (Biggs, 2008). Recent examples in Israel and Greece show self-burning enacted as a means of economic protest. A continuing campaign of self-incinerations by Tibetan Buddhist Monks protests Chinese rule and the erosion of Tibetan cultural and political–economic autonomy: since 2010 there have been a significant number, likely hundreds,[5] of such acts, in Tibet and India, conducted by male and female monks of various ages.

Inasmuch as a wide variety of ideologies, individual aims or collective projects underpin protest self-burnings, the act itself seems associated with diverse political *intentions*; much the same may be said of suicide-bombing or hunger-striking to death (see Gill, 2007; Pedazur, 2005). Equally remarkable is the variance in its apparent effects or political *consequences*. For example, Jan Palach's explicitly political public self-burning in Prague in 1969 had no real consequences beyond the domestic outpouring of grief and public contemplation, in sharp contrast with the international political consequences of Thich Quang Duc's act in Vietnam a year earlier (Suk, 2009). The ongoing Tibetan campaign of self-burning has received only muted coverage, in part due to the control of information flowing out of the region, which contrasts profoundly with the widely documented and apparently revolutionary connotations

OCCUPYING SUBJECTIVITY

popularly assigned to Mohammed Bouazizi's self-burning on 17 December 2010. Given the spectacular consequences associated with Bouazizi's act in various literatures, it is appropriate that this event be subjected to particular study. It appears to be the exemplary recent case of a political self-destruction, and as such constitutes a good case with which to illuminate the ontology of the subject (dis)embodied in such acts.

A young fruit seller from the town of Sidi Bouzid, Mohammed Bouazizi, following an altercation with the local authorities in which his scales or produce were confiscated on the ostensive grounds that he had no permit, and possibly after being physically slapped by a female police officer, went to local magistrate threatening to set himself alight (Schraeder & Redissi, 2011). Being there disregarded, he doused himself with petrol and self-immolated in front of the audience attracted by the commotion (Jacobson, 2011). The police officer accused of abusing Bouazizi was later cleared of wrongdoing, but interviews with family members assert that a highly masculinised sense of personal insult provided part of the, now likely forever opaque, reasons for the act (Amar, 2011; Jacobson, 2011). The intentions standing behind his self-incineration were undocumented, and so could play little role in determining its political consequences.

Indeed, it seems difficult to reach any definitive conclusions about causality. What we do know is that Bouazizi's self-burning became a rallying point for protests throughout the town, centring on poverty and widespread unemployment. As these protests increased in scale, the Ben Ali regime attempted to suppress them, blockading media reports, but aided by the publication and popularisation of Bouazizi's act on Facebook and in other social media, this resulted only in their exacerbation. Protests spread into neighbouring towns (Roy & Merlini, 2012; Schraeder & Redissi, 2011). Western media outlets describing the unfolding events also narrated Bouazizi's act as of central and founding importance. As the protests continued to increase in scale, Ben Ali had himself photographed with the now-dying Bouazizi. This clumsy attempt at retrieving command of the narration of events succeeded only in exacerbating collective opprobrium (Howard & Hussein, 2011; Jacobson, 2011; Schraeder & Redissi, 2011). Bouazizi's death on 4 January sparked nationwide protests. Lethal responses by the authorities were recorded on camera phones and disseminated. In the face of broadening revolt, a series of increasingly cowed speeches by Ben Ali in January culminated in a promise not to seek a sixth term on 13 January. To the chorus of popular rejection on 14 January, gently pushed by the military establishment, Ben Ali departed the country, crowning what was christened the *Jasmine Revolution* by media outlets.

This sudden collapse of an entrenched autocratic regime and security establishment was unanticipated. A spirit of revolutionary excitement spilled over borders, with protests emerging in neighbouring countries (Howard & Hussein, 2011). The collapse of the regime in Tunisia is thus seen as having given birth to what has been termed the Arab 'Spring', explicitly suggesting resonances with Prague 1968 (Dawisha, 1984; Kusin, 1971; Williams, 1997). Revolutionary upheavals swept the region, taking in Libya, Egypt, Yemen, Bahrain, and Syria. Tunisia becomes 'case zero' in an international series, and Bouazizi's act the point of initiation (Schraeder & Redissi, 2011). Commemoration of Bouazizi's act has thus bound him indelibly to the subsequent international events,[6] but it is critical to recognise that Bouazizi himself declared no ideological aims whatsoever. Bouazizi's voice is absent from the signifying regimes that defined the subsequent revolts.[7] It is for this reason that Fierke (2013, p. 220) argues that 'it is less the intentions of Bouazizi, than the effect of his act, and how it was given meaning, that are of interest'. What is critical, Fierke (2013) argues, is that a sacrificial connotation *was assigned to Bouazizi's act* by others, which is what allowed him to unintentionally give birth to an emergent revolutionary condition in the region. The political content of Bouazizi's act was formed through processes of semiotic contestation and capture after the fact.

The Political Subject of Self-immolation

It is widely assumed that only the subsequent assignment of a sacrificial connotation can supply political meaning to self-destructive acts. One indication of this is that self-burning in protest, along with hunger-striking and suicide-bombing, is often referred to as self-immolation (Sweeney, 1993). The term self-immolation is derived from the Latin stem *immolāre*, to sprinkle with sacrificial meal. To immolate is to offer up a sacrifice, with immolation traditionally referring to the slaughter of a sanctified victim. As such, immolation connoted mass or communion before any reference to a 'devotion' to destruction (Simpson & Weiner, 1989). Its most common association today, however, is with fire. The assumption that this term is a fair indication of the meaning of these political subjects draws from a broad tradition of anthropological and sociological research, which stands behind recent work. This section examines the political subject of self-immolation, investigating how the concept of sacrifice allows us to make sense of Bouazizi and other self-burners as political.

As a forceful demonstration of *strength of feeling* about a particular political issue, self-immolation is sometimes interpreted as the direct expression of an experience of suffering (Craig, 2012). The finality of the act clearly directs attention to the embeddedness of the actor in structures outside his or her control (Sarraj & Butler, 2002). Indeed, Crosby et al. argue that self-immolators should be understood in psychological terms as 'bearers' or 'expressers' of a structurally produced 'group desire' (1976, p. 65). Historical clusters of self-immolations are 'epidemics' of behaviour emerging when times are particularly 'unsettled'. We are, therefore, not really talking about political subjects, but a socio-psychological contagion of sorts (Bloom, 2005). This is suggestive of the work of Durkheim et al. (1970), for whom acts of self-immolation may be neatly packaged under the category *altruistic suicide*, who are 'mechanically compelled by society, or the group, to end their lives, with little or no individual will involved', as when an old person commits suicide to avoid 'becoming a burden' on his or her family (Park, 2004). Giddens (1971), reading Durkheim, suggested we might distinguish a unique form of *sacrificial subjectivity* or agency in this context. Where Durkheim's model assumes a mechanical lack of agency on the part of the self-immolator, a conscious intention to further a cause on behalf of others often seems significant in such events. Terming these acts 'sacrifices' allows an 'expansion' of Durkheim's category to articulate the peculiar quality of *consciously choosing* to die *on behalf of* others for a political cause (Park, 2004). This is a straightforward connotation of the term immolation or sacrifice. Framing the act as a sacrificial offering indicates that the political subject is defined by his or her *conscious intention* to die on behalf of any cause.

This cannot, however, provide a satisfying account of Bouazizi as a political subject. It is likely that Bouazizi's act *was* meant as an indictment of the social inequality and limited opportunities provided in Tunisian society under Ben Ali, but there is little or no compelling evidence to suggest this was an act which occurred on behalf of others. Bouazizi seemed to be engaged in a distinctly personal, if very much publically articulated, protest. Indeed, as Fierke notes, all that can be said of Bouazizi's act was that *it was interpreted after the fact as* having been on behalf of society at large, and that this interpretation by others is what gave the act such an enormous political charge. Bouazizi's intentions must remain opaque. Indeed, intentionality is almost always ambiguous in such events, since it is almost always impossible to confirm the motives of self-annihilating subjects after their act.[8]

This question mark over intentionality is unproblematic if we see 'sacrificial acts' as acquiring their content through *subsequent* attachment to the symbolic architecture of social life. In this sense, meaning is identical with a semiotic functionality that is necessarily formed through the wider social interpretation and contestation after the act. Sacrifices glean their social significance by being interpreted as referring to symbols which are 'sacred' inasmuch as they epitomise in some way the values and affective cohesion of a group (Kowalewski, 1980). Intentionality is thus less important than socially assigned sacrificial meaning.

Such an account finds its root in the work of social anthropologists Hubert and Mauss (1964), who claimed that the designation of sacrificial offerings is the *central means by which social norms are created and maintained* in traditional societies. The unity of the 'sacrificial system' is located in a procedure which 'consists in establishing a means of communication between the sacred and the profane worlds through the mediation of a victim, that is, of a thing that in the course of the ceremony is destroyed' (Hubert & Mauss, 1964). The referent 'sacrifice' confers a sacred character on a 'victim', who thereby becomes the means of transmission between divine and profane. The victim separates and unites the profane and divine spheres so that a productive exchange can take place—thus the victim's famous ambiguity (Agamben, 1995). For Hubert and Mauss (1964, p. 88), the institution of sacrifice is intrinsically bound up with the production of the myths and narratives that underpin social life; the genesis of the ideas which are deemed to exist outside, yet condition sociality, and with which individuals seek to enter into relationships with so as to find emotional 'strength and assurance'.[9] Sacrifice is a mechanism of exchange by which the transcendent imaginary or narrative architecture of society is engendered and then sustained through affective identification (Hubert & Mauss, 1964, p. 101).

Andriolo (2006, p. 109) builds directly on this argument in observing that 'the word sacrifice, so often used in reference to protest suicides, correctly points to the premise shared by [self-immolations] and ... ritual or mythical' acts, *an exchange with a figure of transcendence*. Self-immolations, much like ancient sacrifices, establish a 'contract between giver and receiver'. In the operation of sacrifice today, the latter is no longer 'a god or cosmic engine' but rather a 'secular' formation of myth and narrative (Andriolo, 2006, p. 109). We find, in other words, in religious sacrifice the template of political sacrifice, since it is in its relation to the mythic foundations of social life that the constructive force of the practice is located. Immolations are thus not defined via *intentionality*, as illusory personal outputs of theological or ideological fantasy or fanatical over-identification with their social context; they acquire their reality with relation to the 'social facts' which are their result or product. The potency of sacrificial rituals is that they allow imaginary 'social things' to achieve a transcendent reality.

Self-sacrifice is thus seen as an engine for the production of the founding myths or narratives of all sovereign collectivities. As Houen (2010) puts it, sacrifice, whether religious or secular, 'institutes an idealism of transcendent justification for a community' which are central to all political formations, ancient and modern. Sacrificial substitutions reinforce 'pre-existing social relations and spiritual beliefs' but are also '*constitutive* for the community in terms of its particular social dynamic and ideals' (Houen, 2010, p. 116). The point here is straightforward; self-sacrifice is political myth-making, a site for the imagining of community or nation, particularly under conditions of oppression or occupation (Anderson, 1991). Uehling's (2000) work on Crimean Tatar nationalism brings this point to bear on the practice of protest self-burning. Self-immolation amongst Crimean Tatars in the 1970s became the interpretative 'site for the social construction of *vatan* or homeland'.[10] For Craig (2012), the continuing campaign of self-immolations in Tibet are seen as sacrificial rites inasmuch as they sustain sacralised collective identity in the face of the perceived threat to cultural autonomy posed by Chinese control of the region. In affirming a unique Tibetan identity in the face of persecution, monks who conduct self-immolations not only draw international attention to their plight, but also *actively participate in* the imagining of an independent Tibet. Similarly, the Irish Republican hunger strikers construct a narrative body politic through entry into a history of heroic martyrdom (Bolt, 2008; Sweeney, 1993). Bobby Sands explicitly saw himself as in the business of nationalist myth-making (Feldman, 1991; Fierke, 2013). It should be clear, however, that such intentions are at least partly irrelevant to the assignment of political content, for it is the *imaginary social forms constructed through later semiotic capture that gives political meaning to sacrifice, not the intentions of the subjects themselves.* Self-sacrificing subjects acquire political content by being interpretatively folded into an imaginary/mythic totality, and thereby immortalised through memorialisation as martyrs.[11]

Fierke (2013) has published a highly sophisticated, fluent, and systematic articulation of this approach to the political subject of suicide-bombings, hunger strikes, or self-burnings. For this reason her book, *Political self-sacrifice: Agency, body and emotion in international relations*, is given special attention here. For Fierke (2013, p. 22), what identifies a family of 'self-sacrificial political' acts is their role in the 'creation of alternative forms of identity and belonging' through an act of radical communication. For Fierke (2013, p. 37), 'Self sacrifice ... is an "act of speech" in which the suffering body communicates the injustice experienced by the community to a larger audience.' In this context, whilst 'sacrifice in a political context implies a community for which the sacrifice is made and an audience to which it speaks', the self-sacrifice 'is about the restoration of the nation in circumstance in which sovereignty has been curtailed' (Fierke, 2013, p. 38). The speech act becomes political inasmuch as it is received by others as embodying a *desire for communal sovereignty*, emerging in response to the humiliation of its lack (Fierke, 2013, p. 2).

The 'agent of political self–sacrifice, often referred to as a martyr' is political, for Fierke (2013, p. 53), only inasmuch as they can be interpreted as the 'embodiment of the suffering nation'. This is the signature of a 'political self-sacrifice' across different cultural contexts.[12] The politics of self-burning relies on their interpretation as an embodiment of a counter- or restored sovereignty, through an affective re-construction of ontological security: 'The self-sacrifice of the individual body becomes an expression of the loss of collective sovereignty, which materialises the injustice experienced by the community and thereby creates the condition for its restoration' (Fierke, 2013, p. 79). Politics, here, is an emotional 'response to a loss of equilibrium or a loss of value', a sense of 'the need to restore dignity', which is retrospectively read as the connotation of the act of self-incineration by audiences engaged in interpretative contestation around its meaning. In this way, Fierke (2013, p. 92) argues, 'in the Arab Spring, various acts of self-sacrifice contributed to the construction of community and the nation'. Bouazizi's act became political inasmuch as it was interpreted as affirming collective identity, embodying the sovereignty of a repressed 'liminal communitas' that opposed the entrenched autocratic regimes. Mohammed Bouazizi is a self-sacrificial *political* subject because his act was retrospectively understood as having taken place 'on behalf of' a wider community dissatisfied with the Ben Ali regime; his perlocutionary act received as performing a new social imaginary or narrative body politics, promising the restoration of sovereignty.

Self-sacrifices, for Fierke (2013, p. 79), are political inasmuch as they allow 'communities of recognition [to be] constituted and reconstituted through the movement and circulation of emotion, evoked by the bodily self sacrifice, and given resonance and power through memory' (p. 79).[13] Through the construction of memory around the figure of the martyr, a community of desire can take form and re-claim sovereignty over itself (Fierke, 2013, p. 92). Fierke's account is therefore a classically dialectical analysis of political resistance, articulated as the contradistinction of two incommensurable (hegemonic and counter-hegemonic) structures of meaning and authority.[14] Self-sacrificial subjects are political inasmuch as their 'speech act' is interpreted as a declaration of the sovereignty of an affective community that seeks to instantiate an 'anti-structure'. That is to say, the politics of self-sacrifice are wholly a question of their semiotic potential vis-à-vis restoration of the sovereignty of a liminal transcendent community (Fierke, 2013, p. 102).[15]

Fierke (2013, p. 43) argues that the assignment of self-sacrificial content assumes an appeal to pre-existing patterns of meaningfulness (an existing language game).[16] In other words, self-sacrifice, to become political, must tap into a pool of historical memory. This certainly explains how it can be a conservative mechanism for '*restoring* sovereign community' (Fierke, 2013, p. 44), as in Ireland where a historical tradition of struggle through sacrifice was explicitly appealed to by Bobby Sands in his eloquent explanations of the hunger strike in the early 1980s (see also Feldman, 1991). A *transformative or revolutionary charge* is, however, also implied by self-sacrifice inasmuch as it allows the counter-structure of political meaning and rules to emerge in 'opposition to the formalized dominant structures'. This assumes that the 'liminal' affective community will 'by definition [have] a less formal identity, which fluctuates' (Fierke, 2013, p. 99).[17] Fierke's account thus assumes the *retrospective* allocation of politicality to the act of self-destruction, by reference to its potential as an interpretative site for the pursuit of sovereign political projects. Acts of self-sacrifice *become political* inasmuch as communities use them to create a space by which to engage in constructive political conversation about the rules by which they live, and so seek to restore sovereignty in conditions where it is perceived as lost.

If the act is politicised by the patterns of signification and affective resonance that pre-exist and then solidify in the space which succeeds it, the *political subject that self-annihilates* must remain inaccessible and ontologically empty; she gains her politics only through retrospective assignment of a 'martyr' signification. Clearly the political subjects of suicide-bombings, self-burnings, or hunger-strikes are often interpreted as martyrs after the fact and, in this sense, acquire sacrificial political meaning. Martyrs are, as Fierke implies, classical referents in the imagining of sovereign communities, but, whereas self-destructive acts may be assigned retrospective political content via imaginaries that promise alternative rules of social order, *such imaginaries can only be assigned to the act in the aftermath of an immanent challenge to the extant sovereign order of meaning*. The bypassing of the self-annihilating political subject in Fierke's account means that any integral moment of violent rupture with the extant semiotic order becomes inaccessible to political analysis.

Retrospective semiosis simply cannot provide us with an account of the political subject that self-annihilates. This would be to surrender these subjects entirely to the degree to which they are captured by a pattern of affect and signification in consequent interpretative contestation, and in the process eject from political space any number of self-destructive subjects on the consequentialist grounds that they fail to result in the institution of language games that relate to the restoration of sovereignty (Fierke, 2013, p. 80). The differences between the consequences of Jan Palach's act in 1969 and Mohammed Bouazizi's in 2010 are illustrative here. If we assign the politics of the act to its narrative/affective consequences, as Fierke does, we must conclude that Jan Palach is no political subject, since he produced no mythic counter-structure, no language game pursuing the reversal of lost sovereignty, despite explicit hopes for doing so,[18] whilst Bouazizi is a political self-sacrifice despite an apparent absence of myth-making ambitions. The *intentions* of self-immolators, like hunger strikers and suicide-bombers, are necessarily opaque and so can be no adequate guide to politics. *Consequences*, in terms of retrospective semiosis, seem an equally inadequate guide to the political ontology of the self-annihilator. Indeed, our access to a 'political subject of self-annihilation' is simply denied if politicality is limited to the retrospective allocation of meaning.

Political acts of self-annihilation seem to elude our grasp in terms of causal instrumentality, means and ends, intentions, and consequences. Oscillating in the contemporary media space, the narrative and affective consequences of any image or speech act are always uncertain (Devji, 2005). Contingency certainly played a critical role in the interpretation of Bouazizi's act, with key issues, including the apparently gendered element of his protest, absent from most popular narrations. In this context, Bolt (2012) has cogently recognised that for this reason, contemporary suicide-bombings and self-immolations cannot be reduced to their narrative products. Indeed, as noted above, the central problem for propagandists of the deed[19] has always been the *impossibility* of maintaining control over the narratives that emerge from their violent events.[20] Bolt (2008, 2012) notes that propaganda of the deed now occurs in a complex and uncontrollable space of global media interactivity, where the proliferation of meanings and dissemination of images supply the effects of violent acts with accelerated unpredictability (see also Devji, 2005). The significance of symbolic violence seems to reside in its power to give birth to the uncontrollable *proliferation of narratives, myths or affective formations* in a virtual space. Causation is unchained from intention and even from content by the new media: as such, the self-immolator can take on the role of facilitator of revolutionary spontaneity and proliferation through the production of iconic violence, but in abandoning any attempt to control the message, they inevitably have unexpected or even contrary communicative effects.[21] In this way, self-destructive propaganda of the deed is a matter of setting off discursive avalanches that cannot be predicted or mapped in advance, which problematises the sufficiency of reading such act's politicality in their relationship to an affective community construction. It is simply impossible to ascertain in advance whether an act will necessarily garner one signification or another. Fierke (2013, p. 26) recognises this in emphasising the existence of contestation around the meaning of the act, but argues very clearly that the political enters in only with the attribution of a martyr signification.

Fierke thus implies that there is nothing *intrinsically violent* about the *subject* of a political self-immolation (though she acknowledged that such events always *involve* violence): it is, precisely, whether the violence is *interpreted* as 'inflicted by others' or 'self-inflicted' which dictates whether a *political or suicidal* meaning is assigned. Political content relies on assigning responsibility for the death of the 'self-sacrifice' to the existing sovereign regime (Fierke, 2013, p. 131). Only absolving them from responsibility for their death allows the martyrisation of the self-immolator, so she can literally *embody* a community violently excluded from participation in the 'sovereignty game' of International Relations. Any violence intimately associated with the sacrificial subject, as in suicide-bombing, is seen by Fierke (2013, p. 241) to render the emergence of a stable counter-structure out of interpretative contestation less likely, because it renders the act's sacrificial political interpretation as purely embodying a pattern of societal victimisation less stable.[22] This means we need not distinguish a 'self-immolation' from someone murdered by the state. Fierke (2013) views the murder of the Polish Priest Popieluszko as 'resembling' the self-incineration of Quang Duc, or hunger strike of Bobby Sands, because he was retrospectively interpreted as a martyr. Clearly, Quang Duc and Sands, at least in some way, literally chose their deaths in a way that Popieluszko did not, but Fierke's point is that there is no *political* difference here, because sacrificial politicality is retrospective semiosis.

Interestingly, in this context, Sands and Quang Duc provide little evidential support for Fierke's claim that the politicality of these acts of self-destruction can be sufficiently captured by reference to their retrospective interpretation as supporting the affective cohesion of a 'liminal communitas' seeking to instantiate a counter-structure.[23] The immediate result of these two acts of self-annihilation was the emergence of widespread disorganised violence and *social crisis* in Ireland and Vietnam, with little evidence of a cohesive claim to a counter-sovereignty emerging. Following the hunger strike campaign led by Bobby Sand in the early 1980s, there was a substantive *increase* in violence in Northern Ireland,[24] a rise in social tension and an acceleration of conflict. Feldman's (1991) fundamental claim in his definitive and exhaustively researched account of the Irish hunger strikes of the early 1980s is that Bobby Sands did not see his act as distinct from the wider armed struggle. Sands' own articulation of the act in terms of the 'Flight of the Lark' located that violence as a movement of transformation and escape from his prison conditions which were extended to represent the broader socio-political struggle. Whilst Sands clearly engaged in myth-making in advance of his own death, the act was an institution of explicitly violent protest against the injustices of British rule and the conditions in Long Kesh prison. In this way, the hunger strikes, like the dirty protests that preceded them, were bound up in a series of 'formations of violence' around which the struggle against British imperialism circulated (Feldman, 1991).

To render the act as a self-sacrifice, aiming to symbolically reaffirm the Irish catholic myths of collective being, is thus accurate but highly partial. Sands viewed himself as a participant in violent struggle and explicitly intended to spur violent resistance outside the prison. He was, in this regard, highly successful. Though there was no moment of revolutionary spontaneity, the following decades saw the acceleration of the conflict. It was this acceleration of violence which laid the grounds for the later peace process, not any symbolic construction associated with the act of self-immolation. The affective consequences of Sands' act unleashed fury and outrage in a specific community, those already involved in violent struggle. This was a weaponisation, not simply a sovereign reterritorialisation, of desire. It is difficult to interpret this as reflecting increased cohesion of a counter-hegemonic formation or affective counter-structure, since tit-for-tat violence increased not simply vis-à-vis the British state and its Irish supporters, but within and between factions in the Irish Republican community, inside and outside the prison (Feldman, 1991, p. 268). Indeed, Feldman (1991, p. 261) described an *increasingly* disordered mimetic proliferation of violence throughout the Northern Irish milieu following Sands' 'self-sacrifice'.

Much the same may be said of the events which followed the self-burning of Thich Quang Duc in 1968, where a series of similar protests by Buddhist monks created a febrile social condition, leading to mass arrests, sectarian (majority Buddhist) protests and riots, a coup (tacitly sponsored by the USA), the killing of Diem, and a consequent acceleration of the conflict in Vietnam.[25] Quang Duc's self-incineration did not appear to increase capacity for a cohesive counter-claim to sovereignty. The aftermath of Quang Duc's self-annihilation was characterised by disordering and disorganised violence, contextualised by a generalised breakdown of popular faith in the legitimacy of the regime at home and abroad. Quang Duc's self-incineration was read as a negation of the sovereign order, but there is little evidence of an emergent positive counter-structure, liminal community formation, or the interpretative construction of a new sovereign language game, perhaps due to the rapid progression of events.

What this suggests is that the politics of self-destruction cannot be sufficiently contained by its potential for retrospective capture under myth through interpretative contestation. These events may create an 'opportunity space' for sovereign myth-making and for the affective identification of martyrs, but such processes of narrative capture assume the existence of a prior moment of rupture with the extant semiotic regime (see Bolt, 2012). Communities engaging in contestation around the meaning of self-destructive events may well construct a space to engage in political conversation regarding the rules by which they live, but these processes *occur after the fact*, and so cannot explain any violent break with sovereign order integral to the political subject that self-annihilates.

Political Suicide

The sacrificial paradigm averts its eyes from the violent excess and ruptural charge integral to the act of political self-destruction. A broad tradition of thinking on suicide sees its taboo character as indicative of the impossibility of a politics expressed in radical flight from the world. Indeed, as Bauman (1992, p. 2) argued, following Hegel, death is 'the absolute *other* of being, an *unimaginable* other, hovering beyond the reach of communication' that can only be engaged through the cultural production of imaginaries of permanence. Unless mapped onto a broader project of immortalisation or mythic narrativisation that continues after the fact, self-destruction in this account can only be a departure from political space.

When Girard (2005) discussed the sacrificial paradigm, he argued that its function is to construct social order in precisely this sense. His innovation and critique of Hubert and Mauss (1964) rested in observing the circularity in their argument and its consequential deficit of explanatory value.[26] Hubert and Mauss simply failed to recognise that the sacrificial rite functions through substitution to preclude the eruption of social disorder in other forms, most notably as mob violence. The sacrificial rite is thus a socially mediated mechanism for the managed expression of social violence, and this is what allows it to become a means for the symbolic ordering of social life. It institutes imaginaries of stability to contain the ever-present risk of violent disorder that is an inevitable condition for a society of mortals. Ironically, the events marked out as *political sacrifices* by social scientists like Fierke tend to have more correspondence with what Girard (2005) referred to as 'sacrificial crises'—events which, as reminders to primary violence (essentially, death), spark processes of social rupture and disorder, and which in traditional societies elicited sacrificial offerings in the hope of their management through mythic substitution.

Self-burnings, like hunger strikes to death or suicide-bombings, appear to be *inverted sacrifices* in this sense, institutions or formations of primary violence that rupture and break with extant social order, without promising any resolution in an alternative social order or sovereign semiosis. These acts embody or symbolise violent disorder, not its resolution. Any 'counter-hegemonic' myth-making, I have shown above, necessarily comes after the fact, as part of a process of capture and social ordering through, for example, the identification of martyrs by surviving audiences. The object of the sacrificial ritual, from a Girardian perspective, is a pre-social excess that threatens to rupture social order by bringing it face to face with its underlying groundlessness (*qua* death). It is that fatal excess or foundational crisis which is constitutive of the subject that self-annihilates, not any stabilising (hegemonic or counter-hegemonic) semiosis that might be constructed in its aftermath. Indeed, such retrospective semiosis, given the disordered and often violent proliferations that commonly follow acts of self-annihilation, is precisely suggestive of a search for social meaning in the face of its interruption by suicidal death.

Girard (2005) argues that with the onset of modernity, the sacrificial institution is no longer needed for ensuring social stability. It is replaced by law, which is a far more effective tool for managing the threat of violent disorder. Principally law remains, however, a mechanism for the social mediation or *substitution* of violence. The sovereignty of law simply is the assertion that violence (*qua* right to kill) is restricted to the hand of the state (see Foucault, 2004). Inasmuch as legitimate violence is monopolised under law, its generalised social expression is contained (as noted by Weber, 1965). Law is therefore, at its root, a mythic substitution of violence and fulfils the same basic function as the sacrificial institution. Girard's argument here resonates closely with Benjamin's in *Critique of violence* (1986), which provides a conceptual toolbox by which the political subject of self-annihilation can be categorically conceptualised as prior to, and so integrally problematising, any and all sovereign semiosis.

Benjamin also claimed that it is only through myth-making that the sovereignty of law and therefore social order can be sustained. Law must monopolise violence to function, and this reveals law's paradoxical reliance on and foundation in violence. Sovereign law is the continuation of violence as opposed to its denial, a *violence given transcendent or ideal status as myth*. As Derrida (2002) observed, Benjamin suggests that 'the authority of law rests only on the credit that is granted it'. The critical point here is simply that law is always an 'act of Faith ... One believes in it; that is its only foundation' (Derrida, 2002). There is, therefore, something integrally 'mystical' about law, and this is precisely because it is founded on and sustained by violence. For this reason, Benjamin suggested, in some disagreement with Girard,[27] that violence integrally maintains the capacity to shatter, if only momentarily, the force of law.

Benjamin (1986) distinguished the 'mythic violence' of law from what he termed 'divine violence'. The mythic violence of law, which orders, constructs communities, and institutes heroic narratives of sovereignty, is opposed to a *divine violence which destroys law* or more importantly *faith in the sovereignty of law*. Divine violence is law-breaking, anti-mythic violence that creates space for instantiation of a radically new order. It is, as such, fully revolutionary. Benjamin clarifies this distinction via the difference between the 'strike' and the 'general strike'. The strike is a form of political violence that hinges on a withdrawal, generally of labour (for a related argument, see Baudrillard & Grant, 1993). The strike is conditional and grounded in the logic of exchange; it is sustained until a change to the mythic/legal order is negotiated. It challenges, for example, claims of criminality on the grounds that it views that assignation as illegitimate, and so insists upon a change to the law. The general strike, on the other hand, is an absolute withdrawal, and so, Benjamin (1986) argues, 'anarchistic'. It breaks absolutely with the extant social order and asks for no modification of the existing legal code, simply denying the figures of law any legitimacy whatsoever. Unconditional withdrawal frustrates all concepts of defined legal political ends—mobilising violence as a 'pure means'. The refusal of any logic of ends or instrumentality is the marker of divine violence.

The hunger striker unto death or self-burner similarly goes beyond the *alteration* of the law/ mythic order through an exchange or bargaining process; after all, they will never witness any such alteration (Benjamin, 1986, p. 292). Like the general strike these are rites of violence in which no exchange is offered. Death stands unredeemable, and as such institutes a rupture with law *as such*. Understood in this way, self-annihilation is an act without positive or sacred ends: it is violence *as a pure means*. As Benjamin makes clear, only sacred violence leaves positive markers in myth and legal order. Divine violence leaves no traces; it breaks the cycle of myth, embodying an excess that brings social order to its empty origin. Mythic forms may follow, and a new legal order may be created after the fact, but that order is born *in flight from* the radical subject of divine violence. Self-burnings and hunger strikes to death consecrate an offering that embodies crisis without resolution. Mohammed Bouazizi, unlike Bobby Sands, did not even attempt to predetermine his mythic effects, strategically preframing his act within a poetic project of transcendent imagining. He articulated no identifiable ends. It is its radical negativity that gave his act fertility and force. Bouazizi is a political subject of divine violence; his self-burning was a pure means, without heroic ends or positive intentions, which *as such* opened a space for the subsequent proliferation of myth. This suggests the analytical value of the Benjaminian concept of a *suicidal political subject*, introduced at the beginning of this article, as one who needs no transcendent referent or connection to a sovereign semiosis to occupy political space.

Ben Ali correctly identified in Bouazizi's suicide a radical challenge to his authority. We can understand the act in this context as a precise *inversion* of the logic of sacrifice: its political ontology is a function of its exposure of a socially immanent violence (death). As opposed to seeing a political subject given form in the semiotic construction of new myths of sovereign order, a transcendent counter-structure or liminal communitas, Bouazizi's self-immolation embodied and unchained socially immanent disorder. Bouazizi's act shattered popular faith in the Tunisian regime, and in turn led to the establishment, in the surrounding states, of a condition of collective faithlessness. Popular faith in authoritarian law dissolved in the face of an unconditional gift of auto-annihilation. To understand this as a sacrificial offering is to see only the mythic capture of divine violence after the fact and to confuse the political subject of auto-annihilating violence with our attempt to make sense of a politically constitutive excess.

Conclusion

It is not surprising that we moderns wish to render hunger-striking to death and self-burning meaningful, and so assign them after the fact with transcendent sacred/mythic or heroic content. Divine violence, Benjamin argued, is a pure act of negation and leaves no traces in historical memory. It is a fatal rupture with the norms of social order. Theorists map the mythic social products of such events and deem them the markers of a sacrificial political subject. My argument has been that the political subject that self-annihilates is entirely passed over in this gesture. Self-destruction carries no positivity whatsoever. In suicide, the imaginary weight and heft of all law and any sovereign order are punctured, if only momentarily. All authorities are put on hold by the blinding spectacle of the negative.

We see, in the operation of contemporary self-destructive practice, closer to what Devji (2005) has described as accidentological global processes—as indicated in Bouazizi's apparently masculinised sense of personal insult being reinterpreted as an urge to democratic reform. The flight of state sovereignty in the face of global communicative flows naturally leads to the search for new bodies in which such dissolving sovereignties might reside. In declaring the rise of new sacrificial political theologies, however, we risk occluding the uncomfortable fact that acts of self-destruction reveal all our sacred myths for what they are. The willingness to 'go to the edge' only opens the space for a fully revolutionary politics by precisely *making-mythic* every order and all sovereigns.

Morbid excess cannot be excised from the political, nor can it simply be categorically recoded, in modernist terms, as a reach for transcendence under a hegemonic or counter-hegemonic myth-cycle. Martyr-myths may serve in the construction of sovereigns, but they cannot capture the political subject of self-destruction. Not only is the self-annihilating subject never identical to its mythic doppelgangers, in self-destruction we stand witness to the frustration of all sovereign projects. These subjects depart the scene and speak no more, casting aside their right of sovereignty over any myths they come to be identified with. Collapsing the political act of self-destruction into its subsequent heroisation, and so failing to recognise the divine rupture that underpins all myth-making, we avert our eyes from the self-annihilating political subjects themselves. The construction of sacrificial myths in the aftermath of his act was certainly an important part of Bouazizi's politicality, but this retrospective semiosis cannot occlude the disconcerting presence of a suicidal political subject.

OCCUPYING SUBJECTIVITY

Notes

1 This has resonances with what Foucault (1984) referred to as the 'blackmail of enlightenment' in his seminal *What is enlightenment*, referring to the insistence that one must either be *for or against* the modern rationalist project.

2 As Bauman (1992) has noted, it is perhaps constitutive to any true ethic, qua responsibility to an-other, that it cannot stop at the borders of one's life.

3 Like the Russian anarchist group *Narodnaya Volya*, whose preferred method, a hand-thrown bomb, required such intimacy as to almost guarantee death or capture.

4 Recent translations of diaries of individual Kamikaze, however, suggest we are prone to gross oversimplification in this context (see Onuki-Tierney, 2002).

5 Exact figures are difficult to ascertain given the Chinese state's actions to limit information flow from the region.

6 See, for example, *Time Magazine*, Person of the Year 2011. http://content.time.com/time/specials/packages/article/0,28804,2101745_2102139,00.html.

7 The relationship between his international effects and his now opaque intentions suggests something more akin to a natural process. Indeed, the omnipresent rendition of Bouazizi's self-immolation as a 'spark' or 'trigger' for the following international conflagrations implies precisely a role that is broadly incidental or accidental in quality (see, e.g. Bolt, 2012, p. xxii; Howard & Hussein, 2011, p. 43; Jacobson, 2011; Roy & Merlini, 2012, p. vii; Schraeder & Redissi, 2011). As a consequence, authors seek to excavate the 'real' or 'sovereign' causes of these events: socio-economic stress, combined with a youth-heavy population, extremely high food costs, extended economic mismanagement, the rising authoritarianism of the Tunisian regime, and the undisguised rentierism of Ben Ali and his family revealed by Wikileaks (Bolt, 2012; Schraeder & Redissi, 2011). More broadly, the Arab Spring is deemed to have been brewed in the alienation of Arab populations from their governments, and the lack of legitimate channels for voicing grievance. In the context of these 'true' contextual causes, Bouazizi's self-immolation is understood simply as the 'straw which broke the camel's back'.

8 This is true even where 'suicide notes', martyrdom videos or the like are prepared in advance.

9 The act of abnegation implicit in every sacrifice, by recalling frequently to the consciousness of the individual the presence of collective forces, in fact sustains their ideal existence. These expiations and general purifications, communions and sacralisations of groups, these creations of the spirits of the cities give—or renew periodically for the community, represented by its gods—that character, good, strong, grave, and terrible, which is one of the essential traits of any social entity. Moreover, individuals find their own advantage in this same act. They confer upon each other, upon themselves, and upon those things they hold dear, the whole strength of society. (Hubert & Mauss, 1964, p. 102)

10 It is precisely through interpretation of these acts that national selfhood was constructed or sustained in the face of Soviet repression. We see, therefore, in Uehling's (2000) rendition of the Tatar poetic and narrative re-articulations of self-immolation, the classical terms of political theology. The phrase 'homeland or death' became closely linked to the act as the slogan for opposition to the Soviet forces, and the idea of victory through sacrifice takes centre stage in the narrative of national struggle: 'the emblem of their suffering, invoked as both example and ideal'. Self-immolation here is clearly a form of sacrificial myth-making, imagining political being and sustaining it in the face of threats to collective being.

11 The concept of sacrifice implies that what is 'political' in this context is a denial of death, through its replacement by a higher communal life. Self-sacrifice, like nationalist self-sacrifice or Christian martyrdom, is thus essentially a rationalised politics of self-deception. The promise of an afterlife offers consolidatory valence in secularised form, through membership of the transcendent community. An explanatory discourse which views such acts as political because they are transcendentalising obviates the very possibility of a *self-destructive politics*: since the desire for death is really a *desire for immortality* instituted in the sovereignty of the continuing narrative community. Politics simply *is* the desire to counter-death with a secure and stable (i.e. immortal) territoriality: precluding political commitments which reach all the way to self-abolition *whilst remaining political* seems highly problematic if the object of study is political *self*-destruction. The claim that politics is against death is classically articulated by Hannah Arendt, who, as Kateb (1987) has noted, smuggles in precisely this paradoxical obviation of political morbidity.

12 As Fierke (2013, p. 6) puts it: 'The word political points to the objective of the sacrifice, which is the restoration of political community.'

13 This attention to the circulation of emotion is intended to demonstrate the influence of post-modernism on Fierke's account.

14 Contrasting with counter-conduct accounts following Foucault, which assume the continuous re-imbrications of formations of resistance with formations of power.

15 This is what Gilles Deleuze and Felix Guattari refer to as 'Molar desiring-politics', which assumes the construction of identitarian wholes, that may be opposed to other wholes through a binary inside–outside logic, and which thereby operates under the logic of sovereignty (see Deleuze & Guattari, 2004a, 2004b).

16 'Ritualisation is a strategic way of acting in specific social circumstances' (Fierke, 2013, p. 43).

17 After all, a community that has lost sovereignty has 'lost many traditional means of stabilisation' (Fierke, 2013, p. 99).

18 Palach's suicide note read:

> Because our nations are on the brink of despair we have decided to express our protest and wake up the people of this land. Our group is composed of volunteers who are willing to burn themselves for our cause. It was my honour to draw lot number one and thus I acquired the privilege of writing the first letter and starting as the first torch. Our demands are 1) immediate elimination of censorship, 2) prohibition of the distribution of Zpravy. If our demands are not fulfilled within five days by January the 21 1969, and if the people do not support us through a strike of indefinite duration, more torches will burn. Remember August. In international politics a place was made for Czechoslovakia. Let us use it. Torch Number One. (Treptow, 1992)

19 The term coined by the Russian anarchists for the practices discussed here.

20 Thus the reliance on teleology in most theories of revolutionary spontaneity.

21 For example, Jihadist's dismay in response to Al Zakarwi's campaign of suicide-bombings in Iraq.

22 'Various forms of sacrifice are conducive to particular outcomes' (Fierke, 2013, p. 98).

23 Fierke's Polish example does not appear to be a case of *self*-sacrifice, but rather the post-facto martyrdom of a priest *murdered by* an authoritarian state.

24 As Fierke (2013, p. 227) recognises: the hunger strikes were followed by 'a bloody escalation of tit-for-tat violence'.

25 Which again Fierke recognises: in Vietnam as in Northern Ireland 'further war was the consequence' of acts of self-annihilation (2013, p. 190).

26 Imaginary forms explain sacrifice and sacrifice creates imaginary forms.

27 For Girard (2005, p. 23), the juridical system is 'infinitely more effective' in containing violence than the sacrificial system.

References

Agamben, G. (1995). *Homo Sacer: Sovereign power and bare life*. Stanford, CA: Stanford University Press.

Amar, P. (2011). Middle East masculinity studies: Discourses of "men in crisis," industries of gender in revolution. *Journal of Middle East Women's Studies, 7*(3), 36–70.

Anderson, B. R. O. G. (1991). *Imagined communities: Reflections on the origin and spread of nationalism*. London: Verso.

Andriolo, K. (2002). Murder by suicide: Episodes from Muslim history. *American Anthropologist, 104*(3), 736–742.

Andriolo, K. (2006). The twice killed: Imagining protest suicide. *American Anthropologist, 108*(1), 100–113.

Asad, T. (2007). *On suicide bombing*. New York, NY: Colombia University Press.

Barkawi, T. (2004). On the pedagogy of 'small wars'. *International Affairs, 80*(1), 19–37.

Baudrillard, J., & Grant, I. H. (1993). *Symbolic exchange and death*. London: Sage.

Bauman, Z. (1992). *Mortality, immortality and other life strategies*. Cambridge: Polity.

Benjamin, W. (1986). *Critique of violence. Reflections: Essays, aphorisms, antobiographical writings*. New York, NY: Schocken.

Berman, P. (2004). *Terror and liberalism*. New York, NY: W. W. Norton.

Bhugra, D. (1991). Politically motivated suicides. *The British Journal of Psychiatry, 159*, 594–595.

Biggs, M. (2003). *Protest by self-immolation: A global dataset, 1963–2002*. Swindon: Economic and Social Research Council.

Biggs, M. (2008). Dying for a cause—alone? *Contexts, 7*(1), 22–27.

Bloom, M. (2005). *Dying to kill*. New York, NY: Colombia University Press.

Bolt, N. (2008). Propaganda of the deed and the Irish Republican Brotherhood: From the politics of 'Shock and Awe' to the 'Imagined Political Community'. *The RUSI Journal, 153*(1), 48–54.

Bolt, N. (2012). *The violent image: Insurgent propaganda and the new revolutionaries*. London: Hurst.

Craig, S. (2012). Social suffering and embodied political crisis. Hot spot forum, *Cultural Anthropology*. Retrieved from http://culanth.org/fieldsights/97-social-suffering-and-embodied-political-crisis.

Crosby, K., Rhee, J.-O., & Holland. (1976). Suicide by fire: A contemporary method of political protest. *The International journal of social psychiatry, 23*(1), 60–69.

Dawisha, K. (1984). *The Kremlin and the Prague Spring.* London: University of California Press.

Deleuze, G., & Guattari, F. (2004a). *Anti-Oedipus.* London: Continuum.

Deleuze, G., & Guattari, F. (2004b). *A thousand plateaus.* London: Continuum.

Derrida, J. (2002). *Acts of religion.* New York, NY: Routledge.

Devji, F. (2005). *Landscapes of the Jihad: Militancy, morality, modernity.* London: Hurst.

Durkheim, E. (1970). *Suicide: a study in sociology.* London: Routledge & Kegan Paul.

Eagleton, T. (2005). *Holy terror.* New York, NY: Oxford University Press.

Feldman, A. (1991). *Formations of violence: The narrative of the body and political terror in Northern Ireland.* Chicago, IL: University of Chicago Press.

Fierke, K. M. (2013). *Political self-sacrifice: Agency, body and emotion in international relations.* Cambridge: Cambridge University Press.

Foucault, M. (1984). What is enlightenment. In P. Rabinow (Ed.), *The Foucault reader* (pp. 32–50). New York, NY: Pantheon Books.

Foucault, M. (2004). *Society must be defended.* London: Penguin Books.

Giddens, A. (1971). *The sociology of suicide: A selection of readings.* London: Cass.

Gill, P. (2007). A multidimensional approach to suicide bombing. *International Journal of Conflict and Violence, 1*(2), 142–159.

Girard, R. (2005). *Violence and the sacred.* London: Continuum.

Hoffman, B. (1995). Holy terror: The implications of terrorism motivated by religious imperative. *Studies in Conflict and Terrorism, 18*(4), 271–284.

Houen, A. (2010). Sacrificial militancy and the wars against terror. In E. Boehmer and S. Morton (Eds.), *Terror and the postcolonial* (pp 113–140). Malden, MA: Wiley-Blackwell.

Howard, P., & Hussain, M. (2011). The role of digital media. *Journal of Democracy, 22*(3), 35–48.

Hubert, H., & Mauss, M. (1964). *Sacrifice: Its nature and function.* London: Cohen & West.

Husni, M., Koye, N., Cernovsky, Z. Z., & Haggarty, J. (2002). Kurdish refugees' view of politically motivated self-immolation. *Transcultural Psychiatry, 39*(3), 367–375.

Jacobson, A. (2011). *Duality in Bouazizi: Appraising the contradiction.* Independent Study Project (ISP) Collection. Retrieved from http://digitalcollections.sit.edu/isp_collection/1009.

Kantorowicz, E. H. (1951). Pro patria Mori in medieval political thought. *The American Historical Review, 56*(3), 472–492.

Kantorowicz, E. H. (1957). *The king's two bodies: A study in mediaeval political theology.* Princeton, NJ: Princeton University Press.

Kateb, G. (1987). Death and politics: Hannah Arendt's reflections on the American constitution. *Social Research 54*(3), 605–616.

King, S. B. (2000). They who burned themselves for peace: Quaker and Buddhist self-immolators during the Vietnam War. *Buddhist-Christian Studies, 20*(1), 127–150.

Kowalewski, D. (1980). The protest uses of symbolic politics in the USSR. *The Journal of Politics, 42*(2), 439–460.

Kusin, V. V. (1971). *The intellectual origins of the Prague Spring.* Cambridge: Cambridge University Press.

Laqueur, W. (2003). *No end to war: Terrorism in the twenty first century.* New York, NY: Continuum.

Michelsen, N. (2013). Liberalism, political theology and suicide-bombing. *Millennium Journal of International Studies, 42*(1), 198–223.

Onuki-Tierney, E. (2002). *Kamikazi, cherry blossoms and nationalisms: The militarisation of aesthetics in Japanese history.* Chicago, IL: University of Chicago Press.

Park, B. (2004). Sociopolitical contexts of self-immolations in Vietnam and South Korea. *Archives of Suicide Research, 8*(1), 81–97.

Pedazur, A. (Ed.). (2005). *Suicide terrorism.* Cambridge: Polity Press.

Rapoport, D. C. (1984). Fear and trembling: Terrorism in three religious traditions. *The American Political Science Review, 78*(3), 658–677.

Roy, O., & Merlini, C. (2012). *Arab society in revolt.* Washington, DC: Brookings Institution Press.

Sarraj, E. E., & Butler, L. (2002). Suicide bombers: Dignity, despair, and the need for hope: And interview with Eyad El Sarraj. *Journal of Palestinian Studies, 31*(4), 71–76.

Schmitt, C. (1985). *Political theology: Four chapters on the concept of sovereignty.* Cambridge, MA: MIT Press.

Schraeder, P. J., & Redissi, H. (2011). Ben Ali's fall. *Journal of Democracy, 22*(3), 5–19.

Seery, J. E. (1996). *Political theory for mortals: Shades of justice, images of death.* Ithaca, NY: Cornell University Press.

Simpson, E. S. C., & Weiner, J. A. (1989). *The Oxford English dictionary* (2nd ed., Vol. VII). Oxford: Clarendon Press.

Suk, J. (2009). *The rest is silence.* Jan Palach. Prague: Prague House of Photography, o.p.s.

Sweeney, G. (1993). Self-immolation in Ireland: Hungerstrikes and political confrontation. *Anthropology today, 9*(5), 10–14.

Toscano, A. (2010). *Fanaticism: On the uses of an idea.* London: Verso.

Treptow, K. W. (Ed.). (1992). The winter of despair: Jan Palach and the collapse of the Prague spring. *From Zalmoxis to Jan Palach: Studies in East European History* (Vol. 328, pp. 117–136). New York, NY: Colombia University Press.

Uehling, G. (2000). Squatting, self-immolation and the repatriation of the Crimean Tatars. *Nationalities Papers, 28*(2), 317–341.

Weber, M. (1965). *Politics as a vocation.* Philadelphia, PA: Fortress Press.

Williams, K. (1997). *The Prague spring and its aftermath; Czechoslovak politics 1968–1970.* Cambridge: Cambridge University Press.

Maze of Resistance: Crowd, Space and the Politics of Resisting Subjectivity

ANDREJA ZEVNIK

University of Manchester, Manchester, UK

ABSTRACT   *In 1968 the streets around the world saw a rise of a mass political movements. Nowadays, 46 years later, a nostalgic revolutionary aura surrounds that time; as since, such is the impression, the street is yet to emerge as a strong political actor or an effective practice of resistance is yet to take form. It seems as if the old ways of resistance have met their end, and new ways have not quite come in place. However, the most recent protests, as this paper aims to show, might have started a new path of resistance at the centre of which is a particular political subjectivity gaining its power from a space of resistance and appearing in a form of a 'crowd'. By looking at the power of the crowd as a particular embodiment or a cross between a political subject and a multitude this paper explores the constituent power of political gatherings by rejecting race, ethnicity, religion, class or gender as their mobilizing force and instead focusing on the power of coming-together (common) in a particular space. The political capacity of such 'common' mobilising force was fully exposed in the recent protests across Europe and the Arab world (the two examples on which this paper draws). The paper opens with a discussion of the distinct relationship between the sovereign (or state) and political subjectivity. The constitutive moment of subjectivity (the self-other relation) is placed in a political context and by drawing on the examples of sans papiers and Bouazizi's act of self-immolation the difficulties of the act of resistance and their inherent and unavoidable violence are highlighted. These two recent acts of resistance expose the need to think political subjectivity otherwise, and point to vistas (the crowd), which can facilitate such a different thinking. By drawing on the constitutive idea of the common as logic of subjectivation the intricate relationship between the body and the political space as manifested in the most recent against austerity and oppressive political regimes protests is interrogated. In the hope of placing the political subject closer to the driving seat of politics a case is made for a rather distinct relationship between political subjectivity of the crowd and the emerging space of resistance. This is a relationship that amounts to a new 'resisting political subjectivity' and that can bring about a new way of engaging with the politics of oppression and begins to think political contestations otherwise.*

What you aspire to as revolutionaries is a new Master. You will get one. (Lacan, 1977, 24)

The opening quote is rather rare Lacan's commentary on 1968 student protests in Paris.[1] Despite initial appearances, it does not denote pessimism or even dismissal of revolutionary activity. Instead, I suggest, Lacan's statement should be read as a double warning. First, it is a warning against the illusion whereby a change in the seat of sovereignty will automatically come to see the birth of a different world; and second, inter-related, it is a reminder that a change of power institutes a new political relationship affecting not only the sovereign but also the resisting political subject. A revolution, as Žižek (2003) argues, often gives a false impression that a change of a sovereign will automatically institute a new political order. Today, 46 years later, it seems that a revolutionary aura surrounds the year of 1968. The year is often referred to as a year when *the street* outdid the *institutions of the state* and *the university*. Since then the *street* never again emerged as a strong political actor. In fact, post-1990s social movements aimed at imitating the endeavours of 1968, yet to little avail. It appears as if the old ways of resistance have met their end, and new ways have not quite come into place. However, in some of the most recent protests, as this paper aims to show, a new way might have begun.

Yet, every revolution or resistance needs to remain vigilant of its historicity. As Žižek (2003) points out, modern revolutions follow a particular historical passage whereby a pre-revolutionary ancient regime gives way to a modern liberal post-revolutionary new Master who refuses to internalise authority. In the words of Kantorowicz (1998), the new postmodern Master refuses to give birth to its second—symbolic—body alienating the figure of the sovereign from its symbolic power and thus creating a particular impasse in resistant movements, whereby the sovereign can dismiss protests as not being directed towards *him/her* but against some external—divine—source of sovereign power. In doing so, the sovereign de-legitimises the actions taken against him/her, but most importantly, preserves the existing relationship between the sovereign and the subject and creates an illusion that all resistance is futile.

Thus in the opening quote on revolution and resistance movements what Lacan warns us against is a blindness fuelled by the joy that can accompany direct mass political action. The paper argues that recent large political gatherings produce a particular distinct political subjectivity. The space in which large gatherings take place and the sense of togetherness and common purpose that accompanies them lead to a particular, distinct yet temporarily limited political power. The 'emotionally driven' force in such instances takes over reason and established strategic goals of turning the fall of a sovereign into its ultimate and sole goal. No doubt, such political action can force a change in power, but it does not automatically change politics, re-define political space or re-write the political practices producing it. Those that were excluded from the space of politics in the existing regime can remain excluded in the new regime. The perceived impossibility of political action results from the aforementioned gap between the political subjects and the figures of sovereignty. Technocratic procedure (elections) seems to have emerged as the only legitimate means through which governments are to be held responsible. Yet, as Berardi (2011) puts it, 'Peaceful demonstrations are effective in the frame of democracy, but democracy is over as techno-financial automatisms have taken the place of political decisions'. Berardi's observation, however, is not a call to arms or to violence. What recent demonstrations against austerity or for a form of radical democracy have demonstrated is precisely that a new mode of action is necessary. This new mode of action derives from spaces or at the back of political subjectivities that either did not exist before or that were marginalised in the past.

By looking at the power of 'the crowd' as a particular embodiment or a cross between political subject and the multitude, this paper explores the constituent power of political gatherings that are not mobilised around claims of race, ethnicity, religion, class or gender (old sovereign discourses of community, citizenship and the state) but around the phenomena of coming-together (common) in a particular space. The political capacity or the mobilising force of the common was fully exposed in the recent protests across Europe and the Arab world (both examples on which this paper draws). In such strategies space emerges as a particular place which, through its capacity of 'gathering' or bringing people to one place (either in the form of a crowd or as a multitude), produces particular and sometimes distinct political subjectivities.

The paper opens with a discussion of the distinct relationship between the sovereign (or state) and political subjectivity. The constitutive moment of subjectivity, the self–other relation is placed in a political context and by drawing on the examples of *sans papiers* and Bouazizi's act of self-immolation the difficulties of the act of resistance and their inherent and unavoidable violence are highlighted. These two recent acts of resistance highlight the need to think political subjectivity otherwise, and point to vistas, namely the crowd and the multitude as the embodiments of a spatial political entity, which can facilitate such a different thinking. The paper then continues by drawing on the constitutive idea of the *common* as a logic of subjectivation (with the crowd and the multitude as its distinct resisting political subjectivities) and explores the intricate relationship between the body and the political space as manifested in the most recent protests against austerity and oppressive political regimes. In doing so, the paper aims to sketch out a new form of resisting subjectivity. In the hope of placing the political subject closer to the driving seat of politics, the paper makes a case for a rather distinct relationship between political subjectivity of the crowd and the space emerging; a relationship that, amounting to a new resisting political subjectivity, can bring about a new way of engaging with oppressive politics and thinking political contestations otherwise.[2]

Violence and Political Subjectivity

Political subjectivity is commonly understood as an outcome of a relational process between an individual entering a community and a sovereign of that community; the two are co-constitutive, the sovereign is recognised as a sovereign only in the moment when an individual recognises it as such, and equally in this moment of recognition an individual becomes a political subject—a subject of the sovereign. Such a logic of recognition is fundamental to the constitution of democratic political regimes and runs throughout classical social contract theory and the politics of democratic representation. Moreover, its fundaments are further embedded in the discursive formations of the subject. It is through the acceptance of the master signifier that the individual is interpellated, recognised as part of a particular socio-political order; and, as Althussr (2014), Lacan (2006) and Žižek (1999) argue, it is the very same subject who in turn endows the sovereign with legitimate powers to rule.[3] Even modern democratic regimes rest on this particular co-constitutive relationship of recognition and legitimacy between the sovereign and its subjects (community or state). The sovereign holds its powers only for as long as people recognise it as a sovereign and sovereign violence does not outweigh the security individuals gain by living in a community.

The acts of resistance and revolution directly contest this relationship. Yet to affect the ruling powers resistance needs to challenge the constitutive act of political space, which begins with subject's birth in an *institution of law* and culminates in a relationship between a political subject and a sovereign (Legende, 1995, 1997). However, not every act of resistance is strong or *courageous* enough to challenge the fundaments of this relationship. Rabaté (2009, p. 38), for example, acknowledges the difficulty of courage in resistance. He sees it as an act, which contests the sovereign and the subject's place in the socio-political order equally. The subject (as the sovereign) will not know what awaits him at the other end in a new order, and his actions will be met with sovereign's violence. At the moment when an act of resistance exposes the banality of sovereign power (that commonly arrives as a realisation that it is indeed only a contract that endows the sovereign with its powers), as Žižek argues (1993, p. 234), the sovereign is left with no other means but to respond with violence. Any protest or resistance movement (be it in a group or as an individual) that takes as its goal the re-inscription of the relation between the subject and the sovereign will be met by sovereign violence. The question is only of what kind of violence. Tunisia, Egypt or police violence in Greece are only a few most recent instances where the protesters exposed the (il)legitimacy of sovereign order and in doing so, as Douzinas (2013, p. 138) writes, attempted to change the 'parameters of reality'. A radical act of resistance is thus an individual or a collective action that has the capacity to disrupt the existing power structures and again expose the violence of the governing discourses. Douzinas in his analysis of Greek protests points to the struggle of *sans papiers*. Due to the unbearable living conditions and the newly passed laws which would see their deportation and which disregarded their 10 years spent on the Greek labour market, *sans papiers* went on a hunger strike to protest their de-humanisation (Douzinas, 2012, p. 33). 'By persisting in their action, despite the threat of death', as Douzinas (2013, p. 138) puts it, 'they changed the parameters of a reality that presented them as inferior weaklings condemning them and their co-immigrants to invisibility and civil death'. By risking (a symbolic or an actual) death they stated a demand for a recognition of their place in the Greek community, and put their body on the line knowing well that the Greek state needs to respond and that the response might not be favourable. Such an action is a demonstration of the courage mentioned earlier. By tackling the constitutive mutual relationship between the self and the other, the *sans papiers* re-opened political space and demanded a redrawing of the lines of exclusion along the paths inclusive of them.

A similar situation where an individual took action only to expose an implicit violence of the sovereign power took place only a good month earlier, in mid-December 2010. It was the case of Mohamed Bouazizi's self-immolation. Bouazizi, who was a sole income earner for a rather large family, illegally run a vegetable cart for seven years, a rather common practice in Tunisia. On 17 December 2010, a policewoman confiscated his cart and produce; after a failed attempt to bribe the officer and the insults he suffered, Bouazizi went to complain to the local municipality office, to no avail. Frustrated with the situation he left the municipality headquarters only to return an hour later; doused in a flammable liquid he set himself on fire. He died two weeks later in a hospital. Bouazizi's action is significant from two perspectives; on the one hand, it is a painful demonstration of sovereign violence and the powerlessness of a man in the face of it, but on the other, it is also a demonstration of the 'effectiveness' of his radical act. Peaceful marches in support of Bouazizi and the sovereign's inability to deal with Bouazizi's action fuelled the beginning of what was later to be known as the Jasmine Revolution in Tunisia, which saw the end of Ben Ali's regime. But what made Bouazizi's act so powerful was not the radical act itself—the sacrifice of life—but rather the desperation that led him to it. It was the desperation that was shared—in common—by many Tunisians. As Rua Wall (2012, p. 54) writes, 'it was a gesture that marked and traced the everyday injustice shared by all in the situation, but about which all had to remain silent'. The shared experience that led Bouazizi to take his life and the proximity of a death with which everyone can identify gave extra impetus to the initial political uprisings in Tunisia.

The significance of these two struggles for political recognition is twofold. On the one hand they highlight the mobilising force of the common experience (as it will be explained later), whereas on the other hand they call for a re-inscription of the resistant subject in the political order. *Sans papiers* look for a place in the existing order, whereas the supporters of Bouazizi call for a change in power and an institution of a regime that is more attentive to struggles akin to Bouazizi's. When speaking of the common as a form of resistance, the discourse is not about the material commons, which permeate and underpin some of the recent anti-austerity struggles,[4] but of the common as a *commoning* experience that unites resistant subjects in their struggle against an oppressive regime or joins their demands for recognition as political subjects. Thus, *commoning* emerges as a political mobilising force that can spring at any moment and in diverse places yet always under the condition of some shared and *commoning* experience. In recent movements, as I aim to argue in this contribution, the constituent power of the common arises at the back of struggles for political recognition as they emerged within different political spaces. The shared experience of Bouazizi's powerlessness, *sans papiers* or mass political gatherings in the squares, Syntagma in Greece, Tahrir in Egypt or Pearl Square in Bahrain,[5] displaces the initial subject–sovereign relation and instead (re)position the struggle for political recognition away from political action mobilised by the old narratives of the class, race, ethnicity or religion. In recent contestations, which consequently saw the birth of a new resistant political subject, space emerges as a key force of political action and a forum for political subjectivities. As a rather dispersed and horizontal political actor, space produces collectivised rather than individual logics of political subjectivation, such as the crowd and the multitude.

Multitude and Crowd as Spatial Political Entities

> In place of the masses we now have the multitude—which is precisely the always open striving of the multiple singularities within the constitution of the common. (Negri, 2003, p. 205)

A constitutive relation of subjectivation guiding the multitude or the crowd is different to a mutually co-constitutive sovereign–subject relation already described. Moreover, there is, however, a long-standing debate on the two distinct ideas. While political theory, sociology and psychoanalysis/psychology prefer the term crowd, philosophy of the twentieth century (and in the context of this paper this also applies for Negri and Douzinas) opted for the multitude.[6] Yet it is not only that the terms differ as they travel through the different disciplines, but the two also describe different political phenomena, which differentiate between the two—vertical and horizontal—modes of 'subjectivation'. They share a horizontal constitutive logic, yet the crowd maintains a more rigid logic of recognition to that of the multitude. I first draw out the conception of the multitude before moving to a more detailed discussion of the crowd. The relationship between the crowd and the multitude is worth attention because, as I aim to show, it is precisely the question of whether the crowd can maintain the fluidity of the multitude that underlies the possibility of the creation of a new political subjectivity.

The multitude can be described as a multiplicity of singularities that come together in a particular space and that are united by a *commoning* force, as Negri (2003), perhaps the most important thinker of the multitude would argue. Furthermore, the multitude is an expression of the ontological singularities whose individuation does not need to amount to an individual allowing the multitude to operate as a non-human political assemblage. In *A Grammar of the Multitude*, Paolo Virno (2004, p. 74) emphasises precisely the trans-individual elements of the multitude. While nothing prevents the multitude from realising itself in a form of *people* as a distinct political subject, the multitude itself is more than *people* or more than an assemblage of trans-individuals or political subjects. Its generic character orders political space as an open concept, where the relations between singularities are constantly changing, evolving and with it transforming the multitude and its power. Unlike the crowd or the community, the multitude remains at the level of generic organisation, never reaching or consolidating into the 'One' of the *people*. That is, the multitude can work on two levels, as a generic logic ordering singularities and a generic logic of singularities operating in a political space. While the former conceptually remains a multitude, the latter, if one remains faithful to the language of Hardt and Negri (2005), amounts to *people*.

In contrast to the multitude, theorisations about crowd emerged at the back of psychological and sociological studies of mobilisation and crowd control. Theories of sovereignty are particularly concerned with the control of the crowd and preoccupied with fear of what a crowd *can do*. Crowd is not a *demos*. It is in fact almost a pejorative term signifying a group of unruly individuals. It can be with or without a leader, where a leaderless crowd is a crowd that the sovereign fears the most. Le Bon (2002, p. 22), for example, wrote that a/the crowd is idiotic and its members are uncivilised. The crowd fears its dissolution, it is faceless, and thus easily accepts a demagogic leader for its protection. The crowd is a wild unthinking beast or a savage, easily manipulated and waylaid; it follows violently its desires and takes up extreme actions. Or as Canetti (1984, p. 15ff) puts it, a crowd thinks through the body rather than reason and prefers images to ideas and words. A man in a crowd is marked by body and flesh, and cares not about the privacy of its body and thus remains without individuality. The animality of the crowd, if looked at from a historical perspective, derives from its unruliness and is thus of danger to politics/order. Following Freud's (2004) study of civilisation and *Mass Psychology*, one can easily observe that crowd signifies a condition of the *people* before they leave the state of nature behind, enter the social contract and hand over their lives to a sovereign for safeguarding. The emergence of a crowd is thus anti-social and disruptive to the existing sovereign order. For its consequences, such an upright refusal and degradation of the term crowd should come as no surprise; as it is precisely the crowd who has the capacity to re-institute power relations. If we are to follow the above characterisations, an individual is naturally inclined to follow their emotions (rather than reason) and act on them; and it is also the emotion that unites and forms individuals as a crowd. As Douzinas and Freud acknowledge, the emotion is placed in an Oedipal relationship between a leader, an idea or an experience and a crowd. It is the love or emotion individuals experience that brings the crowd together and creates emotional bonds and harmonious relationships (Douzinas, 2013, p. 131; Freud, 1975, p. 70).

In contrast to the multitude for its emotionally charged and affect-driven actions the crowd is a rather controversial political force. Following Freud (2004), Le Bon (2002), or Marcuse (1987, 2008), the crowd then emerges as a relatively close, compact and coherent totality, which is achieved horizontally, through the elements of contagion between its distinct parts or a common space of gathering, and vertically, through a hypnotic identification with a leader, idea or an experience. The crowd achieves its unity through internal transference and common identification/recognition of the 'outside'. At first these accounts quite forcefully distinguish the crowd from the multitude. Such a stark difference (or an up-front rejection of the 'crowd') might also be fuelled by a resemblance between the theory of the crowd and the mass gatherings under totalitarian systems (fascism and Nazism, for example, where people 'come together' bound in unity in the face of a charismatic leader as Marcuse (2008) argues). Yet, if separated from associations with totalitarian mass gathering there is an element in crowd that can lead to a more positive reading of the idea. While the crowd remains heavily reliant on emotional investment and common experience (horizontal level), at the other end (on the vertical level) a charismatic leader can be absent. That is, in crowds, both vertical and horizontal levels can work on emotion, common experience and affect to create a form of *people*. Inevitably, such a leaderless yet emotionally charged crowd produces a space where the crowd meets and shares emotions and experiences. In hindsight, recent resistance movements and protests were indeed driven by the occupations of space, mass public manifestations of grief and rallies in support of injustices (or deaths) occurring to a member of a community. The space coupled with the emotiveness or affect of large gatherings emerges as an even stronger political factor. As resistance movements and protests seem to create horizontal (internal to the group) and vertical lines of identification (often in relation to the space and longevity of the action) a debate as whether these actions resemble a multitude or a crowd took off. For a leaderless nature and yet rather strong vertical identification with an idea, I maintain the reference to the crowd.[7]

The acting out of the crowd in a political space was evident in the case of anti-austerity protests in Greece. Douzinas identifies Syntagma square, a place that was occupied in May 2011 and that saw many violent struggles between the police and the protestors, as the centre of resistance. Syntagma, as Douzinas (2012, p. 43) writes:

> [T]urns the square into a public space where different singularities exist in common, discuss, decide and act together.[...] The square allows the coming together of the multitude [crowd], in a material co-existence of bodies with a common political desire.[...] Its strongest characteristic is the lack of a common ideological or political line, the absence of organised parties and political groupings, the banning of party banners, the wide nature of the slogans and the wide ranging nature of the popular assembly debates.

Thus, it is not a leader but an idea, a grievance or a feeling of solidarity that acts as emotional libidinal glue bringing the crowd together, and it is the space of the square where the crowd receives its material embodiment. Such a crowd, however, is not entirely removed from the reality of everyday politics or from their everyday social identities and roles. The people coming together in a crowd are members of different political parties, factory workers, university professors, bankers, pensioners, students and so on, but in the realm of the square they leave their other political/social identities aside and act as a crowd united in their common political desire (Douzinas, 2012, pp. 35–45). People come to Syntagma, as Douzinas (2012, p. 45) continues, 'as singular unique persons with their views and beliefs and not as representatives of political positions of ideologies. But when they address the crowd, they are encouraged to speak for themselves and leave the party badges behind'. Such a new political formation acts as a leaderless political force, a subject of a kind, which escapes the party-like or ideological political divisions and exclusions. It is also a political entity, which dismisses political authority and remains speechless on their demands. Instead, it is strategically positioned in a political space so that its demands for recognition cannot remain ignored, as it was seen in the examples of *sans papiers* or in Bouazizi's act of self-immolation. From the position of exclusion (*sans papiers*) or from political margins (Bouazizi), a protest that transgresses the limits of the individual acts of political power is staged and places under question the legitimacy and sovereignty of the state authority. These acts of resistance were acts that exposed sovereign violence. They were not calls to surrender the power, but demands for political recognition. In fact, both cases epitomise the story of most recent political struggles: as instead of voicing particular demands these struggles present a sovereign with a task it cannot address. They stand for a refusal of a sovereign; that is, they present a simple claim for recognition (as in the cases of Bouazizi and *sans papiers*) or voice their presence by re-claiming the space (as is the case with Syntagma).

In these struggles, a particular political entity emerges. As discussed, that entity is a form of crowd that is heavily invested by emotion and experience. In theorisation of such a political entity, the idea of the common is central for the existence of a leaderless crowd, for crowd can only be bound together by forms of common or shared experience that translates into common—yet not necessarily unified—political action. It is the crowd that brings individuals in common on Syntagma square, it is the common experience of Bouazizi's despair that gives life to the Tunisian revolution and it is *sans papiers*' claim for humanity/political recognition that brings recognition of their struggle and aligns (commons) it with other existing political struggles. It is, however, not a common of political demands, but of a political position from which different actions are taken: a common position of a refusal or a common claim for space. Or as Negri (2003, p. 205) puts it, 'in the place of the [political entity] we now have the multitude—which is precisely the always open striving of the multiple singularities within the constitution of the common'. To understand the political potential of such a common I continue by looking at common political actions as they manifest in a particular political space, with a focus on the body of the crowd that emerges from and as a result of a different ordering of political space.

The Common and the Space

> The common name is the teleological trace [...] that unites the events in the construction of a community; it is thus the ontological composition of the events that expresses itself as power and imagines itself as a reality *to-come*. (Negri, 2003, p. 205)

The common as a political idea bears in itself a significant political power; aside of the private and public, the common stands for the 'third order' excluded from the dominant political imaginaries. To look at the social contract, for example, the contract recognises individuals on the grounds of their property or possession. It draws a distinction between that which is private (and belongs to a particular individual) and that which is public (and is within limits and under the sovereign eye put for public use). By acknowledging that which belongs to me and that which is yours (or someone else's), individuals constitute each other as political subjects living in a particular community. In other words, with their actions and recognitions they draw a unified political space, which excludes those who—for the lack of property—do not fit the image of their political space. Recent political actions that came from the excluded sites (*sans papiers*), from the margins (Bouazizi), or that contested the use of public space (Syntagma) thus challenged the existing political power relations and brought to life different collective political agents. By looking at the manifestation of the bodily appearance in the space of politics I attempt to make another step in drawing out the limits of new common and collective political entity.

The struggle of *sans papiers* and Bouazizi comes down to a question of 'do I count as a political subject?' Negri in his writings on the revolution notes that claims for recognition coming from those excluded—the proletariat or the poor—are claims that derive from a common space par excellence. He writes: 'The poor are the common of the common. [...] Their resistance and their struggles have opened the eternal to the immeasurableness of the to-come' (Negri, 2003, p. 183). The outcome of such struggles is unknown and left open. Butler (2011) in her reflections on the Occupy Movements around the world and resistance/protests across Europe and the Arab World continues to point to the role space has in everyday politics of recognition. In her analysis, she acknowledges that space is seen as given, as if it exists per se, independently of subjects occupying it, and is thus *there* to be put to political (or any other) use. However, the reality is rather different as the Occupy Movements in London or New York testify well. Legal evictions, which threatened the Movement, were to stop the physical occupations of the space and public enactments of resistance; that is, law was to put an end to the expression of resistance as well as to its material effect—namely a re-appropriation of public space (Butler, 2011). The presence of a somewhat alien body in the space between the private and the public called for a legal action to stop the expression of a demand that was not only 'said', voiced or put on paper, but that persisted through its corporeal visual presence. In other words, the occupations, with their persistent visual presence, disturbed the existing political space and thus could not have been left ignored.

When crowd gathers, as Butler (2011) discusses, the very public character of the space is disputed and fought over. The fighting for the control over the Tahrir Square and police interventions and the closure of Syntagma Square are direct illustrations that a claim for public space is indeed central to a modern political struggle. But in a struggle for the space another division, as Butler (2011) continues, is at play:

> [W]hen crowds move outside the square, to the side street or the back alley to the neighbourhoods where streets are not yet paved, then something more happens. At such a moment politics is no longer defined as the exclusive business of public sphere distinct from a private one, but it crosses that line again and again, bringing attention to the way that politics is already in the home, or on the street, or in the neighbourhood [...] that are unbound by the architecture of the public square. So when we think about what it means to assemble in a crowd, a growing crowd, and what it means to move through public space [...] we see in some way that bodies in their plurality lay claim to the public, find and produce the public through seizing and reconfiguring the matter of material environments.

These struggles for the space are struggles that do not only test the limit of that which is to be public, but also they challenge that which are to be a sphere of a family and a sphere of a street. Social roles, gender relations, exclusions or inclusions are re-inscribed alongside the changes in the political space. The space per se is never a neutral category.

The nature of space—and its political—has always been of interest for politics. Arendt, for example, asks whether space is given or whether it results from a political activism of bodies. Drawing on Greek philosophy she concludes that the Polis is not a city-state in its physical location but rather 'the organisation of the people as it arises out of acting and speaking together, and its true space lie between people living together for this purpose, no matter where they happen to be' (Arendt, 1958, p. 198). The true space lies between people for, as Butler (2011) reminds us, all assembling and mobilisations of space need to happen in common, with other bodies. As much as any action is spatially bound—it takes place in a location—it also establishes a space, which belongs to the alliance itself, to a crowd that came together and (re)claimed the space. This duality or a reciprocal relationship between a space and a common political action of bodies is crucial for two reasons. It creates a space for political action and it transforms this space into a space of recognition/appearance. The space for political action is not given in advance, it comes into existence with particular political action, reminding us that space is not a blank page devoid of divisions and exclusions, but on the contrary, as Arendt (1958) notes, political space is drawn on exclusions. Knowing who does not belong marks politics and political action. In Ancient Greece, slaves, women and foreigners were the excluded crowd, those without a political voice. In today's Greece those are *sans papiers*, in Tunisia these are those who share the grievance/poverty that led Bouazizi to self-immolate. A political action then challenges the lines of exclusion and the borders of the existing political space with political recognition as its goal.

If space defines political actions, then how does one appear politically (or in space)? The appearance always comes from the Other. It is impossible for one to create an image of one's body alone. One cannot see or relate to itself without there being an-other body. Who we are bodily, as Butler (2011) writes: 'is already a way of being for the other, appearing in ways we cannot see, being a body for another in a way that I cannot be for myself, and so dispossessed perspectively by our very sociality'. Then, the space of appearance must be a common space where, as put by Arendt (1958, pp. 197–198), 'I appear to others as others appear to me, when men (sic) exist not merely like other living or inanimate things but make their appearance explicitly'. The force creating political space derives from the plurality of bodies—a collective body—rather than from the individual body. Butler in particular acknowledges the importance of the multiple/collective body over the subject. The body, as Butler (2011) argues, has its material existence that cannot be taken away from it. Thus a political space designed around the materiality of the body is an inclusive political space, where other divisions such as identity, foreignness and citizenship play no role. The body is not primarily located in space but with others brings about a new space. And the space that is created is precisely between those who act together. Just as Arendt pointed out, it is the locality of the action as well as the space between those in action that matters politically. Thus the body only acts in concert with other bodies and as such demands its recognition, its reality (Butler, 2011). In a crowd (or in multitude) an-other body is not the sovereign, but a body that stands next to 'us'. In Tahrir Square, for example, the recognition of different bodies comes through in the organisation of space. Men, women and members of different religions organised their life on the street in an egalitarian way; they all cared for those sick, they all cleaned the sanitary facilities and they all cooked and secured their sleeping arrangements. In Tahrir, it was the common and equality that permeated the space created between bodies. In all these cases, bodies occupy space: a street, a building or a square and with such action they 'liberate' space and redraw political power relation. But with their act/presence they also immediately re-occupy that very same space and alter its political meaning. Sleeping on the pavement, as Butler (2011) continues,

> was then not only a way to lay claim to the public, to contest the legitimacy of the state, but also [...] a way to put the body on the line, [to overcome] the distinction between public and private for the time of revolution.

A Politics of Resisting Subjectivity

Throughout this paper, I tried to redefine the notion of the crowd as a common and collective political entity by positioning it somewhere in-between hierarchical and horizontal relations between the sovereign and its political subject, and a horizontal generic logic of multitude. The key in maintaining both spectres of relation while escaping the aftertaste of crowd's old totalitarian lineage was the idea of the unified practice of common or shared experience and emotion. A crowd when brought together by emotions and manifested in a public square stands for the power of popular sovereignty. It is an expression of the popular will that needs an 'outing' or a carnival for its expression. Already Rousseau (2004) pointed out that civil festivities are theatres of popular sovereignty. People become actors who through speeches and acts perform their sovereignty. It is not that people live in the illusion that their acts will become a dominant political discourse, on the contrary. With such an act people symbolically reclaim their sovereignty, withdraw their consent to the existing social contract and take away the legitimacy of the government. An act does not say how things should be, but rather that they cannot continue on its current path. In such an outing space is mobilised; and as the paper aimed to show, it is precisely the bondage between space as a place of common experience that creates crowd as a particular collective resisting political entity. On the one hand, crowd unites people solely on the grounds of their responses to the situation (their coming together to oppose), but on the other hand it also redefines the limits of what it means to be a political subject and what such a political subjectivity entails. By looking at these two implications and sketching out a new politics of a resisting subject I conclude this paper.

A common or shared affect, an experience and emotion as a force supporting political manifestations of the crowd have been identified as key, but what remained somewhat illicit is a question of what drives such *coming-togethers*. In particular, how the horizontal level is maintained as an open and fluid assemblage of relations. Negri writes about love as the constitutive force enabling the emergence of the common and the individual's persistence in their common struggle leading to a multitude-like form of political organisation. For Negri (2003, p. 196), 'Love is the desire of the common, the desire that traverses physics and ethics'. It is thus not a physical love—love for a person or a thing—but rather love in its pure sense, love as *filia*.[8] Following Aristotle here, *filia* is peculiar; it is fulfilled when those who feel *filia* for one another, desire good things for one another for they regard each other as good and for they wish the other person good. One desires good for another person from purely selfless reasons and there is nothing that the person wishing good receives in return (Aristotle, 2009, p. 145). Love independent of individual concerns and interests is traditionally an ontological condition of politics. In this observation Aristotle or Negri are of course not alone. Lacan (2007) points to love as the only force that enables the movement between different social orders. Thus, a revolution, as an attempt to move from one order to another, must be driven by a form of love: be that love for the cause, demand, a way of life or as in the case of the recent protests, love for democracy, solidarity or social justice, which all manifest in an act of *refusal*.

But why is love so significant or such a powerful tool for political unification in particular when the language of crowd and multitude is mobilised? Arguably, love opens one to the singularity of the other. In love one is prepared to accept the other as such other is, with all its peculiarities. However, that other is always an imaginary other, one that does not exist, one that cannot directly receive love. The readiness to open oneself to the other—to re-position one's body in relation to other bodies in a community, to rethink one's own subjectivity and to emerge as a different political body—is the work of love. Love creates a capacity for new political entities to command themselves differently. To somewhat simplify, it is just as those taking part in the protests testify: 'I came out a different man, this experience changes me as a person' (Mason, 2012, p. 13–14). Such common, which is not an abstraction of individual interests, but, is as Negri (2003, p. 202) continues, 'a circulation of singular needs [stresses] that the public is not a juridical category but biopolitical; that politics (law, government, etc.) are not above, but within life'.

OCCUPYING SUBJECTIVITY

Two political sites come to view, one of the sovereign and the other of the common struggle. If the former is a space of *existing authority*, the latter is the space of humility or humbleness. Instead of individual concerns the community steps forward in common (in *filia*). As Berardi (2011) observes, solidarity is about love:

> [I]t is about the pleasure of sharing the breath and the space of the other. [... It is the] ability to enjoy myself thanks to your presence. [...] This is solidarity. As solidarity is based on the temporal proximity of social bodies, you cannot build solidarity between fragments of time.

In other words, solidarity depends on the linearity of time and the corporeal presence of bodies in a particular space. Such moments can include neighbourhood assemblies, primary unions and groups of solidarity with people we would have never imagined standing next to us. Such actions in matter of moments do away with the existing social, political and normative exclusions. Living an egalitarian moment leads, as Douzinas (2013, p. 140) points out, to a rapid change of terms of political inclusion and exclusion. We have 'transformed from invisible solidarity figures rambling around in our urban misery into political subjects who managed to challenge, not the solutions that has to be applied to the situation, but the situation itself', as Douzinas (2013, p. 140) continues. How is such a new and transformed political actor—a new political and resisting subject—constructed? The form of a body (and what the body can do) and the question of the limits of the new political self are the two sites of a resisting subject.

The body gives material support to the claims and manifestations of individuals' wills. When the resisting body is put on show—becomes visible and does not disappear from TV screens (as, for example, has been the case in the coverage of the protests on the Tahrir Square)—a common form of political entity, which is defined by its presence in a space of appearance, emerges. In mass demonstrations, such as those discussed here, those bodies came to the forefront and with their uninterrupted persistence gave voice to their presence. As Butler (2011) observed, the revolutions took place because the bodies refused to go home and because, even when asleep, they never stopped speaking, imposing their presence and opposing the existing regime. The body with its presence makes a claim for the space and for a political recognition that cannot remain ignored.

The self, in contrast, relies on the materiality of the body. It is unique and its uniqueness derives from the interactions one has with other bodies in a crowd. The subject instead of 'looking up' at the sovereign or at an idea (which would recognise him/her as a part of the existing political community or as a member of a sovereign political space) looks at those standing next to him/her. It is still 'the other' that makes one appear and count, but that other comes from the crowd. These others are neighbours, rather than subjects to some higher idea or authority. From such a neighbourhood springs a new politics, which initially aims to dislocate the existing sovereign forms of inclusion and exclusions.[9] The new politics springs from a difficult struggle between singularities as they enter a space of resistance with different histories and memories. They are everything but blank canvases. A sovereign discourse in the form of social norms, accepted political practices, etc. is inscribed on the bodies of these singularities; laws, conventions and social (in)security hold these singularities imprisoned in the existing power structures. Thus, the initial task of a crowd is to dislocate and re-evaluate the existing individual subjectivity and political space. The questions central to such a struggle concern frameworks of inclusion and exclusion, solidarity and acceptance of those that are different. The Syntagma square and Indignados testify of the (re)openness of political space as foreigners, asylum seekers and seasonal workers were all welcomed to join in. Such attitude to those that otherwise do not belong pointed to a different politics at stake. The new resisting political subject that emerges in spaces of resistance then fathers its own political space and political subjectivity; it determines where new lines are to be drawn (if at all)

111

and who is to be part. That it cannot be an all-inclusive political space, Freud (1975, p. 70) already warned us when he said that the crowd unites in force for as long as there is something that remains outside of it. In cases discussed here, what, however, seems to be left outside a new political space is not another human being (an excluded and depoliticised being) but rather an idea of austerity (in the case of Europe), a figure of an authoritarian sovereign (Egypt or Tunisia) or a particular experience which the crowd wishes to denote as foreign.

If the first task of the crowd is to dislocate the existing normative structures inhabiting political subjects and the existing delimitations of a political space, the second task is to re-claim the opened space and to re-configure its new limits. That is, of course, a much harder task commonly associated with the most daunting question revolution or resistance has to face: that is, what is to be done the day after the revolution? Is such a fluid political entity or resisting subjectivity at all sustainable outside the space of the square or beyond the times of struggle? Its strength certainly fluctuates. It is stronger when the movement is flourishing, when optimism, joy and a feeling that a change is possible dominate; however, when the movement is weakening, pessimism takes over, as Douzinas (2012, 2013) alludes to in his recent work. But not all is lost in a movement of such unrest. Relatively short and unpredictable political interventions have the capacity to make a point, disrupt, or destabilise the sovereign political space more abruptly than a slow gradual movement and to a different degree alter it. In Greece, Egypt or Tunisia, affectionate coming-togethers produced enough force to at least temporarily dislocate the existing power structures. There is of course never a guarantee that such action will be effective at a different place and in a different time. Yet in Syntagma direct democracy was enacted and performed as a demonstration of the power of the crowd. The crowd acted, as Douzinas (2013, p. 161) puts it, '[out of] determination to stop the social catastrophe, in the imagination of new ways of organising the social bond. The [crowd] was thinking and deliberating, speaking, and self-governing'. The crowd dislocated and at least temporarily broke with the vertical *institution* of political subjectivity and with the sovereign logic of counting those belonging to a particular community and excluding those who for whatever reason cannot be counted. Such an act is a move away from a revolutionary cyclical reproduction of master discourse Lacan warns us against in the opening quote. The crowd—even if only temporarily—does not need another master. Such a disturbance of political space and of a resisting political subjectivity is what a mass political movement acting in common affect can provide for. The crowd with fluid horizontal and vertical forms of identification centred around the ideas of the common and the space, as I have sought to show in this contribution, provides a fruitful ground for a re-thinking of political subjectivity and for re-evaluating the individual and collective actions in current political struggles.

Acknowledgements

I thank Samo Tomsic, Bostjan Nedoh, Maria Drakopoulou, Davide Tarizzo, Andrea Mura, Emmy Eklundh, Henrique Tavares Furtado and the two anonymous reviewers for helpful comments on earlier drafts and Chris Rossdale for the opportunity to be part of this exciting set of contributions.

Notes

1   Jacques Lacan was a French psychoanalyst who at the time of 1968 student protests refused to stop his seminars. He insisted that such an act is not an expression of his reluctance to support the protests, he fully embraced them as many of his students including his soon to be son-in-law sympathised with left ideology and were supporters/members of

Maoist movement. However, Lacan's support of the movement did not prevent him from being cautious and from voicing concerns about the foolish embracement of everything of the street, new power structures and political activism. The above quote made during his visit at Vincennes is a response to a provocation asking him to come clean and publicly voice whether he supports or opposes the protests.

2   As it will be discussed later on, space is a key political category that has played an important role in re-definition of resistance and protests movements already in the past: the Situationist movement or Autonomia movement are just two of the examples. However, the most recent movements draw attention to space in a different way; the relation is in particular interesting for general absence of leftist ideological discourse and for a particular emotional investment that space in current political struggles manifests.

3   For a more details explanation of subject's placements in the socio-political order, see Lacan's theory of the Graph of Desire explained in the essay 'Subversion of the subject and the dialectics of desire', in *Écrits* (2006) and Žižek's extended explanation of it in *The Sublime Object of Ideology* (1999, pp. 87–129).

4   The struggle for material commons is in the heart of Italian anti-austerity movements and occupations. In most instances, these relate to the cultural commons and the occupations of artistic space (e.g. Teatro Valle), or the 'commoning' of water and other natural resources that are perceived as basic human resources (and that fall under basic human rights).

5   Pearly Square in Bahrain is a much less popularised image of resistance yet its significance is vast perhaps not for the success of the protest, but on the contrary, for the brute force with which resistance was silenced. The square situated near the financial district of Bahrain's capitol Manama was a site of anti-government protests and occupations; the Square was forcefully cleared of protestors on 16 March 2011 and with its 'pearl' statue completely demolished two days later, on 18 March 2011. For its symbolic capital in the uprisings and anti-government protests the square was put under heavy surveillance. From a roundabout, the square has been turned into a junction with traffic lights and remains sealed off by security forces. See: Bassiouni, Rodley, Al-Awadhi, Kirsch, Arsanjani 'Report of the Bahrain Independent Commission of inquiry' (2011) or Bahrain Observer 'The Story of Bahrain's Pearl Roundabout' (2013) I also thank Luke S.G. Bhatia for drawing my attention to Pearl Square.

6   Here it is worth emphasising that the distinction between mob, crowd and the multitude is rather recent. In the writing of Hobbes, for example, the mob and the multitude (or what has been interpreted as such) seem to appear rather interchangeably.

7   See also Illan Rua Wall's project *Crowded Sovereignty: Law and Disorder* for another attempt at re-reading the idea of a crowd as a positive, emergent and resistant political subjectivity [*crowdedsovereignty.com*].

8   In Ancient Greek *filia* or *philia* [φιλία] is an idea introduced by Aristotle. It stands for friendship, the love for the family or the community, or a desire or enjoyment derived from a particular action or activity. Thus *filia* is a dispassionate virtuous love. It is either an emotion or a disposition, as Konstant (2008) argues. (Konstant, 2008). http://www.nsu.ru/classics/schole/2/2–2-konstan.pdf; accessed on December 22 2013.

9   Recent political developments, particularly in Spain but also in Italy, move towards a neighbourhood political model, where neighbourhood assembly decides on political actions and on everyday running of its communities. A similar model of governing through an assembly is in place in a number of occupied spaces (such as Teatro Valle).

References

Althussr, L. (2014). *On the reproduction of capitalism: Ideology and ideological state apparatuses*. London: Verso.

Arendt, H. (1958). *The human condition*. London: University of Chicago Press.

Aristotle. (2009). *Nicomachean ethics*. Oxford: Oxford University Press.

Bahrain Observer: democratic movement in Kingdom of Bahrain. (2013). *The story of Bahrain's pearl roundabout*. Retrieved June 28, 2014, from http://www.bahrainobserver.com/en/page/761/The+Story+of+Bahrain's+Pearl+Roundabout.html

Bassiouni, C. M., Rodley, N., Al-Awadhi, B., Kirsch, P., and Arsanjani, M. H. (2011, December 11). *Report of the Bahrain independent commission of inquiry*. Retrieved June 28, 2014, from http://www.bici.org.bh/BICIreportEN.pdf'

Berardi, F. (2011). Collapse and uprising in Europe: The right to insolvency and the disentanglement of the general intellect's potency. *Theory & Event, 14*(4). doi:10.1353/tae.2011.0062

Butler, J. (2011). *Bodies in alliance and the politics of the street*. Lecture held in Venice, September 2, 2011.

Canetti, E. (1984). *Crowds and power*. New York, NY: Farrar, Straus and Giroux.

Douzinas, C. (2012). Stasis Syntagma: The name and types of resistance. In M. Stone, I. Rua Wall, & C. Douzinas (Eds.), *New critical legal thinking: Law and the political* (32–45). Abington: Routledge.

OCCUPYING SUBJECTIVITY

Douzinas, C. (2013). *Philosophy and resistance in the crisis*. Cambridge: Polity.

Freud, S. (1975). *Group psychology and the analysis of the Ego*. New York: W.W. Norton.

Freud, S. (2004). *Mass psychology: And other writings*. London: Penguin.

Hardt, M., & Negri, A. (2005). *Multitude: War and democracy in the age of empire*. London: Penguin Books.

Kantorowicz, E. H. (1998). *The King's two bodies: A study in medieval political theology*. Princeton, NJ: Princeton University Press.

Konstant, D. (2008). Aristotle on love and friendship *ΣΧΟΛΗ II* (2), 207–212.

Lacan, J. (1977, février). L'impromptu de Vincennes. *Le Magazine littéraire 121*, p. 24.

Lacan, J. (2006). In B. Fink (Ed.), *Écrits: The first complete edition in English*. New York: W.W. Norton.

Lacan, J. (2007). *Seminar XVII: The other side of psychoanalysis*. New York: W.W. Norton.

Le Bon, G. (2002). *The crowd: A study of the popular mind*. London: Dover.

Legende, P. (1995). The other dimension of law. *Cardozo Law Review, 16*(3–4), 943–961.

Legende, P. (1997). The masters of law: A study of dogmatic function. In P. Goodrich (Ed.), *A legendre reader* (pp. 98–133). Basingstoke, London: Macmillan Press.

Marcuse, H. (1987). *Eros and civilisation*. London: Routledge.

Marcuse, H. (2008). *A study on authority*. London: Verso.

Mason, P. (2012). *Why it's kicking off everywhere: The new global revolutions*. London: Verso.

Negri, A. (2003). *Time for revolution*. London: Continuum.

Rabaté, J.-M. (2009). 68 + 1: Lacan's Année Érotique. *Parrhesia, 6*, 28–45.

Rousseau, J.-J. (2004). *Letter to d'Alembert on the theatre* [Collected writings of Jean-Jacques Rousseau]. Dartmouth: Dartmouth College.

Rua Wall, I. (2012). A different constituent power: Agamben and Tunisia. In M. Stone, I. Rua Wall, & C. Douzinas (Eds.), *New critical legal thinking: Law and the political* (pp. 46–64). Abington: Routledge.

Virno, P. (2004). *A grammar of the multitude*. Los Angeles: Semiotext(e).

Žižek, S. (1993). *Tarrying with the negative: Kant, hegel and the critique of ideology*. Durham: Duke University Press.

Žižek, S. (1999). *The sublime object of ideology*. London: Verso.

Žižek, S. (2003). Homo Sacer as the object of the discourse of the University, *Lacan.com*. Retrieved July 15, 2014. http://www.lacan.com/hsacer.htm

Dancing Ourselves to Death: The Subject of Emma Goldman's Nietzschean Anarchism[†]

CHRIS ROSSDALE

Royal Holloway, University of London, Egham, UK

ABSTRACT *This article draws together two lively and provocative radical theorists, Emma Goldman and Friedrich Nietzsche, and suggests that a reading at their intersections can inspire political thought, action, and resistance in particular ways. The argument is framed through and productive of a particular archetype which emerges from a reading of these thinkers, that of The Dancer. Both Goldman and Nietzsche have been noted for their affect-laden reflections on dance, as an image of the subject which evades capture within the frameworks of discipline, morality, and* ressentiment *and which instead commits to a ceaseless and creative insurrection of- and- against the self. Here, I argue that through this image of The Dancer we can conceptualise a form of critical or anarchic subjectivity which can provocatively interpret and inspire radical political action. In the article I look at some of the ways in which dance has formed an important component of radical politics. However I also argue that dance as understood in the terms established through Goldman and Nietzsche moves beyond corporeal performance, indicating a more general ethos of the subject, one of perpetual movement, creativity, and auto-insurrection. I also reflect on the difficulties involved in the idea of 'self-creation'; as we can see from the more problematic dimensions of Goldman's thought, creation is an ethically and ontologically ambiguous concept which, when affirmed too easily, can serve to mask the subtleties by which relations of domination persist. With this in mind, the article goes on to discuss what it might mean to 'dance to death', to negotiate the burden of transvaluation, limitless responsibility, and perpetual struggle which these two thinkers evoke, in the service of a creative and limitless radical political praxis.*

[†]Various drafts of this article were presented at the 'Confronting the Global' conference at the University of Warwick in 2011, the 'A New Initiative' reading group at the University of Warwick in 2012, and the 'Anarchism Research Group' at Loughborough University in 2014. It is far stronger for the generous contributions of colleagues at these events, as it is for the suggestions of Aggie Hirst and James Brassett.

Only in the dance do I know how to speak the parable of the highest things. (Nietzsche, 1997, p. 110)
To dance to death—what more glorious end! (Goldman, 1970a, p. 19)

Dance-time is here folks, the artistic ballet of fucking it up, and shaking the old world to the ground. (Vaneigem, 1983)

I begin from a problem that has become familiar in contemporary radical political theory, that is, that purported discourses, practices, and projects of liberation have so readily coalesced into forms of domination, produced tyrannies which sport and distort the mask and mantle of emancipation. The force of calls to urgency or to pragmatism readily deflects attention from the subtleties by which relations of power and domination operate, such that the most ardently revolutionary or cautiously poised strategies for change so often signify a perpetuation of the same. For all the changes and all the revolutions, too much remains undisturbed. Diagnoses abound, citing inadequate attention to micropower, modernity, intersectionality, privilege, class composition, and more. This is, of course, a challenge with which many of the articles in this special issue are contending.

My contribution engages with the work of one important anarchist thinker, Emma Goldman. More specifically it focuses on the specifically Nietzschean dimensions of her thought, suggesting that it is through her encounter with Friedrich Nietzsche that we can read Goldman's most provocative contributions to radical thought and practice, and her most acerbic critiques of established orthodoxies. I argue that an encounter between Goldman and Nietzsche provides an important account of the limitations of radical politics, and of pathways forward which might disrupt some of these limitations. The argument is framed through and productive of a particular archetype which emerges from a reading of these thinkers, that of The Dancer. Both Goldman and Nietzsche have been noted for their affect-laden reflections on dance, as an image of the subject which evades capture within frameworks of discipline, morality, and *ressentiment* and which instead commits to a ceaseless and creative insurrection of- and- against the self. Here, I argue that through this image of The Dancer, we can conceptualise a form of critical or anarchic subjectivity which can provocatively interpret and inspire radical political action.

I begin by outlining Nietzsche's contested relationship with anarchism, before looking in some detail at Goldman's Nietzschean anarchism. Goldman argued that a meaningful project of liberation must take seriously Nietzsche's critique of morality and suspicion of mass politics, and his emphasis on self-creation; these strains collect around both thinkers' use of dance. As such, I turn to look at instances and examples of dance in the conduct of political resistance, suggesting that they demonstrate the place and importance of play, festival, and minor composition. However, I also argue that dance as understood in the terms established through Goldman and Nietzsche moves beyond corporeal performance, indicating a more general ethos of the subject, one of perpetual movement, creativity, and auto-insurrection. Before outlining this conception of the subject, however, I reflect on the difficulties involved in the idea of 'self-creation'; as we can see from the more problematic dimensions of Goldman's thought, creation is an ethically and ontologically ambiguous concept which, when affirmed too easily, can serve to mask the subtleties by which relations of domination persist. With this in mind, the final section examines what it might mean to 'dance to death', to negotiate the burden of transvaluation, limitless responsibility, and perpetual struggle which the two thinkers evoke, in the service of a creative and limitless radical political praxis.

Nietzsche observes that philosophy tends to consist of 'the confession on the part of its author', that in writing we offer an 'involuntary and unconscious autobiography' (2003, p. 37). The implications and complexities of such a claim are beyond the scope of this article. However, I feel I must begin with a small confession of my own: I have absolutely no idea how to dance.

Nietzsche and Anarchism

Nietzsche was famously suspicious of anarchists. He referred to them as 'the mouthpiece of the decaying strata of society' (2007a, p. 65), and claims that it 'is quite justifiable to bracket the *Christian* and the *anarchist* together: their object, their instinct, is concerned only with destruction' (2007a, p. 156). This suspicion emerged from what Nietzsche saw in anarchism to be a reactive dimension which encountered the world only on the terms of that which was hated, rather than through the impulse or instinct to create the world anew: 'A word in the ear of the psychologists, assuming they are inclined to study *ressentiment* close up for once: this plant thrives best amongst anarchists and anti-Semites' (2006, p. 52).

Despite this mistrust on Nietzsche's part which, as Nathan Jun notes, probably came neither from reading anarchist thinkers such as Bakunin or Proudhon, nor from actual engagement with anarchist movements, but from sensationalist denunciations in newspapers (2012, p. 151), Nietzsche's work has been influential on a number of anarchist thinkers. Of the early twentieth-century figures, alongside Goldman, it is perhaps Gustav Landauer's readings which stand as the most prominent (Landauer, 2010, p. 64), though Nietzsche's thought clearly influenced elements of Rudolf Rocker's *Nationalism and Culture* (1937). Indeed Rocker, a prominent anarcho-syndicalist, also translated *Thus Spake Zarathustra* into Yiddish. More recently a number of treatments have reflected on the similarities, differences, and productive tensions between anarchism and Nietzsche, which provide lively analyses of libertarian worker movements (Colson, 2004), the state (Call, 2002, pp. 31–60), epistemology (Koch, 1993), the role of *ressentiment* in anarchism (Newman, 2004), and more.

There is insufficient space here to do justice to either the complexity of the relationship between Nietzsche and anarchism, or the richness of contemporary scholarship on this subject. My concern in this article is not with Nietzsche and anarchism per se, but with Goldman's interpretations. The discussion clearly resonates with debates about the place of Nietzsche for anarchists (and radicals of all stripes), but does not seek to treat anarchism in its entirety. Similarly the concern is not to examine the totality (or 'truth') of Nietzsche's thought, nor to become bogged down by Nietzsche's particular (and frequently problematic) political opinions. Rather, it is to ask how a Nietzschean encounter can enliven our sense of the possible, without allowing this sense of the possible to coalesce into some general or grand theory (of either anarchism *or* Nietzsche).[1] It is on such terms that we move to Goldman's Nietzschean anarchism.

Emma Goldman: The Dancing Anarchist

As Hilton Bertalan makes clear, Goldman has been largely overlooked as an anarchist theorist, attention focused on her personal and political life at the expense of her theoretical contributions (save somewhat patronising acknowledgements that she 'introduced' a feminist element to anarchism) (2011, pp. 209–211). Goldman's absence from most surveys of anarchist theory (or, rather, her presence as a perpetual footnote) is conspicuous. Despite this, her insistence on self-transformation, on creativity, and on a radical politics which infuses and embraces all

OCCUPYING SUBJECTIVITY

areas of life remains potent. Kathy Ferguson argues that the moves to see Goldman as an 'emotional' rhetorician and propagandist, rather than as a theorist in her own right, represent

> an implicit and highly conventional gendering in the distinction between the emotional activist and the theoretically sophisticated intellectual, a recapitulation of patriarchal gender codes that inhibits both our reading of Goldman's political thinking and our ability to engage theories as kinds of practices. (2004, p. 31)

Against this marginalisation, I argue that we should view Goldman as an important anarchist theorist. That she expressed ideas not just in her writing, but also in her speeches, her activism, and in her life more generally does not render her ideas less important—indeed, it precisely asks important questions about how we view boundaries between ideas and practices, calling to mind Nietzsche's response when faced with a scholarly book:

> We are not among those who have ideas only between books, stimulated by books—our habit is to think outdoors, walking, jumping, climbing, dancing, preferably on lonely mountains or right by the sea where even the paths become thoughtful. Our first question about the value of a book, a person, or a piece of music is: 'Can they walk?' Even more, 'Can they dance?' (2001, p. 366)

Goldman could dance.

Despite scepticism towards Nietzsche from much of the anarchist community of the late nineteenth and early twentieth century, Goldman was fascinated by his ideas. She called him 'the intellectual storm center of Europe' (Starcross, 2004, pp. 37–38) and gave at least 23 lectures across the USA between 1913 and 1917 on the relevance of Nietzsche's thought for topics including atheism, anti-statism, and anti-nationalism (Starcross, 2004, p. 29). Unfortunately, as Leigh Starcross notes in her attempt to reconstruct Goldman's ideas about Nietzsche, the papers for these lectures were seized in a police raid on the offices of *Mother Earth*, the anarchist newspaper which Goldman co-edited (Starcross, 2004). Whilst a full account of Goldman's thoughts on Nietzsche no longer exists, his influence on her thinking is evident across much of her work. More important than his direct influence on Goldman, for the purposes here, are the ways in which she provides a lively interpretation of important Nietzschean ideas.

Goldman's most substantive remaining comment on Nietzsche can be found in her autobiography, *Living My Live*, where she recalls debating his ideas with some friends and her lover, Edward Brady:

> One evening we were gathered at Justus's place at a farewell party. James Huneker was present and a young friend of ours, P. Yelineck, a talented painter. They began discussing Nietzsche. I took part, expressing my enthusiasm over the great poet-philosopher and dwelling on the impression of his works on me. Hunecker was surprised. 'I did not know you were interested in anything outside of propaganda,' he remarked. 'That is because you don't know anything about anarchism,' I replied, 'else you would understand that it embraces every phase of life and effort and that it undermines the old, outlived values.' Yelineck asserted that he was an anarchist because he was an artist; all creative people must be anarchists, he held, because they need scope and freedom for their expression. Huneker insisted that art has nothing to do with any ism. 'Nietzsche himself is the proof of it,' he argued; 'he is an aristocrat, his ideal is the superman because he has no sympathy with or faith in the common herd.' I pointed out that Nietzsche was not a social theorist but a poet, a rebel and innovator. His aristocracy was neither of birth nor of purse; it was of the spirit. In that respect Nietzsche was an anarchist, and all true anarchists were aristocrats, I said. (1970a, pp. 193–194)

Brady's dismissive response to this statement moved Goldman to end their relationship soon after the conversation, such was her depth of feeling on the subject. For Goldman, anarchism is first and foremost a creative philosophy, and though it sets itself against (and works to defeat) multiple forms of domination—whether in the form of capitalism, militarism, patriarchy, and more—it was imperative that it do so from a desire to build something new, something better. It is on such terms that she insisted that Nietzsche's 'master idea had nothing to do with the vulgarity of station, caste, or wealth. Rather did it mean the masterful in human possibilities, the masterful in man that would help him to overcome old traditions and worn-out values, so that he may learn to become the creator of new and beautiful things' (1996, p. 233).

In accordance with these ideas about the creative spirit, Goldman also outlined a Nietzschean critique of morality and of mass politics predicated upon the subordination of the individual. These ideas were, for her, mobilised as indistinct from the political struggles in which she was tirelessly engaged, ranging from anti-militarist agitation (for which she spent time in prison for the attempt to convince people to resist the draft), to providing information and support about contraception (for which she was also jailed).

Goldman was uncompromising in her critique of morality. She argued that morality has been a tool by which the rich have convinced ordinary people to accept the naturalness and even desirability of their poverty and dispossession; for instance, it 'is Morality which condemns woman to the position of a celibate, a prostitute, or a reckless, incessant breeder of hapless children' (1996, p. 171). Using language reminiscent of Nietzsche, she argues that:

> the Lie of Morality still stalks about in fine feathers … it is safe to say that no other superstition is so detrimental to growth, so enervating and paralyzing to the minds and hearts of the people, as the superstition of morality. (1996, p. 169)

Just as religion 'paralyzed the mind of the people … morality has enslaved the spirit', providing security for the rich more successfully 'than even the club and gun' (1996, p. 170).

Crucially this disavowal of morality did not for Goldman entail a rejection of ethical responsibility and interconnection, nor the impossibility of taking particular positions. As Bertalan argues, hers 'is not an apathetic, detached, apolitical theoretical exercise lacking a consideration for consequences. Positions *are* taken, identities *are* asserted, injustices *are* addressed, and conceptual and logistical spaces *are* occupied' (2011, p. 218). What is crucial is that these positions are not raised to the metaphysical level of absolute standards, a gesture which will always work to subordinate humanity beneath it. Rather than establishing new idols, the task, for Goldman, must be to engage in an ethics of self-creation:

> The 'beyond good and evil' philosopher, Nietzsche, is at present denounced as the perpetrator of national hatred and machine gun destruction; but only bad readers and bad pupils interpret him so. 'Beyond good and evil' means beyond prosecution, beyond judging, beyond killing, etc. *Beyond Good and Evil* opens before our eyes a vista the background of which is individual assertion combined with the understanding of all others who are unlike ourselves, who are different. (Goldman, 1996, p. 214)

As I outline in more detail below, this sensibility translates directly into the theme of perpetual movement and the archetype of dance through which we can read Goldman.

Alongside this suspicion of morality came a contemptuous response to any form of radical politics which allowed abstracted or over-strategised notions of 'The Cause' to subordinate individual and affective experience. One famous example here (from which comes the apocryphal quote 'if I can't dance it's not my revolution') concerns Goldman's recollection of a particular evening dancing in New York:

> One evening a cousin of Sasha,[2] a young boy, took me aside. With a grave face … he whispered to me that it did not behoove [*sic*] an agitator to dance. Certainly not with such reckless abandon, anyway. It was undignified for one who was on the way to become a force in the anarchist movement. My frivolity would only hurt the Cause.

I grew furious at the impudent interference of the boy. I told him to mind his own business, I was tired of having the Cause constantly thrown into my face. I did not believe that a Cause which stood for a beautiful idea, for anarchism, for release and freedom from conventions and prejudice, should demand the denial of life and joy … I want freedom, the right to self-expression, everybody's right to beautiful, radiant things. Anarchism meant that to me, and I would live it in spite of the whole world—prisons, persecution, everything. Yes, even in spite of the condemnation of my own closest comrades I would live my beautiful ideal. (1970a, p. 56)[3]

This is not to imply that Goldman was unaware of the potential pitfalls of foregrounding the insistence on 'beautiful things' in a context of struggle against poverty and domination. Recalling a conversation with Alexander Berkman, Goldman acknowledges his criticism of spending money on luxuries when so many people were living in poverty:

'But beautiful things are not luxuries,' I insisted; 'they are necessaries [*sic*]. Life would be unbearable without them.' Yet, at heart, I felt that Berkman was right. Revolutionists gave up even their lives—why not also beauty? Still the young artist [Fedya—who had raised the issue] struck a chord with me. I, too, loved beauty. (1970a, p. 32)

I would suggest that it is precisely at the fold of this contradiction that we might interpret Goldman's project. She was certainly no apolitical aesthete, and sacrificed money, comfort, and even her citizenship in the name of political agitation.[4] Despite this, she retained her insistence on an anarchism which embraced and sought life and beauty. Whilst particular choices and priorities must be made, excising politics, or beauty, in the name of the other, in more general terms, fundamentally missed the purpose and content of both.

This suspicion of the ways in which ideals of 'The Cause' could be used to subordinate more particular experiences did not rest at Goldman's insistence on the role of affective experience. On a number of occasions she distanced herself from her comrades by supporting causes or expressing opinions that they felt worked against wider strategic interests. Most notable was her decision to criticise the Russian Revolution following her stay in Russia (2003), though her comments about homosexuality are particularly telling:

Censorship came from some of my own comrades because I was treating such 'unnatural' themes as homosexuality. Anarchism was already enough misunderstood, and anarchists considered depraved; it was inadvisable to add to the misconceptions by taking up perverted sex-forms, they argued. Believing in freedom of opinion, even if it went against me, I minded the censors in my own ranks as little as I did those in the enemy's camp. In fact, censorship from comrades had the same effect on me as police persecution; it made me surer of myself, more determined to plead for every victim, be it one of social wrong or moral prejudice. (1970b, p. 555)

For Goldman, an anarchism which dismissed particular struggles in the name of The Cause was both objectionable and, ultimately, doomed to fail.

As she sought to criticise such strategised formulations of struggle, Goldman also turned her critical focus on what was often felt to be the axiomatic subject of revolution, 'the mass'. In her most controversial (and, perhaps, most Nietzschean) passage, she wrote:

That the mass bleeds, that it is being robbed and exploited, I know as well as our vote-baiters. But I insist that not the handful of parasites, but the mass itself is responsible for this horrible state of affairs. It clings to its master, loves the whip, and is the first to cry Crucify! the moment a protesting voice is raised against the sacredness of capitalistic authority or any other decayed institution. Yet how long would authority and private property exist, if not for the willingness of the mass to become soldiers, policemen, jailers and hangmen.

[…]

OCCUPYING SUBJECTIVITY

> Not because I do not feel with the oppressed, the disinherited of the earth; not because I do not know the shame, the horror, the indignity of the lives the people lead, do I repudiate the majority as a creative force for good. Oh, no, no! But because I know so well that as a compact mass it has never stood for justice or equality. It has suppressed the human voice, subdued the human spirit, chained the human body. As a mass its aim has always been to make life uniform, gray, and monotonous as the desert. As a mass it will always be the annihilator of individuality, of free initiative, of originality. (1969, pp. 77–78)

In this unnerving statement we see many of the above-mentioned features of Goldman's Nietzschean anarchism at their most acute. She qualifies it by citing Emerson: 'I wish not to concede anything to [the masses], but to drill, divide, and break them up, and draw individuals out of them' (1969). Her critique is not levelled so much at individuals within as it is at the perpetual folding of these individuals into the collectivity, whereby the only meaningful expression of political action is one which compels self-denial.

Goldman acknowledges that her perspective here will not be popular ('no doubt, I shall be excommunicated as an enemy of the people' (1969, p. 44)), but nonetheless insisted that at the heart of radical subjectivity must be a commitment to an ethos of dissent and creativity; without this, revolution would only prolong misery and domination under a new idol. It is on such terms that the politics of her Nietzscheanism is most apparent. Chastising poor reading (incidentally an issue which also preoccupied Nietzsche), she condemned 'the shallow interpreters of that giant mind' who did not understand that Nietzsche's 'vision of the *Uebermensch* also called for a state of society which will not give birth to a race of weaklings and slaves' (1969, p. 44). A politics of the mass, for Goldman, can never be the creative force which will give birth to a society beyond the slavery and cruelties of the current one.

This emphatically does not mean that Goldman did not support collective political projects; she spent her life producing propaganda precisely advocating for them, and shortly after writing the above passage arrived in Russia full of hope for the revolution. She cannot be criticised as an inward-looking individualist in the same vein as Nietzsche. Rather, Goldman's critique was not of collective projects as such, but of the traditional dichotomies between individualism and collectivism which presume that one must eclipse the other.[5] In particular, where the (image of the) collective was allowed to dominate and subordinate the individual, rather than reflect and build on the desires and creativities of those within, then the project of liberation begins to wither.

For Goldman, nothing was more pressing than the need to overthrow capitalism and the state. She saw them clearly for what they were (and are): a means of organising society which kept the majority poor and enslaved whilst enriching a small minority. However, for her, a response which was not creative, or which demanded the subordination of the individual to the mass, would only trap us in this world or foster a new tyranny. Energetic and ethical self-creation must be at the heart of any radical project. In this sense, though she targeted her ire at particular processes, moralities, and tendencies, her critique was not limited to these particular forms. She embraced the unknown and insisted on perpetual movement, arguing that 'finalities are for gods and governments, not for the human intellect' (1996, p. 49). Bertalan connects Nietzsche and Goldman on this point through the metaphor of dance. Citing Deleuze, he notes that 'throughout his work, Nietzsche makes use of dance to explain perpetual and creative epistemological shifts ... for Nietzsche, 'dance affirms becoming and the being of becoming' (2011, p. 214, citing Deleuze, 2006, p. 183). As Zarathustra proclaims, 'Only in the dance do I know how to speak the parable of the highest things' (1997, p. 110). Nor should we do Nietzsche the disservice of limiting his statement here to an offhand metaphor—he took it seriously, made sure to note that his dancing was both a spiritual and corporeal concern (2007a, pp. 235–236) and, apparently, could be seen dancing and singing naked in his room (Nietzsche, 2007b, p. 112n70). Emma Goldman's love of dance was noted in the above discussion of 'beautiful things'. In another passage she breathlessly recounts a different evening:

> At the German Club everything was bright and gay. We found Helena's employer, whose name was Kadison, and some of his young friends. I was asked for every dance, and I danced in frantic excitement and abandon. It was getting late and many people were already leaving when Kadison invited me for another dance. Helena insisted that I was too exhausted, but I would not have it so. 'I will dance!' I declared; 'I will dance myself to death!' My flesh felt hot, my heart beat violently as my cavalier swung me round the ball-room, holding me tightly. To dance to death—what more glorious end! (1970a, p. 19)

To dance to death—this was Goldman's project. Perpetual movement, endless self-creation, and an affective experience of the world which refused to draw lines between the micro-politics of desire and domination and the macro-politics of social change. Whether on the dance floor or shuttling around the USA and Europe delivering incendiary speeches and lectures, Goldman never quite stood still; whether consumed with joy at the news of revolution or with grief in the face of suffering, her encounter with radical politics was a deeply affective one. Zarathustra tells us that, 'though there be on earth fens and dense afflictions, he who hath light feet runneth even across the mud, and danceth as upon well-swept ice' (1997, p. 284). Engaging in perpetual political action, and enlivened by the sense that 'it is the *struggle* for, not so much the attainment of, liberty, that develops all that is strongest, sturdiest and finest in human character' (1996, p. 49), Goldman danced.

Are You Ready for a Brand New Beat?

> Organizing to undermine the state, capitalism, and all forms of social domination does not mean that one is faced with a choice between the joys of dancing and revelling and the serious work of class struggle. Far from it. Indeed, if one wants to be a revolutionary, perhaps it is the dancing that one should take more seriously. (Shukaitis, 2009, p. 79)

Examples of dance playing a diverse role in political resistance, both historical and contemporary, are plentiful. Enslaved people in Brazil developed capoeira as a martial art which incorporated dance elements, as a means by which to develop skills that would be needed when attempting to escape colonists without raising suspicion. Elsewhere in this issue, Adam Barker highlights the role of the Round Dance in asserting a specifically indigenous form and identity during the Idle No More protests in Canada in 2012.[6] In 1982, women involved in the Greenham Common Women's Peace Camp broke into RAF Greenham Common and danced on top of the missile silos. In the 1990s the 'Reclaim the Streets' movement in the UK saw thousands of people take over major roads and hold huge street parties, both as an assertion of collective ownership of public space and as a challenge to mass car ownership. It is rare to come across a political demonstration of even moderate size that is not accompanied by a sound system, samba band, or other musical accompaniment, followed by a mass of rhythmically energised activists. Of course, the specific nature and purpose of these (and other) examples of dance in resistance vary with context, representing and performing very different sensibilities. Without wishing to posit a general theory, I would suggest that many contemporary examples demonstrate the centrality of joy, festival, and play to the present-day understandings of creative political change.

Authors like David Graeber have suggested that, over the past 20 years, radical politics across much of the Western world has developed in a direction which has sought to avoid the clichés associated with much of twentieth-century Marxism; po-faced marches, endless factional debates and cleavages, and a strict separation between the serious work of political organising and the desires of everyday life (2007, pp. 375–418). Though this cliché is something of an over-statement, the desire to do radical politics differently remains important. It represents a move to overcome what Simon Critchley has called the 'active nihilism' which plagues forms of protest which are always constituted only through opposition, and which do not focus on creative and immediate transformation (Critchley, 2008, p. 124), and to respect Raoul Vaneigem's infamous charge, that people 'who talk about revolution and class struggle without referring explicitly to everyday life, without understanding what is subversive about love and what is positive in the refusal of constraints—such people have a corpse in their mouth' (Vaneigem, 1994, p. 26). In this sense, it represents precisely the affect-laden and creative politics advocated by Goldman.

Stevphen Shukaitis places these ideas in the context of what he calls 'minor composition'. He argues that political action (whether in the form of protest, occupation, workplace assembly, or otherwise) marked by dance, humour, and conviviality has a particular series of resonances, insofar as it reshapes the relations between subjects at the micro-political level. Protest 'becomes a space where intensive forms of social engagement occur as an integral part of the developing of the collective self of the organising campaign as well as an intervention within the symbolic labour process' (2009, p. 72). He offers an evocative example of one particular (and, up to this point, dour) Mayday demonstration which was rescued from its own trudging monotony by the appearance of a sound system, which created 'an affectively richer composition of relations for those involved' (2009, pp. 78–79). Such moments are not confined to their immediacy: '[m]oments of minor mutation, while often occupying a seemingly insignificant role within the larger social fabric, act as a fulcrum on which larger transformations in collective imagination are initiated' (2009, p. 14). This faith in the importance of minor composition comes from the sense, shared by Goldman, that a change in macro-level political structures which does not emerge from or alongside a shift in everyday social relations will not fundamentally unsettle the place or nature of domination.

The image of festival has been important in understanding the role of these forces in contem-porary resistance. Gavin Grindon highlights the ways in which the alter-globalisation movement foregrounded a sense of festival or carnival as a means by which to bring desire, joy, and dance into the heart of tactical thinking (2007, pp. 94–95). Of course, as Marieke De Goede demon-strates, the role of festival is not a new phenomenon, though its role has undoubtedly expanded over the previous 20 years (2005). De Goede notes one central dimension of political resistance which involves festival; it is, to a certain extent, content with its own irrationality. That is, it does not define success only in terms of policy achievements or the discovery of new hegemonic ideals, but also recognises that political transformations are less easily conceptualised or realised.

As dance and festival perform a frivolous irrationality, they also have a deeply playful dimen-sion. Playfulness is a key component of Goldman's dance. Refusing the imperative to be incor-porated within a systemic rationality, it is valuable precisely on its own terms; nonetheless (and precisely for this reason) play also has deeply subversive implications. Rose Pfeffer, following Nietzsche, suggests that 'play represents an activity that does not aim at any practical utilitarian need and ends, being unconcerned with good and evil, truth and falsity' (1972, p. 207). In one particularly spectacular example, in 2007 a group of anarchists known as the 'Space Hijackers' protested against an arms fair in London by attempting to auction a tank outside the exhibition.

Their (hilarious) account of allowing themselves to be chased around London in their tank, out-manoeuvring the police at every turn, and successfully arriving at the arms fair in East London, evokes the sense of dance in a playful manner which simultaneously satiates the anarchists' desire for fun whilst highlighting the skewed priorities of the state's hapless security forces, who are playing games with anarchists instead of contending with the violence of the arms fair (Space Hijackers, 2007). Sandra Jeppesen argues that:

> [a]narchist theory, like anarchist practice, at its rhizomatic roots, is about play. From playing anarchist soccer to sex and gender play and playing with words to playing with a diversity of tactics, playing with the legalities of border-crossings, or playing with fire—play has always been an anti-authoritarian practice. (2011, p. 158)

None of this is to suggest that any one particular example of dance, festival, and playfulness is necessarily good, ethical, revolutionary, or even particularly creative. Instead, it is to make the more modest suggestion that the presence of these elements in forms of contemporary resistance signifies a certain understanding about the place of creativity and affect, and of the importance of everyday transformation. How these dynamics work out cannot be determined in advance. As Shukaitis argues, 'the politics of carnival do not have any particular set direction *a priori*, whether radicalizing or stabilizing, but are only determined within particular historical conjunctions' (2009, p. 72).

This remains slightly unsatisfying, however. The conception of dance that I take from Nietzsche and Goldman demands more than that we bring an affective and creative spirit into the project of social change. It poses important questions and challenges to the nature of radical subjectivity. The creativity and joyfulness it demands is not a frivolous performance, even though frivolity may be its manifestation; its affirmation cannot be simple—creativity is too ambiguous and too fraught a task for this. It calls for a ceaseless and creative insurrection of the self. It challenges us to dance ourselves to death. Nowhere is this necessity more apparent than in the complications and contradictions we might identify in Goldman herself. In the following section I suggest that, rather than hold Goldman up as an idol, we might focus on her shortcomings and violences, as a means by which to think about the ambiguities of self-creation and the demands which accompany the Nietzschean imperative to dance.

Ambiguities of Self-creation

Thus far, this article has taken Goldman and Nietzsche's pronouncements about dance at face value and has proceeded with a certain series of assumptions about the creative potentials of the dancing subject. However, we can also identify a series of problematic forms or manifestations of dance, which exhibit reactionary, disciplining, or conservative tendencies.

William McNeill's anthropological study *Keeping Together in Time: Dance and Drill in Human History* examines the ways in which the development of military training and military strategy has drawn on the human affectation for rhythmic solidarity (or what he calls 'muscular bonding'), using the affective pleasure which comes from collective movement as a means by which to craft militarily effective social units. He essentially argues that militarism as we know is ontologically rooted in precisely the same human interaction as dance (1995, pp. 101–150). Franz Fanon criticises the way in which dance provides a collective catharsis which saps the energy from more focused revolutionary activity, arguing that:

> . . . any study of the colonial world should take into consideration the phenomena of the dance and of possession. The native's relaxation takes precisely the form of a muscular orgy in which the most

OCCUPYING SUBJECTIVITY

> acute aggressivity and the more impelling violence are canalized, transformed and conjured away.... When they set out [to the dance], the men and women were impatient, stamping their feet in a state of nervous excitement; when they return, peace has been restored to the village; it is once more calm and unmoved. (2001, pp. 44–45)

Shukaitis warns against a confidence which obscures the ways in which spectacular manifestations of dance and festival can be recuperated within a capitalist system always working to commodify popular expressions of dissent, cautioning that 'it is important to not allow the giddiness of line of flight and seemingly endless deterritorialization to obscure the very real line of command of appropriation that capitalist valorization uses precisely in ... networks of coding, decoding and overcoding' (2009, p. 73). And Michel Foucault's work in *Security, Territory, Population* demonstrates clearly how contemporary liberal governance functions precisely through the conduct of creativity and movement (2007). Indeed, several working within dance studies have identified the ways in which a Foucauldian gaze reveals the forms of discipline operating in the studio (Ann Ness, 2011; Green, 2002–2003). And so, against the evocation of dance as a liberatory, creative endeavour, we have a militaristic, depoliticising, readily recuperated, neoliberal framework. What, then, insulates the form of dance outlined here from these important, even fatal challenges?

I would suggest that, to an extent, there can and should be no insulation, and that the radical Dancer must remain perpetually alive to the dangers of her movement. To dance in the footsteps of Goldman and Nietzsche, we need to take the conception of dance beyond corporeal or metaphorical practice, framing it as an ethos of the radical subject. The Dancer is she who is committed to a perpetual project of self-creation. For her, liberation comes when people 'refused to be dazzled by superstitions' of morality and of the necessity of domination and poverty, and instead build their own values and create their own worlds (Goldman, 1996, p. 432). However, the form of radical subjectivity evoked by The Dancer must remain open to and in continual struggle with the reality of those difficult features outlined above. Nietzsche's mobilisation of dance, whilst playful, is also deeply demanding, and not affirmed easily; to engage faithfully, one must contend with the ambiguities of what it really means to 'self-create'. Whilst Goldman was to some extent aware of the difficulties that may be encountered here, there are also certain aspects of her thought which were deeply problematic—principally, elements of cruelty, misogyny, racism, and essentialism. In the following discussion I suggest that is through attention to these features that we might gain a broader perspective on the ambiguities of self-creation.

Goldman has received widespread admiration from anarchists, feminists, and beyond. The eloquent, passionate, and ferocious manner in which she castigates her political opponents for their duplicity, cruelty, or stupidity to this day sends shivers down a host of radical spines. However, and particularly when taking seriously the affective dimensions of Goldman's projects, there is something uncomfortable about the ways in which there has been a tendency to cherry pick the parts of Goldman's thought which are more easily affirmed, leaving other more troubling features in the past. As Clare Hemmings has argued, doing so can serve as a sort of cleansing process, by which we reassure ourselves of our own distance from these problematic perspectives whilst obscuring the ways in which these features can persist (however quietly) in our own practices and movements (2013, pp. 337–340). If political radicalism is to avoid the traps of coalescing into new forms of domination, it must take this process (and the ways in which it reveals the ambiguities of self-creation) seriously.

Hemmings highlights a certain, cruel, misogyny in Goldman's thought. It is true that Goldman differed from many of her contemporaries in refusing to leave the work of women's liberation until 'after' the revolution, and in recognising that dominant relations of production depended precisely on a certain gendered subservience—that is, that women occupied a particular position which situated them as important revolutionary subjects. She also recognised that the form of femininity which rendered women as passive and subservient was not tied to women's natural condition, and that 'true emancipation of women ... will have to do away with the absurd notion of the dualism of the sexes, or that man and woman represent two antagonistic worlds' (1996, p. 167). When encouraging women to reject the subservience and consumerism which dominant ideas about gender compelled, however, Goldman exhibited elements of misogyny. She made 'full use of an affective repertoire that includes humour, rage, irony, and rapture, as she positively will[ed] the women she baits to become subjects and not objects of history' (Hemmings, 2012, p. 533); her concern was to 'shake bourgeois women out of their contentment with gilded cages, and to encourage poor women not to risk all for the false promises of consumerism, marriage security and giving birth to sons' (Hemmings, 2013, p. 341). Nonetheless, Goldman's passionate style betrays more than this analysis, and 'she frequently moves into characterising women themselves—rather than womanhood as a position, or femininity as a capitalist mode—as stupid and superficial to the core', exhibiting a 'vitriol bordering on misogyny' (Hemmings, 2012, pp. 537, 541). What is particularly disquieting is the apparent delight Goldman found in making this case; 'the sheer pleasure she takes in her subject—women's dependency, greed and stupidity—means that this has considerably more liveliness than her suggestions for alternatives' (Hemmings, 2013, p. 341). In her affective and passionate style, Goldman 'risks getting caught up in the sadistic pleasures of humiliating those to whom humiliation already attaches' (Hemmings, 2012, p. 537).

Similarities can be drawn between Goldman's chastising of women and her comments on the 'mass' noted above. In criticising 'the inertia, the cravenness, the utter submission of the mass ... [which] ... wants but to be dominated, to be led, to be coerced', and arguing that 'the majority represents a mass of cowards, willing to accept him who mirrors its own soul and mind poverty', Goldman was engaging in a similar project of trying to excite individuality, movement, disobedience, and creativity (1969, pp. 71–73). However, there is an indulgence in her style which establishes her own terms (and shortcomings) as self-evidently superior, in a manner which perhaps closes her mind to other manners of insurrection. As Hemmings argues:

> in the purity of her position and extremity of her feeling, Goldman is unable to consider that the excessive modes she finds so enraging—manipulation, duplicity, nagging—might be resources women take up in a hyperbolic mode not entirely unlike her own. (2012, p. 538)

There is in Goldman a hierarchisation of quality and authenticity, by which certain examples of creativity or genius are held above others as idols of liberation; and so, frequent references to 'the beauty and genius of an Emerson, Thoreau, Whitman; an Ibsen, a Hauptmann, a Butler Yeats, or a Stephen Phillips' (Goldman, 1969, p. 71) set a certain standard of taste. Moreover, she sees such figures as struggling *against* forms of oppression in order to express their individuality, failing to consider the ways in which these (mostly white, mostly male) figures also benefited from those very same structures of oppression. The problem here is not in Goldman's call for an insurrection against stultifying, moralising, and submissive modes of being, but in the ways she establishes such insurrections from a privileged vantage point. Her attempted redemption of Nietzsche's aristocrat, as manifesting an aristocracy of the spirit rather than of wealth or caste, nonetheless retains an imaginary predicated on and produced through social hierarchy.

This is not to suggest that Goldman was not capable of being self-critical; indeed, she was very hard on herself when she felt that she had fallen short of her own standards. On one level, it is simply to point out certain important shortcomings in her analysis, many of which persist in contemporary political thought. And so, to the above issues of hierarchisation and misogyny we can point to the ways in which Goldman evaded more difficult questions about American race politics by highlighting her Jewishness (Hemmings, 2013, p. 337), or the optimism (however cautious) Goldman placed in the idea of 'human nature' (1969, pp. 61–62).[7] I want to suggest, however, that these problematic perspectives might to some extent stem from the overconfident manner in which Goldman invokes self-creation. In one sense, this is a rhetorical move, a challenge for people to defy the conventions of the age ('how many women are strong enough to face ... condemnation, to defy the moral dicta?' (1996, p. 174)). It also has an onto-political component, rooted in the understanding that 'man has as much liberty as he is willing to take' (1969, p. 65), and that it is important 'to begin with ... inner regeneration, to cut loose from the weight of prejudices, traditions, and customs' (1996, p. 167). However, Goldman does not pay a great deal of attention to the ways in which creation is an ambiguous concept which, despite poetry and promise, never simply removes us from the world in which we have been made. Attempts to create new values, new systems, and new subjectivities never quite shake off their heritage; in the face of confident pronouncements about women's liberation we find misogyny; in the call for liberation we have familiar images of social hierarchy.

Whilst he was himself uncompromising about the need for self-creation, Nietzsche was more circumspect about its ontological content. In Karl Jaspers' terms, he was '*necessarily* indefinite':

> Nietzsche always treats creation as though it were self-evident, but virtually never takes it as his theme. He does not develop and explain its nature. It is never a possible goal of the will. But his formulations have all the power of an as yet indefinite appeal to recall and to come to grips with authentic being. (1980, p. 145, emphasis in original)

Firm or confident proclamations about creation too easily trap us within the dominant order, and blind us to the ways in which we are always produced through and implicated in the violences of the world; as such, a more delicate series of manoeuvres may be necessary:

> Nietzsche's stern earnestness paralyzes every sort of moral pathos. His kind of thinking can not rest content with, or even find edification in, any proposition, demand, law, or specific content. It proceeds indirectly by demanding that one take seriously those profound inner depths that would simply be obstructed by appeal to any derived law and any fixed standard. (1980, pp. 147–148)

The Nietzschean-inspired anarchist Gustav Landauer expressed similar sentiments when he argued that '[w]hat most anarchists like to present to us as an ideal society is too often merely rational and stuck in our current reality to serve as a guiding light for anything that could or should ever be in the future' (2010, p. 89).

This caution about firm prescriptions and recognition of the ways in which purportedly new social forms so frequently reflect that which they supposedly displaced does not mean that we should therefore abandon concrete creative tasks of the sort that Goldman, Landauer, and many others were (and are) involved in. It does, perhaps, mean that we might take more seriously Nietzsche's best known aphorism:

> He who fights with monsters should look to it that he himself does not become a monster. And when you gaze long into an abyss the abyss also gazes into you. (2003, p. 146)

Whilst there is no shortage of interpretations of this statement, in the context here I suggest that it might be read both more obviously as a warning against becoming that which one opposes, but more substantially as a reflection of the demands that self-creation poses; seemingly trapped between the overbearing presence of where we have been and the dizzying, potentially danger-ous possibilities of where we might go, the imperative to create stands without ground or content, and yet remain crucial. As Nietzsche points towards the unnerving nature of the abyss, he also draws us towards it; preparing to encounter the idea of eternal recurrence, Zar-athustra proclaims to himself 'Now only dost thou go the way to thy greatness! Summit and abyss—these are now comprised together!' (1997, p. 149). The impossible trauma of self-cre-ation, in which we seek to remake the world knowing that we can never quite escape it, and knowing that our (necessary) attempts will always themselves (re)produce forms of oppression, place a heavy and urgent burden, both to continue creating, and to subject these creations to the utmost interrogation. This is not a straightforward waltz into the future, but a dancing on the margins which finds little resting space. As the examples at the outset of this section made clear, dance is not innocent, and can be found in or turned to the service of life-denying forces. The argument I outline here does not diminish this danger, but instead insists that The Dancer in Goldman and Nietzsche's terms proceed precisely with a lively and active sense of the possibility of these dangers, and with an understanding that this makes stasis an unconscion-able choice. The Dancer must dance herself to death.

Dancing Ourselves to Death

> Ye higher men, the worst thing in you is that ye have none of you learned to dance as ye ought to dance—to dance beyond yourselves! What doth it matter that ye have failed!

> How many things are still possible! So learn to laugh beyond yourselves! Life up your hearts, ye good dancers, high! higher! And do not forget the good laughter. (Nietzsche, 1997, p. 285)

In this article dance has been used to signify both a corporeal, affective practice of resistance, and as a metaphor for a mobile and creative radical subjectivity. The latter has been somewhat compromised by the recognition that creativity is a deeply ambiguous concept, both necessary and fraught with problems. However, this recognition and its accompanying caution are not intended to constitute a limitation on or dulling of the dancing subject, but are themselves imbued with a certain creative force. Three final comments on the nature of The Dancer serve to situate her as a subject of ceaseless insurrection, creative responsibility, and cheerful irony.

What is striking about Goldman's conception of radical subjectivity is that it is a ceaselessly mobile one, never resting, always creating, and never arriving:

> The 'arrived' artists are dead souls upon the intellectual horizon. The uncompromising and daring spirits never 'arrive'. Their life represents an endless battle with the stupidity and the dullness of their time. They must remain what Nietzsche calls 'untimely,' because everything that strives for new form, new expression or new values is always doomed to be untimely. (1996, pp. 223–224)

This is an endless dance which permits few resting spaces and which allows no part of life to excuse itself from the imperative to recognise domination and to create anew. Her challenge is to render oneself vulnerable to this experience, to evade the stasis of morality and superstition and embrace the unknown, to acknowledge and even delight in the fracturing of one's subjec-tivity. The Dancer is a courageous figure, practicing what Nietzsche refers to as the 'art of sep-arating without creating enemies; not conflating, not 'reconciling' anything; an immense multiplicity which is nevertheless the opposite of chaos' (EH, *Why I Am So Clever*, 9). Bertalan cites Butler, who argues that the 'unitary subject':

is the one who knows already what it is, who enters the conversation the same way as it exits, who fails to put its own epistemological certainties at risk in the encounter with the other, and so stays in place, guards its place, and becomes an emblem for property and territory. (Bertalan, 2011, p. 222, citing Butler, 2004, p. 228)

Instead, we may choose to hold less tightly to our impressions of who we are:

Nietzsche views humans not as finished beings but as works of art, and specifically works in progress. The philosophy of becoming implies a single ethical imperative: become who you are, create yourself as a masterpiece. And as Nietzsche argues, this involves creating one's own law (Call, 2002, p. 51).

There is, for Lewis Call, a powerful synthesis between the micro- and macro-political implications here, insofar as an ethic of self-creation undermines the conditions of possibility of statist/totalitarian thought. He cites Rolando Perez, who argues that 'the overman or over (wo)man is she who no longer needs the State, or any other institution, for that matter. She is her own creator of values and as such the first true an(archist)' (Call, 2002, p. 52).

These flighty evocations of a multiple, dancing subject are, however, only part of this story. Their cheerful optimism about the space and opportunities for creativity must be read alongside those trends in Nietzsche and Goldman which point towards a weighty responsibility. It is only through engaging with this dynamic that we can really grasp what it might mean to dance to death. Responsibility is a fundamental concept for Nietzsche (though, as with creativity, under-discussed). Jaspers lays out the challenge well:

Thus Nietzsche's freedom without transcendence is by no means intent upon simply returning to mere life; it aspires to the life of authentic creation. Just as Nietzsche's denial of morals does not mean the annulment of all morality but a laying hold upon what is *more than merely moral,* so here his sole intention is to stimulate man to higher achievement. To be sure, without God, Nietzsche's purpose seems to lead to the radical loss of all bonds: what remains is just to live as before and to allow life to continue as always. But this is to turn Nietzsche's idea into its very opposite. Its challenge is tremendous, for the entire burden is laid upon the individual ... Nietzsche is asking those who abandon morality to bind themselves by still higher and more inexorable bonds. (1980, pp. 149–150)

The responsibility here is twofold: firstly, we must create something meaningful, something which does not simply replicate past forms or flee towards nothingness. Secondly, we must undermine ourselves seriously. To affirm the challenge of transvaluation whilst believing it to be easy is to fail, indeed, to not even begin. Nietzsche makes this clear when discussing the idea of cheerfulness; as Ansell-Pearson argues, a shallow cheerfulness is really miserable, because it:

does not see the sufferings and monsters [it] purports to see and combat ... tries to convince us that things are easier than they really are ... The cheerfulness we can respond to must come from one who has thought most deeply and who loves what is most living. (2005, p. 37)

An easy affirmation of Nietzsche's freedom is a chimera, a fraud which misses what is most challenging, profound, and productive. This is a challenge which Goldman made to other anarchists in her injunctions to draw anarchism into every phase of life—though, as we have seen, it is also a challenge with which she herself struggled.

It is here that the seriousness with which Nietzsche took self-reflection contextualises his cheerfulness in important ways—his was the cheerfulness of one who has thought most deeply. And so, he cheekily proclaims:

OCCUPYING SUBJECTIVITY

> His step betrayeth whether a person already walketh on *his own* path: just see me walk! He, however, who cometh night to his goal, danceth ... Life up your hearts, my brethren, high, higher! And do not forget your legs! Lift up also your legs, ye good dancers: and better still, if ye stand upon your heads! (1997, pp. 283–284)

However, he also writes that 'The most intellectual men, provided they are also the most courageous, experience the most excruciating tragedies: but on that very account they honour life, because it confronts them with its most formidable antagonism' (2007a, p. 57). Amongst these tragedies involves the recognition that we are more tied to our superstitions, more desiring of domination, and more faithful to our idols, than we might wish to acknowledge.

This simultaneously joyful and painful encounter with the world (which one also finds in Goldman) evokes an ironic subject, a perpetually disruptive and partial self. Ansell-Pearson points towards:

> the self-referential aspects of Nietzsche's philosophy, which mock his own authority and draw attention to the personal nature of his principal thoughts and teachings (that the will to power is *his* interpretation of existence; that eternal return represents *his* formula for the highest affirmation of life possible, etc.) ... Nietzsche conceives himself, not as another ascetic priest, but as a *comedian* of the ascetic ideal. (1994, pp. 58–59)

Nietzsche pulls himself apart gleefully and self-consciously. As he proclaims 'I am Dynamite', he simultaneously ponders 'Maybe I am a clown' (2007a, p. 253). He challenges us to cheerfully, seriously cheerfully, dance our way through life, learning to recognise the ways in which we remain faithful to superstition and domination such that we might create ourselves anew:

> By teaching us that we must pursue a perpetual project of self-overcoming and self-creation, constantly losing and finding ourselves in the river of becoming, Nietzsche ensures that our subjectivity will be fluid and dispersed, multiple and pluralistic rather than fixed and centered, singular and totalitarian. (Call, 2002, p. 33)

Call suggests that a Nietzschean might criticise anarchism because it constructs itself as a particularistic sect, 'a political theory which would replace the nations of Germany and France with a "nation" of Bakuninites'. He argues that 'The dominant figure in Nietzsche's utopian political imaginary is much more profoundly non-sectarian. She is indeed *nomadic* in character' (2002, p. 41). The explorations here have suggested that Goldman might be read in just this nomadic light, arguing that a radical politics that will truly change the world must dance, must be creative, joyful, multiple, and must take seriously the challenge of an ethos of self-creation which truly seeks to unsettle our endless complicity in domination, and which recognises that this task is never fully complete, that we must dance to death.

Notes

1   Cautioning against focusing too much on the specifics of Nietzsche's political pronouncements, Lewis Call suggests that we think more generally in terms of the 'Nietzsche effect'. Call cites Ansell-Pearson arguing that the most fertile spaces are not Nietzsche's 'overt pronouncements ... but rather in their "style(s)", in their attempt to communicate a philosophy of the body, in their disclosure of the metaphoricity of philosophical discourse, and in the exemplary way in which they are seen to deconstruct the logocentric bias of western thought and reason' (Call, 2002, p. 35, citing Ansell-Pearson, 1993, p. 29).

2   Sasha was Goldman's name for Alexander Berkman, her lover, and closest comrade.

3   On the origin of the quote 'if I can't dance it's not my revolution', see Shulman (1991).

4   Goldman was deported from the USA in 1919.

5   See Goldman (1970a, pp. 402–403) and also Ferguson (2013, pp. 164–166).

OCCUPYING SUBJECTIVITY

6   Indeed, a recently published book reflecting on the Idle No More protests is entitled 'The Winter We Danced' (The Kino-nda-niimi Collective, 2014).

7   For a carefully nuanced account of Goldman's problematic encounter with race, see Ferguson (2013, pp. 211–241). On the contested relationship between anarchism and 'human nature', and for critiques of this humanism, see Newman (2007), May (1991), and Jun (2012).

References

Ann Ness, S. (2011). Foucault's turn from phenomenology: Implications for dance studies. *Dance Research Journal, 43*(2), 19–32. doi:10.1017/S0149767711000039

Ansell-Pearson, K. (1993). Nietzsche, woman, and political theory. In P. Patton (Ed.), *Nietzsche, feminism, and political theory* (pp. 27–48). New York: Routledge.

Ansell-Pearson, K. (1994). *An introduction to Nietzsche as a political thinker: The perfect Nihilist.* Cambridge: Cambridge University Press.

Ansell-Pearson, K. (2005). *How to read Nietzsche.* London: Granta.

Bertalan, H. (2011). When theories meet: Emma Goldman and 'post-anarchism'. In D. Rousselle & S. Evren (Eds.), *Post-anarchism: A reader* (pp. 208–230). London: Pluto Press.

Butler, J. (2004). *Undoing gender.* New York: Routledge.

Call, L. (2002). *Postmodern anarchism.* Oxford: Lexington Books.

Colson, D. (2004). Nietzsche and the libertarian workers' movement. In J. Moore (Ed.), *I am not a man, I am dynamite! Friedrich Nietzsche and the anarchist tradition* (pp. 12–28). Brooklyn, NY: Autonomedia.

Critchley, S. (2008). *Infinitely demanding: Ethics of commitment, politics of resistance.* London: Verso.

De Goede, M. (2005). Carnival of money: Politics of dissent in an era of globalizing finance. In L. Amoore (Ed.), *The global resistance reader* (pp. 379–391). London: Routledge.

Deleuze, G. (2006). *Nietzsche and philosophy.* (H. Tomlinson, Trans.). London: Continuum.

Fanon, F. (2001). *The wretched of the earth.* London: Penguin.

Ferguson, K. (2004). E.G.: Emma Goldman, for example. In D. Taylor and K. Vintges (Eds.), *Feminism and the final Foucault* (pp. 28–40). Urbana: University of Illinois Press.

Ferguson, K. (2013). *Emma Goldman: Political thinking in the streets.* Plymouth: Rowman & Littlefield.

Foucault, M. (2007). *Security, territory, population: Lectures at the Collège de France, 1977–1978.* (G. Burchell, Trans.). New York: Picador.

Goldman, E. (1969). *Anarchism and other essays.* Mineola, NY: Dover.

Goldman, E. (1970a). *Living my life* (Vol. 1). Mineola, NY: Dover.

Goldman, E. (1970b). *Living my life* (Vol. 2). Mineola, NY: Dover.

Goldman, E. (1996). *Red Emma speaks: An Emma Goldman reader.* Amherst, NY: Humanity Books.

Goldman, E. (2003). *My disillusionment in Russia.* Mineola, NY: Dover.

Graeber, D. (2007). *Possibilities: Essays on hierarchy, rebellion, and desire.* Oakland, CA: AK Press.

Green, J. (2002–3). Foucault and the training of docile bodies in dance education. *Arts and Learning, 19*(1), 99–126.

Grindon, G. (2007). The breath of the possible. In S. Shukaitis & D. Graeber (Eds.), *Constituent imagination: Militant investigations//collective theorization* (pp. 94–108). Oakland, CA and Edinburgh: AK Press.

Hemmings, C. (2012). In the mood for revolution: Emma Goldman's passion. *New Literary History, 43,* 527–545. doi:10.1353/nlh.2012.0030

Hemmings, C. (2013). Considering Emma. *European Journal of Women's Studies, 20,* 334–346. doi:10.1177/1350506813502022

Jaspers, K. (1980). Man as his own creator. In R. C. Solomon (Ed.), *Nietzsche: A collection of critical essays* (pp. 131–155). Notre Dame, IN: University of Notre Dame Press.

Jeppesen, S. (2011). Things to do with post-structuralism in a life of anarchy: Relocating the outpost of post-anarchism. In D. Rousselle & S. Evren (Eds.), *Post-anarchism: A reader* (pp. 151–159). London: Pluto Press.

Jun, N. (2012). *Anarchism and political modernity.* New York: Continuum.

Koch, A. (1993). Poststructuralism and the epistemological basis of anarchism. *Philosophy of the Social Sciences, 23,* 327–351. doi:10.1177/004839319302300304

Landauer, G. (2010). *Revolution and other writings: A political reader* (G. Kuhn, Trans.). Oakland, CA: PM Press.

May, T. (1991). *The political philosophy of poststructuralist anarchism.* University Park, PA: Pennsylvania State University Press.

McNeill, W. H. (1995). *Keeping together in time: Dance and drill in human history.* Cambridge, MA: Harvard University Press.

Newman, S. (2004). Anarchism and the politics of ressentiment. In J. Moore (Ed.), *I am not a man, I am dynamite! Friedrich Nietzsche and the anarchist tradition* (pp. 107–126). Brooklyn, NY: Autonomedia.

Newman, S. (2007). *From Bakunin to Lacan: Anti-authoritarianism and the dislocation of power.* Plymouth: Lexington Books.

Nietzsche, F. (1997). *Thus Spake Zarathustra.* (T. Common, Trans.). Ware: Wordsworth.

Nietzsche, F. (2001). *The gay science.* (J. Nauckhoff, Trans.). Cambridge: Cambridge University Press.

Nietzsche, F. (2003). *Beyond good and evil.* (R. J. Hollingdale, Trans.). London: Penguin.

Nietzsche, F. (2006). *The genealogy of morals.* (C. Diethe, Trans.). Cambridge: Cambridge University Press.

Nietzsche, F. (2007a). *Twilight of the idols, with the antichrist and Ecce Homo.* (A. M. Ludovici, Trans.). Ware: Wordsworth Editions.

Nietzsche, F. (2007b). *Ecce Homo: How to become what you are.* (D. Large, Trans.). Oxford: Oxford University Press.

Pfeffer, R. (1972). *Nietzsche: Disciple of dionysus.* Cranbury, NJ: Bucknell University Press.

Rocker, R. (1937). *Nationalism and culture.* Los Angeles, CA: Rocker Publications Committee.

Shukaitis, S. (2009). *Imaginal machines: Autonomy & self-organization in the revolutions of everyday life.* London: Minor Compositions.

Shulman, A. K. (1991). Women of the PEN: Dances with feminists. *The Women's Review of Books, 9*(3), 13. doi:10.2307/4021093

Space Hijackers. (2007). Tuesday, September 11th—Tank Day [webpage]. Retrieved from http://spacehijackers.org/html/projects/dsei07/tuesday.html

Starcross, L. (2004). 'Nietzsche was an anarchist': Reconstructing Emma Goldman's Nietzsche lectures. In J. Moore (Ed.), *I am not a man, I am dynamite! Friedrich Nietzsche and the Anarchist tradition* (pp. 29–39). Brooklyn, NY: Autonomedia.

The Kino-nda-niimi Collective. (2014). *The winter we danced: Voices from the past, the future, and the idle no more movement.* Winnipeg, MB: Arbeiter Ring.

Vaneigem, R. (1983). *The book of pleasures.* (J. Fullerton, Trans.). Retrieved from http://theanarchistlibrary.org/library/raoul-vaneigem-the-book-of-pleasures

Vaneigem, R. (1994). *The revolution of everyday life.* (D. Nicholson-Smith, Trans.). London: Rebel Press.

Liberation for Straw Dogs? Old Materialism, New Materialism, and the Challenge of an Emancipatory Posthumanism

ERIKA CUDWORTH & STEPHEN HOBDEN

University of East London, London, UK

ABSTRACT *The term 'new materialism' has recently gained saliency as a descriptor for an eclectic range of positions that question the human-centred and human-exclusive focus of scholarship across the humanities and social sciences. In turn these emerging perspectives have been subject to critique by those writing in the established materialist tradition, who argue that new materialism ignores the unique specificity of human agency and the transformatory capabilities of our species. Our previous interventions have endorsed a particular account of posthumanism that draws together complexity influenced systems theory with elements of political ecologism that have incorporated aspects of established materialist and humanist thinking. This article rejects the old materialist critique that denies the emancipatory potential of posthumanist thinking, and explores the potential for an emancipatory posthumanism.*

Introduction

In Tom Robbins' comic novel, *Skinny Legs and All*, a series of inanimate objects—a sock, a can of beans, a silver spoon, and two ancient and spiritually invested things, a painted stick (or self-described 'navigational instrument'), and a conch shell—find themselves brought together by events and destined to travel together from the American Midwest to Jerusalem. The reader should allay disbelief, cautions Robbins, because:

> The inertia of objects is deceptive. The inanimate world appears static, 'dead' to humans only because of our neuromuscular chauvinism. We are so enamoured by our own activity range that ... We regard the objects that polka-dot our daily lives as if they were rigid, totally predictable solids, frozen inferiority in time and space. (Robbins, 1991, p. 62)

OCCUPYING SUBJECTIVITY

But lo and behold:

> A gentle nudge from Conch Shell's spire punctured the bean can's musings. 'We must depart now',
> Conch Shell said. 'Painted Stick has taken his fix on the guide star. '
> 'Hey' yelled Dirty Sock. 'Round 'em up and head 'em out!' He was certainly enjoying himself.
> Spoon popped up tentatively over the gully edge. She was nervous but under control.
> Very well, thought Can o' Beans. On to Jerusalem ...
> Under cover of darkness they scooted, toddled and bounced along ... (Robbins, 1991, p. 63)

Of all the complicated interwoven narratives that make up the book, the travails of the internationally travelling objects are most hilarious. We think that some of the 'old' and some of the 'new' materialists discussed in this paper might also laugh at the antics of these plucky and determined things. They would do so, however, for different reasons. For new materialists, accounts of agency that are human-centred and human-exclusive fail to attend to the powers of the non-human world in making and remaking our shared world. Robbins, like theorists working within new materialism, is perfectly clear that shells and cans of pork and beans cannot speak as we humans do, but challenges us to imagine what they might have to say. Yet, there have been strong criticisms of such a position of distributed agency. If we humans are simply another node in the relational net of lively matter then how exactly can we be seen to act in and on the world, in particular, in the pursuit of human projects of emancipation? For old materialists, the laugh is that the contents of a comic novel and a book on political theory might show such striking resemblance.

We have recently made a call for a *Posthuman International Relations*. As such, our work has been associated with 'new materialism' (Chandler, 2013a, 2013b). It is worth noting that ideas about which ideas and positions might be 'posthumanist', and which might be 'new materialist', are often used interchangeably by many authors identifying with such positions, and also by their critics (Braidotti, 2013; Schmidt, 2013). Whilst we are not quite convinced that the overlap is as tight as some suggest, in this paper we examine some examples of posthumanist/new materialist positions and their challenge to human-centred notions of the political.

As Coole and Frost suggest (2010, p. 1), in the light of the 'massive materiality' that makes us up in our embodied condition as human animals—embedded in webs of dependencies and relations with myriad other species and forms of 'matter', produced and reproduced by social and economic structures that shape our everyday existences—how could we be anything other than 'materialists'? The new materialist turn has also been given added impetus by the development of controversial political issues which involve the politics of matter—such as climate change or applications of biotechnology. We see this broadening out of concern with the material as a positive move towards more inclusive and less parochial social science. Yet whilst we might concur with Coole and Frost that we are increasingly 'all' materialists now, they underplay the contention around the notion of the material.

For some, perhaps 'old materialists', the increasing influence of new materialism has been a matter for concern. In particular, the eclectic and often slippery perspectives that constitute new materialism have been seen to undermine the potency of older more established materialist positions, particularly those associated with Marxism. Here, we consider arguments that new materialism ignores the unique specificity of human agency and the transformatory capabilities of our species. Interestingly, for some advocates of posthumanism, and for some critics, the division between 'old' and 'new' materialism is dichotomous—it concerns ontological incompatibility. Criticisms of our own work have alluded to this and suggested that we are 'bolting on' complexity analysis to a normative political project that is decidedly humanist (Edelmann, 2012). Our previous interventions have certainly endorsed a particular account of posthumanism that draws together complexity influenced systems theory with elements of political ecologism that have incorporated aspects of established materialist and humanist thinking. This article explores the potential for a number of political projects within a posthumanist frame. In doing so, we reject the old materialist critique that denies the emancipatory potential of posthumanist thinking; and question those positions in new materialism that tend towards biological determinism and which have been largely responsible for generating these critiques.

Varieties of New Materialism and the Challenge to Humanist Politics

At one level, the intellectual project of new materialism is to insist on a reconfiguring of our ideas about the social, economic, and political as a result of developments in the natural sciences that have disturbed nineteenth century certainties about the nature of the material world (Coole & Frost, 2010, p. 5–7). This project is a broad and a contested one. In this section, we discuss the range of approaches in posthumanism/new materialism, but first, we begin by considering what might be common strands.

'Ten Tenets of the New Materialism'

While Connolly (2013a, pp. 399–402) suggests that there are 10 distinguishing features which unite the various very different new materialist approaches, we suggest that these can be grouped under three main headings.

First, the radical ontological claim of the new materialism is the priority given to matter. Matter, and in particular its self-organising capabilities, becomes the centre of attention. This leads to a rejection of a mind and body distinction. All things, living and non-living, are constituted of the same basic elements. Connolly describes this ontological position as a 'protean monism'. Matter is therefore (drawing on complexity thinking) imbued with a dynamic quality which contains self-organising capacity, such that there is a tendency for ever more complex formations to appear. Matter is not seen as 'dead' but as containing energy–matter complexes which are constantly in flux.

A second area of concern relates to the implications of thinking within new materialism. Connolly advocates a 'speculative realism'. This rejects postmetaphysical approaches (that is, those demonstrating reflexivity in their use of Enlightenment categories such as 'reason') in favour of a 'contestable metaphysic and cosmology'. This stresses the dynamic character of matter such that an awareness is demonstrated of '*differential periods of stability, being and relative equilibrium in this or that zone while coming to terms with periods of real disequilibrium and becoming*' (Connolly, 2013a, 2013b, p. 400, emphasis in original). This disjuncture between periods of stability and instability has epistemological issues which challenge traditional approaches for understanding human and non-human processes. As a result a 'problem orientation' is needed. Likewise the new materialism challenges human-centred ways of thinking. While humans may not be the centre of things, Connolly argues that they think more profoundly about their situation than other species. This, he argues, does not excuse humanity from thinking about its position in the context of a wider set of relations with the rest of nature; rather, it heightens this responsibility.

Third, the acknowledgement of the subjectivity of humanity in a world where the human is not *necessary* prompts Connolly to advocate the development of an 'ethic of cultivation'. Such an ethic needs to be located both at the level of the individual and within institutions. Additionally our focus of attention needs to be wider than the local, which Connolly describes as 'the sufficiency of cultural internalism'. While the focus cannot be everything, all of the time, there is a requirement to be aware of the embedded character of phenomena and the levels of analysis in which it is possible to investigate. Ultimately our concerns should be at the planetary level. Such a focus also prompts us to be aware that there may be things beyond our comprehension—and such issues, politics being one, oblige experimental action.

As noted, Connolly advocates a speculative realism. This is a philosophical realism as opposed to a political realism. And it is a realism of a very specific sort. While it maintains that there is a physical world of which we can have knowledge, it denies a separation between us as observers and material objects. The mind is an emergent feature of the body. It is *speculative* in the sense of acknowledging an awareness to the limits of our knowledge. This acknowledges a central unknowableness to existence related to the difficulties in understanding processes of self-organisation. Connolly (2013b, p. 77) argues that 'we are beings flopping around in one corner of a cosmos that exceeds our capacity for knowledge, self-awareness, and mastery'. As a result speculative realism 'folds a fungible element of mystery into its philosophy' (Connolly, 2013b, p. 9).

Connolly is keen to emphasise the common underpinnings of new materialism and we concur with his 'ten tenets' as a useful definitional starting point. Yet these ten tenets have given rise to a plethora of positions, and these have marked differences. There is a spectrum of approaches to posthumanism that might be considered to be more or less critical in focus and give rise to rather different political projects. One of the reasons for this is that Connolly's ten tenets do not indicate the divergences between different ontological positions implied by the divergences in, for example, complexity thinking. As we have found, there is 'no unified theory of complexity' (Bertuglia & Vaio, 2005, p. 315). The term can be used to describe a variety of theoretical positions which draw upon a similar conceptual lexicon while having radically different epistemological and ontological perspectives. Elsewhere we have identified four different ways in which complexity theory has been applied in the social sciences (Cudworth & Hobden, 2009).

Our own engagement with complexity has been general and philosophical, and built around three interdependent concepts we have found particularly useful: complex adaptive systems, self-organisation, and emergence (Cudworth & Hobden, 2011). Our selection of these concepts has a number of motivations which have led us to develop a particular perspective within new materialism. While Connolly uses complexity in a reinvention of pluralism, we use it to very different ends. There is then, we suggest, a plurality of posthumanisms, some of which, we will now explore.

Varieties of Posthumanist Political Theory

The term posthumanism has been understood in a variety of different ways (Wolfe, 2010, p. xi). In line with Connolly's 'ten tenets' however, a clear common theme in posthumanist scholarship would be to say that it represents a reaction against the view of human exceptionalism (or anthropocentrism). This view understands humanity to be marked off from the huge diversity of non-human animal life due to 'exceptional characteristics', such as the possession of syntactical language or of 'free will'.

One strand of new materialism/posthumanism might be referred to as 'new vitalism'. The latter has been particularly associated with the influence of Gilles Deleuze, who did not consider himself a materialist but rather was concerned that his work be understood as vitalist (Coole & Frost, 2010, p. 9). In political work, this position is best illustrated by the 'enchanted' or 'vital' materialism of Bennett (2010) who argues that inorganic matter such as kerbside litter (trash) or an electricity grid, all exhibit force and vitality rendering them active, productive, and self-creating. Bennett argues for a vital materialism in order to recognise the role of apparently inanimate matter affecting and configuring situations and events. In vital materialism there is a tendency to minimise the differences between subjects and objects with this notion of a vitality which runs through both human and non-human matter. The end in view is the development of a more environmentally aware and cautious politics, but the elevation of the 'shared materiality of all things' does seem to be a rather blunt instrument in securing this end. Bennett's notion of 'thing power' understands agentic capacity as distributed, apparently equally, 'across a range of ontological types' (2004, pp. 347–372).

There are difficulties here of both conceptual conflation and lack of clarity. For Bennett, non-human assemblages can act. However, what she actually seems to mean is that assemblages can have an impact or effect on humans and non-humans. Here, Bennett is conflating the idea of the properties and powers of beings and things, and the notion of action and the idea of agency, and there are serious questions to be raised about her assumption that a distributed concept of agency will be effective in unsettling humancentric politics (2010, p. 13).

The second approach, hybridisation, is best illustrated by the contributions of Bruno Latour, for whom the social world is an assembly of material entities and processes which is constituted through the interactions of all kinds of matter (human and non-human) in the form of networks. Latour (1993) describes the emergence of apparently modern Western societies through the interaction of two processes—purification and hybridisation. The processes of purification involve the separation of the human world from the world of things and the construction of the world of nature and its scientific study; separate from the study of the social world with its selves, cultures, and politics. Yet, Latour argues, the human social world has never been pure, despite all the attempts to extricate it from the world of nature. However 'modern' we think we are, our world is one of relative degrees of hybridisation as we are caught in networks of interactions and relations between what Latour would understand as more or less natural and more or less social phenomena. Within these networks, non-human matter can be understood as 'actant'. This is both a counter to humancentric prejudice, and reflects our reality as one of the multitude of species situated in a range of 'attachments' on planet earth (Latour, 2009, pp. 72–84).

Latour's actor network theory (ANT) holds that agency may be attributed to any object or 'actant', temporarily constituted by the emergent web of 'materially heterogeneous relations' (Law, 2009, p. 71). Here, as with the vital materialist position, agency is inflated conceptually (so that it becomes simply a capacity for action) and extensively (so that anything that has an effect on something else is seen as an actant, from fishermen to scallops). However, the difficulty with Latour is that in his broad sweep, all agency is understood as of the same quality. In addition, it is a property of 'things' rather than, as complexity thinking suggests, of systems in relation. Like Latour, we want to be able to discuss the ways that all kinds of creatures, beings, and things, bound up in relations of complex systems and relations with their system environments, and are agential in the sense that they might 'make a difference in the world' (Giddens, 1984). Both Latour and Bennett can be seen as subscribing to a position of agential realism. Here, the agency of matter, distributed across the world of 'being', makes up the beings, things, and relations of which our world is composed. In both hybridity and vitalism, there is a tendency to horizontalism—relations are not understood to exist in a context of hierarchies of power. The flat, non-hierarchical networks for ANT cannot deal with power because it cannot make distinctions between nature and society, or between humans, other animals, plants, and objects. In theorising power, we consider that need such distinction between different kinds of being and objects in the world in order to recognise, for example, that distinction such as those between humans and all other 'animals' are forged through and continue to carry, relations of inequality and domination. It is this flattening of social relations which old materialists find so objectionable in new materialist approaches.

Our own complexity engagements have led us down a very different route wherein we have been interested in the relations between stability and change, and the resilience of complex systems. We have remained committed to many of the insights of the varieties of political ecologism and have advanced a notion of 'complex ecologism' in trying to understand the current social formations of what, after Haraway, we would call 'naturecultures'. This uses complexity theory with its notions of co-existing, interrelated, multi-levelled systems to capture the ontological depth of relational systems of social domination (of colonialism, capitalism, patriarchy, and so on) and their intersections. Complex ecologism assumes the co-constitution and co-evolution of social and natural systems in dynamic configurations (Cudworth & Hobden, 2011, pp. 110–139). Whilst we have acknowledged that human communities of all kinds live in relations of dependency and reciprocity within complex natural/social systems with non-human beings, things, and processes, we have stressed the domination of non-human nature under certain kinds of relations and the ways in which certain groups of relatively privileged humans are able to assert domination over certain other kinds of human, other animal, and life forms.

Drawing on Archer's (2000) discussions of primary and corporate agency, and on Nickie Charles and Bob Carter's use of Archer's work (Carter & Charles, 2011), we have developed a threefold approach to thinking about structure and agency that allows us to think about agency beyond the human (Cudworth & Hobden, 2013). First, reproductive agency acknowledges the way in which agential beings, both human and non-human, emerge into a pre-existent web of social relations and unequally distributed power and resources and their practices over time reproduce those situational constraints with relatively minor alterations. Second, there is transformative agency where humans and possibly some other creatures engage in a struggle over resources and social organisation to effect differences in that distribution. The human world overlaps with innumerable non-human systems, both animate and inanimate, which can impact and influence, and indeed radically change the structures of the human world. We describe this as 'affective agency'. As we will later see, some consider an understanding of our embedding in 'natural' systems as subjecting humanity to the rule of blind necessity. This is reflected in some posthumanist work. The title for John Gray's controversial *Straw Dogs* comes from the Tao Te Ching, wherein 'Heaven and Earth are ruthless and treat the myriad creatures as straw dogs' to be trampled on and destroyed similarly to the straw effigies offered to the gods in ancient Chinese rituals (Gray, 2002, pp. 33–34). We would concur with Gray that exclusive humanism is arrogant and ignores our shared vulnerability with other creatures, but do not think that humans are 'straw dogs'. Rather, we consider the agency of non-human species to be constricted in the extreme and that privileged groups of humans exercise considerable power over the lives of human and non-human animals and intervene dramatically and often disastrously in non-human lifeworlds.

We have argued for a conception of differentiated agency in which the agential being of non-human animals, particularly mammals is countenanced, and the possibilities for agency very much depends on the relational systems which produce such being. We would use affective agency to discuss the significant effects of natural systems and the beings and things caught up in them and in their relations with other systems. This is not simply the causal powers of a being or thing but a systemic impact that is collective and significant. By significant, we mean that it 'makes a difference in the world', that it alters the systemic conditions, the agential landscape, for other beings and things. The impact of global warming or the effects of a viral pandemic would be examples here. Whereas hybridity and vital materialism consider agency simply to be a quality of material existence, our conception of agency incorporates the idea that non-human life and non-human animals are social actors able to exercise agency without seeing agency simply as a capacity that material beings can exercise. We need a situated and differentiated notion of agency that understands the ability of creatures and things to 'make a difference in the world' as a question of *situated relations* rather than *intrinsic capacity* alone.

These discussions of theorising the social, and potentially political, agency of beyond-human life have posed a challenge to politics-as-usual. Perhaps not unsurprisingly, the challenge has been resisted and it is in our view most unfortunate that some critics seem set on constituting a dichotomy rather than a continuum of positions on 'the material' and in straight-jacketing certain perspectives to either a politics of stasis, one of neo-liberalism or one of emancipation.

Resisting the Challenge to Humanist Politics

There are some very set against the challenge of 'new' materialism. In many cases, these appear to be 'old' materialists disturbed by the apparent uncertainty implied by post-materialist analyses. As Connolly suggests, this lies in a partial reading of the range of new materialism(s):

> A philosophy of becoming set on several tiers of temporality does not, though some fools project such a conclusion into it, postulate a world in which every-thing is always in radical flux. That would mean that you could never act upon one desire before it was replaced by another. The projection of such a judgement into the new materialism means that the projector has so far only heard one part of the thesis being advanced. (2013a, p. 401)

However, this track has been the chosen route of critique. New materialists, David Chandler argues, celebrate human embeddedness in the non-human world. Their perspective is to engage with an ethics of becoming, where knowledge can only illuminate what is happening rather than predict what is to come. This, for Chandler (2013a, p. 527) is 'far too high' a price to pay, and one for which 'the prize on offer is a false one'. The reason for this, Chandler (2013a, p. 528) argues, is because it removes our subjectivity as human beings; 'we can never be human subjects, collectively understanding, constituting and transforming our world'. New materialist approaches suggest that we live in a world of becoming, where it is the connections and inter-relations that take priority, as a result the ontological focus is 'objects transforming objects—rather than subjects transforming objects' (2013a, p. 529).

There are two interrelated implications Chandler highlights. First is that we are subject to the 'rule of blind necessity', where our options become those of a micro politics, the transformation of the self as a more ecologically aware embedded being. Second, and most importantly, this move, Chandler claims, puts us beyond the world of the knowable. Drawing on Hannah Arendt, who argued that the world that could be understandable marks the limits of what we should consider, he argues that the unpredictability implied by New Materialism leads to 'a desert', and as such removes 'the meaningfulness of the world itself' (Chandler, 2013a, p. 534). When we lose the possibility of engaging meaningfully in the world 'we lose the freedom of the goal-determining subject' (Chandler, 2013b, p. 18). In a world where the predictability of our actions is limited we become incapable of action (Chandler, 2013a, p. 525). Human freedom is only possible through the overcoming of necessity, and for this, Chandler (2013b, p. 6) argues we need fixed understandings: 'it is through these fixed structures of meaning that we understand ourselves as able to master necessity—the relations of cause and effect'.

If only our political intentions were so straightforwardly realisable in their outcomes! Surely, even if one has never chanced upon any of the ideas of complexity theory, new materialism, posthumanism, and the like, the simple point that political ends are often at odds with the intentions of actors has become abundantly clear in the impact of radical politics in the last century, whatever the quality of the understandings of the world on which political interventions were founded. It is interesting that Chandler endorses Lenin's engagement with questions of freedom and necessity somewhat approvingly. The outcomes of the Russian Revolution of October 1917 are well-debated, but the notion that the revolution was in many aspects 'betrayed' by consequent developments is now widely accepted—albeit that Emma Goldman's contemporary observations were harshly received:

> Try as I might I could find nowhere any evidence of benefits received either by the workers or the peasants from the Bolshevik régime.
>
> On the other hand, I did find the revolutionary faith of the people broken, the spirit of solidarity crushed, the meaning of comradeship and mutual helpfulness distorted. (Goldman, 1923, p. 8)

That the outcomes of our actions may be different from our intentions, or in Morin's (2008, p. 96) terms that 'action escapes the will of the actor', is far from a novel idea. Yet while complexity thinking has often focussed on the problems confronting policy-makers (Forrester, 1971), there is a developing literature on policy-making under conditions of complexity. Mitchell (2009), for example, suggests replacing traditional 'predict' and 'act' policies with processes of scenario evaluation and 'adaptive management'. In a similar vein, Axelrod and Cohen (1999) argue that not only is it possible to make policy under conditions of complexity, complexity itself can be actively harnessed in pursuit of goals. While the analysis of policy-making, and the development of policy-making when confronted by complexity is a recent development, the point is that this would be a rejection of the idea that in complexity we confront a situation of 'blind necessity'.

Chandler's claim is that the 'rule of blind necessity' prescribes our options in terms of a micro politics. This, he suggests, involves the transformation of the self into a more ecologically aware embedded being. This individualist response to ecological crises is certainly present in the literature on political ecology, associated particularly with the work of Naess (1973) and Fox (1995) but has been effectively critiqued by left and feminist political ecologisms (Gorz, 1994; Soper, 1996). Part of the problem is the narrow selection of new materialists on which Chandler focuses his attention (Bennett, Connolly and Latour). In addition, he over-compares the similarities between approaches and the political projects they advance. Whilst his arguments about a politics of being and stasis might work for Bennett, they do not work so well for Latour, for example. Schmidt (2013, pp. 177–178) makes no distinction at all between the 'general positions and assumptions' of the wider range of posthumanist positions she references.

A better example for Chandler's argument for posthumanism as a politics of being-in-the-world in face of ecotastrophe would be John Gray, who, following Lovelock and his ilk, considers that the current impact of humanity on patterns of change in natural systems, means that we might be simply tossed aside as a species unfit for purpose in the earth system. Gray (2002) smirks at the demise of arrogant humankind, and the flawed humanist political projects we insist on holding onto; dismissing what we would call critical posthumanism as 'green humanism' that reflects the same naïve doctrine of the possibilities for human salvation. For

Gray, we, along with Schmidt and Chandler, are like poor deluded and despairing Nietzsche, 'trapped in the chalk circle of Christian hope' (2002, p. 48). Gray, however, is not quite the secularist he often considers himself to be. More recently, and drawing on non-Western political thought, Gray (2013) suggests that we might address our arrogant humancentredness by learning silence and the art of simply 'being'. This, certainly, is a recommendation for doing nothing in the face of potential calamity.

Chandler suggests that such a politics of stasis is the outcome of new materialism and an intrinsic element of a posthumanist position. But it is not. There are as many political paths for posthumanisms as for the humanisms of modernity. This is something that neither Chandler nor Schmidt can acknowledge, for it is on a homogenous new materialism that any argument rests. Both the politics of humanism and of posthumanism can be deployed for liberal, left, and other forms of political project. For neither Latour, nor Connolly, nor those with more radical perspectives (feminist or de-development, or indeed, our own) accept that creatures are straw dogs. We are all acutely aware, however, of the 'fragility' of human and non-human lifeworlds, it is this shared vulnerability of the living which is the grounds of separation from the humancentric modernism of Chandler, Schmidt, Lenin, and Francis Fukyama! Schmidt (2013) is obviously hostile to environmental politics, using some ideas about climate change policy (drawn entirely from liberal international institutions) 'in dialogue' with new materialism in order to assert that the epistemological underpinnings of the latter make it possible for it to 'become aligned' with neo-liberal international governance. The ontology of modernity and the certainties of realist or positivist epistemologies led to a range of contested pathways towards very different futures. The future may be less certain for new materialisms but the notion of desirable change is still as deeply contested, and what might be done is not easily read-off from a new materialist and posthumanist analysis in the way which Schmidt suggests, but depends on what kind of posthumanist position we are speaking of.

Some Posthumanist Political Projects

The posthumanist critique raises vital questions for human beings in the world and demands qualitative and quantitative shifts 'in our thinking about what exactly is the basic unit of common reference for our species, our polity and our relationship to the other inhabitants of this planet' (Braidotti, 2013, p. 2). While we might endorse Rosi Braidotti's sentiments, it needs to be acknowledged that both the analyses emerging within posthumanism/new materialism and the political projects these positions imply or endorse cover a range of political positions.

A Conservative Politics of Attachments

For Latour (2005a, 2005b), a huge, unknowable multiplicity of realities exists. Each actor has their own 'world' and this provides the source of agency and their inspiration for action. In turn, Latour is sceptical of political claims for the existence of overarching systemic relations of power and inequality around which emancipatory politics has coalesced.

Latour's most obvious attack on emancipatory politics is contained in his 2004 paper on the problems of critique within science and technology studies. Here, he suggests that around 90% of social critique fall into two approaches 'the fact position and the fairy position' (2004a, p. 237). The fact position holds that 'objects of belief' are merely concepts onto which power is projected; while the fairy position argues that individuals are dominated by external forces

OCCUPYING SUBJECTIVITY

(such the operation of capitalism or of gender relations) that may by covertly effective without the awareness of those whose behaviour is affected (2004a, p. 238). In the latter, critique is straightforward, and any evidence which might contract a theoretical certainly is explained away by unseen forces so that 'You're always right!' (2004a, p. 239). While both positions have their attendant difficulties, it is the 'fairy' position which seems most irksome to Latour.

We require a new way of conceptualising 'nature'. Nature is not an obvious domain of reality, and we have a false dichotomy between the non-human and human that needs to be reassembled (Latour, 2004b). In doing this, we need to constitute a political community incorporating humans and non-humans and building on the experiences of the sciences as they are practiced. Moving beyond the modernist institutions of 'mononaturalism' and 'multiculturalism', Latour develops the idea of 'multilateralism'. This is Latour's notion of the 'good life', one which in an interview he described as 'the composition of a common world' (Latour & Navaran, 2011). Latour has more recently moved away from issues of representation and deliberation to political culture and in particular, seeing if traditional ways of seeing the world might shed light on and add legitimacy to arguments for a non-modern posthuman politics. Latour has invoked a more traditional conservatism drawing on ideas about 'respect for creation' within the Orthodox Christian tradition of Central and Eastern Europe (Latour & Naravane, 2011). For Latour, the threat of environmental collapse is strong, and engendering public emotion is necessary to secure the political consideration of our attachments to the non-human lifeworld and thereby secure ourselves. This return to religion however seems a retreat to a cultural politics of engendering ecological selves. Rejuvenating declining cultural mores to invigorate concern about the more-than-human world would appear to be a project doomed from the start.

Complex Pluralism

William Connolly echoes in some ways the earlier project of Latour—using new materialism as a frame within which to recast a liberal pluralist political project. Here, he is very much attuned to the concern of political alienation highlighted by Schmidt and Chandler. For Connolly (2013b, pp. 181–182), the desire to abandon electoral politics is understandable given how dysfunctional it is—yet deserting democratic means leaves the field to the right who consistently attempt to depict politics as a dysfunctional realm. Hence while forsaking democracy for Connolly is not an option, at the same time, working within democratic systems as currently constituted only allows limited possibilities for change.

The resolution to this conundrum lies, Connolly (2103b, p. 182) argues, in a politics of 'micro-experimentation on several fronts'. Here he is advocating the possibilities that aggregated small changes to behaviour can result in large political changes. When role behaviour conforms to expectations this can act to legitimise current sets of arrangements, whilst 'large-scale role experimentations can make a difference on their own *and help to set preconditions for constituency participation in more robust political movements*' (Connolly, 2013b, p. 184, emphasis in original). It is the cumulative power of such role experimentation and challenges to the existing order that is significant in creating a 'pluralist assemblage'. At critical moments, such as political disorder or economic chaos movements appear which reveal further the cracks within the existing order—promoting yet further role experimentation.

We can see clear overlaps with Latour's liberal project here, although these pluralist assemblages appear more open to the influence of social movement activity and the engagement of extra-parliamentary pressure in policy fora. In thinking about the presence of cracks in political order and the insertion of scientific (and other) expertise, these ideas could be linked to (neo)liberal forms of environmental governance. This is not to be associated with new materialism (as per Schmidt) but with liberalism. Current policy initiatives reflect the concerns of complex pluralism as articulated by Connolly. For example, in the UK the creation of what might be seen as a 'new' posthuman political settlement has been advocated by Stern (2009). Stern's argument for a new 'global deal' via which we move to a carbon neutral economy can be read as a reflection of neo-liberal governance, guided by common-sense principles of effectiveness, efficiency, and fairness, and an overarching framework of the 'greening' of the capitalist system and the liberal state. At the heart of his work is the simple calculation that, if the science of climate change is right, the cost of doing nothing about global warming would be very high, while the cost of transforming our energy system would be relatively low. Stern's policy measures are a series of corrections to market failures and externalities by using regulations to encourage market mechanisms to reduce emissions.

The 'greening of capitalism' is Stern's project, perhaps shared by Connolly. Even these ideas of low-carbon development and re-invigoration of democracy for ends both human and beyond represent however, not the cultivation of the environmental self, but a re-orientation of public policy. They do not represent the incapacity of politics. Other posthumanist positions lend themselves to progressive political projects outside the liberal frame. Here, it has been suggested that exploitative and oppressive relations exist and must be taken seriously, and that their challenge has seen the emergence of a posthumanist polities allied to the politics of emancipation, albeit one which stresses the notion that 'freedom' is both embodied and embedded.

Critical Posthumanism

We would define critical posthumanism as approaches to more-than-human politics which draw on aspects of critical theory and thereby contain an agenda for transformation. In developing a politics of emancipation however, it is important to remember that much radical politics of liberation draws very heavily on the same European Enlightenment humanism which informed a model of political and cultural universalism that has had disastrous consequences for many peoples and non-human lifeworlds. But does a problematising of the liberal and Enlightenment foundations of emancipatory agendas mean that they cannot be disentangled from the imperialist mission of Western civilisation? Does a new materialism involve the rejection of any kind of emancipatory agenda as Chandler and Schmidt suggest?

Many of us working within the posthumanist critique wish to advance an agenda which opposes the domination of life in all its variety. Yet as emancipatory politics has learned to its cost, there are many dangers in universalist schemas of all kinds and conceptions of liberty, rights, wellbeing, and so on are fraught with contradiction. This is why in our own work, we have emphasised the importance of social intersectionality as an analytic frame. Our use of posthumanism is to indicate the understanding of 'humanity' as embedded in networks of relations of dependency with the non-human lifeworld, to emphasise the fragility of embodied life. In addition, we want to emphasise the importance of a posthumanist lens in examining phenomena which, in international politics, are often seen as exclusively human such as the practice of war, the delivery of welfare and security, the distribution of resources, and so on. Humanism might sensibly appreciate the qualities of the human animal, but we would hope it might radically consider the extent to which these are entirely unique given the multiplicity of species. A critical humanism must also abandon its history of humancentrism and be highly attuned to the domination of the animal that is not human, in addition to the animal which is.

Work in the areas of de-development and eco-feminism provides a starting point for our own perspective. From a de-development perspective, such as advocated by Sachs (2008a, 2008b), there is a need to completely re-think forms of social organisation. For Sachs (1992) the notion of development 'stands like a ruin in the intellectual landscape'. In its place there is a need for a radically different path, particularly in the wealthier parts of the world. This way of life requires a prioritisation of the carrying capacity of the planet, and the envisioning of life-styles within that capacity. Val Plumwood shares Sachs' concerns with the impacts of develop-ment on the planet and its capacity to support life. In terms of our relationship with the rest of nature her view is that notions of human domination over nature 'must end either with the death of the other on whom he relies, and therefore with his own death, or with the abandonment of mastery, his failure and transformation' (Plumwood, 1993, p. 196). While Sachs advocates a de-development agenda, Plumwood argues for a reconsideration of our place within the rest of nature. Drawing on the political frameworks of indigenous Australian and North American cultures she argues for a non-colonial posthuman politics which develops a culture of belonging and community (as opposed to a prioritisation of conquest and private property), and on flour-ishing (to replace a western obsession with wealth). For Plumwood, a posthuman politics is not some form of pre-modern exchange with the modern, but rather a re-working of elements of humanist politics of emancipation alongside non-Western and non-capitalist conceptions (Plum-wood, 2002; Salleh, 1997).

Paraphrasing probably the most quoted sentiment in International Relations, Booth (2011, p. 329) has described Critical Theory as '*for* the potential community of mankind and *for* the purpose of emancipation'. A critical posthumanism, we would suggest is *for* all that lives, and *for* the purpose of eliminating multiple forms of oppression. How might this be considered part of an emancipatory programme?

First it provides a form of analysis which stresses the common constitution of all living things. A systems analysis derived from complexity theory allows for the analysis of the interactions between human and non-human systems and between animate and inanimate systems. This forms the basis of an ethic of care and responsibility which does not cease at the species border. One of the central contributions of posthumanist work has been to question the character of these boundaries, and in particular to raise questions about those features which humans have declared indicate their uniqueness, such as tool use, or use of language. The intention here is to de-centre the position of the human. This is not to deny the planetary significance of human activity, but to indicate that many other species also possess capabilities once thought the sole preserve of humans.

While we do not regard our particular position to be one directed towards policy-making, the implications of thinking about our actions are part of the emancipatory programme. In particular in thinking about policy issues we have suggested that a precautionary principle should domi-nate, a greater humility in terms of our embeddedness in non-human nature, and a priority towards the building of resilience within systems rather than the undermining of resilience. Both the de-development literature and the eco-feminist literature alluded to above indicate a requirement for a total re-constitution of our economic and social arrangements. This is a view with which we would concur. Intra-human and inter-species forms of domination are exacerbated by the capitalist systems and a more equitable form of social system could be a sig-nificant move towards alleviating both of these. How such a transition would be achieved is more problematic, and the posthuman perspective would not envisage a programmatic overthrow of capitalism, but rather change through small actions particularly as a result of increased aware-ness about forms of intra and inter-species domination. In this sense we see the posthuman move as being at home within the discipline of International Relations—which is a discipline which takes change at a global level as a central concern, though which to date, in our opinion, has been weak in terms of its contribution to understanding global environmental issues.

Conclusion

This article refutes the claim that in a complex world we confront blind necessity and that in acknowledging complexity we are incapacitated from moving towards a more just and equitable world. Certainly one conclusion that can be drawn from complexity is that any action is futile because we confront a situation of radical unpredictability. Indeed, this would appear to be the standpoint of John Gray who would see human attempts to improve their position as misguided. However, that is not the only conclusion; rather, there is a growing body of literature on policy-making under complexity as well as some radical ideas for the re-invention of our world. Without a doubt it would be easier to make progress in a world where there was a predictable link between our actions and their outcomes. Yet, we argue, it is better to try to learn with complexity than to pretend that it is not there.

The claim that we exist in a condition of complexity is an ontological one, not an ethical one. However, an ethical position can be derived from a starting point in complexity. Complexity points to the overlapping and inter-connected character of human and non-human systems. This, we suggest, indicates the embedded character of human activity. Humans are not the independent separated beings of some religious and humanist claims. Furthermore an embeddedness in the rest of nature implies a need not only to prioritise our relations to the rest of nature, but also of our common origins with the rest of non-human nature. While it may be in human self-interest to protect the rest of non-human nature, our shared heritage with the rest of lively matter points to a responsibility to minimise forms of oppression with the other forms of life on the planet. In most posthuman perspectives, creatures share vulnerabilities but they are not 'straw dogs'. For critical posthumanism there can also be emancipation and, indeed, this is its ethical project.

References

Archer, M. (2000). *Being human: The problem of agency*. Cambridge: Cambridge University Press.

Axelrod, R. M., & Cohen, M. D. (1999). *Harnessing complexity: Organizational implications of a scientific frontier*. New York, NY: Free Press.

Bennett, J. (2004). The force of things. *Political Theory, 32*, 347–372.

Bennett, J. (2010). *Vibrant matter: A political ecology of things*. Durham, NC: Duke University Press.

Bertuglia, C. S., & Vaio, F. (2005). *Nonlinearity, chaos & complexity: The dynamics of natural and social systems*. Oxford: Oxford University Press.

Booth, K. (2011). *Realism and world politics*. London: Routledge.

Braidotti, R. (2013). *The posthuman*. Cambridge: Polity.

Carter, B., & Charles, N. (2011). Human–animal connections: An introduction. In B. Carter & N. Charles (Eds.), *Human and other animals: Critical perspectives* (pp. 1–30). Basingstoke: Palgrave.

Chandler, D. (2013a). The world of attachment? The post-humanist challenge to freedom and necessity. *Millennium, 41*, 516–534.

Chandler, D. (2013b). *Freedom versus necessity in international relations: Human-centred approaches to security and development*. London: Zed.

Connolly, W. (2013a). The "new materialism" and the fragility of things. *Millennium, 41*, 399–412.

Connolly, W. (2013b). *The fragility of things: Self organizing processes, neoliberal fantasies, and democratic activism*. Durham, NC: Duke University Press.

Coole, D., & Frost, S. (2010). *New materialisms: Ontology, agency, and politics*. Durham, NC: Duke University Press.

Cudworth, E., & Hobden, S. (2009). Complexity theory in the social sciences. *The International Journal of Interdisciplinary Social Sciences, 4*(4), 59–69.

Cudworth, E., & Hobden, S. (2011). *Posthuman international relations: Complexity, ecologism and global politics.* London: Zed Books.

Cudworth, E., & Hobden, S. (2013). Of parts and wholes: International relations beyond the HUMAN. *Millennium Journal of International Studies, 42*(3), 430–450.

Edelmann, F. (2012). *Complex social system thinking beyond posthumanism: The exclusion of subjectivity and possibilities for human agency.* Paper presented at the Millennium Annual Conference, Materialism in World Politics, London.

Forrester, J. W. (1971). Counterintuitive behavior of social systems. *Technology Review, 73*, 52–68.

Fox, W. (1995). *Towards transpersonal ecology.* Dartington: Green Books.

Giddens, A. (1984). *The constitution of society.* Cambridge: Cambridge University Press.

Goldman, E. (1923). *Preface to the first volume of the American edition of My Disillusionment in Russia.* New York, NY: Doubleday, Page and Co.

Gorz, A. (1994). *Capitalism, socialism, ecology.* London: Verso.

Gray, J. (2002). *Straw dogs: Thoughts on humans and other animals.* London: Granta.

Gray, J. (2013). *The silence of animals: On progress and other modern myths.* London: Allen Lane.

Latour, B. (1993). *We have never been modern.* Hemel Hempstead: Harvester Wheatsheaf.

Latour, B. (2004a). Why has critique run out of steam? From matters of fact to matters of concern. *Critical Inquiry, 30*, 225–248.

Latour, P. (2004b). *The politics of nature: How to bring the sciences into democracy.* (C. Porter, Trans.). Cambridge, MA: Harvard University Press.

Latour, B. (2005a). *Reassembling the social: An introduction to actor–network theory.* Oxford: Oxford University Press.

Latour, B. (2005b). From realpolitik to dingpolitik or how to make things public. In B. Latour & P. Weibel (Eds.), *Making things public* (pp. 14–43). Cambridge, MA: MIT Press.

Latour, B. (2009). A plea for earthly sciences. In J. Burnett, S. Jeffers, & G. Thomas (Eds.), *New social connections: Sociology's subjects and objects* (pp. 72–84). Basingstoke: Palgrave.

Latour, B., & Naravane, V. (2011, January 4). I would define politics as the composition of a common world, interview with Bruno Latour, *The Hindu.* Retrieved from http://www.thehindu.com

Law, J. (2009). Practising nature and culture: An essay for Ted Benton. In S. Moog & R. Stones (Eds.), *Nature, social relations and human needs: Essays in honour of Ted Benton* (pp. 65–79). Basingstoke: Palgrave Macmillan.

Mitchell, S. D. (2009). *Unsimple truths: Science, complexity and policy.* Chicago, IL: University of Chicago Press.

Morin, E. (2008). *On complexity.* Cresskill, NJ: Hampton Press.

Naess, A. (1973). Self-Realization in mixed communities of humans, bears, sheep and wolves. *Inquiry, 16*, 95–100.

Plumwood, V. (1993). *Feminism and the mastery of nature.* London: Routledge.

Plumwood, V. (2002). *Environmental culture: The ecological crises of reason.* London: Routledge.

Robbins, T. (1991). *Skinny legs and all.* London: Bantam.

Sachs, W. (1992). Development: A guide to the ruins. *New Internationalist.* Retrieved from http://newint.org

Sachs, W. (2008a). *Zukunftsfähiges Deutschland in einer globalisierten welt (Sustainable Germany in a globalized world).* Frankfurt: Brot für die Welt, eed and BUND – Fischer.

Sachs, W. (2008b). Climate change and human rights. *Development, 51*, 332–337.

Salleh, A. (1997). *Ecofeminism as politics: Nature, Marx and the postmodern.* London: Zed.

Schmidt, J. (2013). The empirical falsity of the human subject: New materialism, climate change and the shared critique. *Resilience: International Policies, Practices and Discourses, 1*, 174–192.

Soper, K. (1996). Feminism, ecosocialism and the conceptualisation of nature. In T. Benton (Ed.), *The Greening of Marxism* (pp. 81–102). London: Guilford Press.

Stern, N. (2009). *The global deal.* New York, NY: Public Affairs.

Wolfe, C. (2010). *What is posthumanism?* Minneapolis, MN: University of Minnesota Press.

Index

Please note that page numbers relating to Notes will contain the letter 'n' followed by note number.

Abbas, M. 37
abnegation, act of 96n9
aboriginal political claims 46
Ackerman, P. 39n3
active nihilism 123
activism: in Canada 55, 61n12; community 49;
    deconstruction as 16; Indigenous 43, 49, 51;
    online 43; political 108, 113n1; post-politics 67,
    68, 69; queer 18; radical 66, 68; social/social
    media 51, 68; textual 17
actor network theory (ANT) 137–8
acts: and decisions 68; political 69, 70; of
    resistance 6, 7, 8, 102, 103, 107; suicide *see*
    suicide, political
Adams, T. 40n6
Adorno, T. 12, 15, 23n6
affective agency 138
affective process/resistance 46
Afghanistan 26, 36
Agathangelou, A. 25, 40n6
agency 134, 137; affective 138; differentiated
    138–9; reproductive 138
agent/actor of resistance 6, 7, 8, 9, 12
Alberta, Canada 47
Alfred, T. 44–5, 52, 53, *54*, 55, 60n1
Ali, Ben 86, 89, 95, 96n7, 104
Allooloo, S. 50–1
alter-globalisation movement 123
Althusser, L. 102
altruistic suicide 87
ambivalence, colonial 47, 55
American Indian Movement (AIM) 27, 45
American University School of International
    Service 33
analysis of resistance 13, 14
analytic auto-ethnography 39n1
anarchism 25; of Goldman 116; Goldman as
    dancing anarchist 117–22; of Nietzsche 116,
    117, 121; *ressentiment* in 117; 'Space Hijackers'
    group 123, 124

Ancient Greece 109, 113n8
Andriolo, K. 88
Ansell-Pearson, K. 129, 130, 130n1
ANSWER (Act Now to Stop War and End Racism)
    32
anti-austerity protests 67, 106, 113n4
anti-capitalism, and religious pacifism 25–42
Anti-Capitalist Convergence 33
anti-militarism 40n6
anti-nuclear protests 27, 29, 35
anti-war groups/movements 26, 27, 28, 31, 32, 35,
    40n6, 71
aporias: deconstruction 11; defined 68; Occupy
    protest movement 66, 68, 77–9; unity and
    singularity 66, 78, 79
appropriation of resistance 6, 7
Arab League 27, 37
Arab Spring (2011) 35, 36, 37, 89, 96n7
Archer, M. 138
archeo-genetic motif 14
Arendt, H. 96n11, 139
Aristotle 110
assemblages, human 137
Assembly of First Nations (AFN), Canada 49, 57,
    59
Atleo, S. A. 49, 59, 61n23, 62n23
attachments, conservative politics of 141–2
Attawapiskat First Nation (reserve community,
    northern Ontario) 48
Austin, D. 61n20
auto-annihilation 95
auto-ethnography, expressive 25–42; and analytic
    auto-ethnography 39n1; benefits 26; distance
    between author/subject and 'big events' of
    history 40n6; and journalistic auto-ethnography
    39n1; newspaper entries 26–39, 40n6;
    paradoxes, exploring 40n6; recurrence of issues
    and actors 40n6; self-investigation 40n6
Autonomia movement 113n2
Axelrod, R. M. 140

INDEX

Bahrain 86, 104, 113n5
Bakunin, M. 117, 130
Barack, E. 37
Barker, A. 3, 122
Baudrillard, J. 12
Bauman, Z. 93, 96n2
Begin, M. 27
Behar, R. 25, 40n6
Ben Ali *see* Ali, Ben
Benjamin, M. 32
Benjamin, W. 82, 95; *Critique of Violence* 83, 94
Bennett, J. 137, 140
Berardi, F. 101–2
Berkman, A. 120, 130n2
Berlusconi, S. 35
Bertalan, H. 117, 121, 128–9
Bethlehem, Church of Nativity 37
Bill C-45, Canada 47, 49, 57, 58
binary politics 56–7
biological determinism 135
bisexuality 19
blackmail of enlightenment 96n1
Bleiker, R. 8, 13–14
Blevis, M. 59
blind necessity, rule of 139, 140, 145
blockades, Canada 48, 49, 58
Bloc Quebecois (nationalist party) 61n16
'blue dot' protest movement 62n23
Bochner, A. 40n6
body, the 111, 130n1, 136; of crowd 107; and space 100, 102, 109
Bolt, N. 91
Booth, K. 144
Boston Tea Party 56
Bouazizi, M. (self-burning in Sidi Bouzid, Tunisia) 4, 82, 83, 86–91, 94, 95, 100, 102–4, 107, 109; *see also* self-immolation; suicide, political
Bourdieu, P. 12
Bowman, P. 10, 11, 12, 13, 15, 17–18
Brady, E. 118
Braidotti, R. 141
Brazil 122
Breivik, A. B. 37
bricolage 40n6
British Columbia, Canada 58
British imperialism 92
Bruyneel, K. 44, 46–7, 55
Bryce, C. 46
Buddhism 33
Bush, G. H. W. 31
Bush, G. W. 34, 35
Butler, J. 7, 108, 128–9

Cairo 27, 36
Call, L. 129, 130, 130n1
Campaign for Nuclear Disarmament (CND) 29

Camp David Accords 27
Canada 43–65; activism in 55, 61n12; Assembly of First Nations (AFN) 49, 57, 59; Bill C-45 47, 49, 57, 58; colonial geography 50; as colonial 'structure of invasion' 44; emergence of Idle No More (winter, 2012) 43; Guswenta/Two-Row Treaty 52–4, 53; police 45; 'Round Dance Revolution' 48, 51; Settler identity/politics *see* Settler Canadians; sovereignty 43, 44, 52, 54; *see also* Conservative Party of Canada (CPC); Harper, S. (Canadian Prime Minister); Idle No More (Canadian political protest movement); Indigenous people, Canada
Canadian Nurses Association 55
Canetti, E. 105
capitalism 69, 118, 121, 125, 142; 'greening' of 143
Caputo, J. 11
Carter, B. 138
Carter, J. 27
Catholicism 32
Cause, The 119, 120
Chandler, D. 139–40, 141, 142, 143
Charles, N. 138
Chernobyl, Ukraine 29
Choudry, A. 57
Christianity 26, 30, 31, 32, 33; and anarchism 117; *corpus mysticum* 84; Orthodox 142
Christoyannopoulos, A. 39n4
Church of Nativity, Bethlehem 37
civilisation 105
civil society 8
civil war 36
class war 26
Coalition of the Willing, US 35
Code Pink 32
Coe, D. 27, 28
Cohen, M. D. 140
Coleman, L. M. 7
collectivism 121
colonialism 19; colonial ambivalence 47, 55; Indigenous resistance to Settler colonialism, in Canada 44–7; *see also* post-colonialism
common, the 107, 108, 109
communism, revolutionary 25, 26
Complete Programs and Confident Answers 32
complexity theory 135, 136, 138, 140, 144, 145; complex pluralism 142–3
Comprehensive Test Ban Treaty 28
concrete interventions 8, 9, 18, 22n2
concrete praxis 6, 8, 17, 22n2
Connolly, W. 135, 136, 139, 141, 142, 143
Conservative Party of Canada (CPC) 44, 56, 61n16, 61n17
Coole, D. 134
Cork, Ireland 66, 68, 74

148

INDEX

Corntassel, J. 44–5, 46, 60n1
corpus mysticum 84
Coulthard, G. 58, 59
Council of Canadians 55, 57
counter-conduct 7, 14, 97n14
counter-genealogy 14
counter-hegemonic social movements (Gramscian) 7
counter-structure 91
Craig, S. 88
Crimean Tatar nationalism 88
Critchley, S. 123
critical posthumanism 143–5; and 'green
   humanism' 140
Critical Theory 144
Critique of Violence (Benjamin) 83, 94
Crosby, K. 87
crowd 102, 104–7, 112
Cuba 31, 32–3
Cudworth, E. 4
Culp, A. 52, 56
cultural revolution, Maoist 10
cultural theory 12

dance 128–30; The Dancer 4, 115, 116, 125, 128;
   'dance to death' 115, 116, 128–30; Goldman as
   dancing anarchist 117–22; playfulness 116, 123;
   'Round Dance Revolution', Canada 48, 51
Day, D. 39
Days of Action, Canada 48, 50, 51, 59
death 21
"Death of God" 12, 22n4
decision-making 66, 70, 77, 78, 80; and acts 68;
   undecidability 68, 72, 73; and violence of law
   72–4
deconstruction 3, 6–24; as activism 16; Anglo-
   American 10; animating drive/momentum of 11;
   aporia underpinning 11; auto-deconstructionist
   mode of resistance 22n2; conceptualising as
   form of political resistance 8–12; consequences
   17; criticism 9; "Death of God" 12, 22n4;
   enactment of 11; first-order engagement 14;
   genealogy, as mode of resistance 13–14;
   interventionary potential 9–10, 11; as 'martial
   art' 17; micro-politics 16; misreadings 17;
   movements of, resistance to 13; and onto-
   political 6, 7, 8, 11, 15, 19; otherness/'something
   other' 11, 13; as political praxis 16–19;
   radicalism of 10, 15, 19; second- and third-order
   political critiques/resistance 6, 7, 14, 15, 17;
   subject of resistance 7, 8, 19, 20; sufferance,
   involving 11–12; *see also* Derrida, Jacques;
   resistance, political
De Goede, M. 123
Deleuze, G. 25, 26, 40n6, 41n7, 97n15, 121, 136
democracy: assault on in name of 67; democracy-
   to-come 77–8; democratic deficit 35; direct 66,

68, 70, 75; and Occupy movement 77–9;
   participatory 68; Real 78–9; representative 69, 77
Denzin, N. 40n6
depoliticisation, non-intentionality and
   hyperpoliticisation as 68–9
Derrida, Jacques: on Benjamin 94; on decisions
   and Occupy movement 4, 66, 67, 68, 73, 74, 77,
   79; and deconstruction 3, 6–24; and political
   resistance 12–16; *see also* decision-making;
   Lacan, J.
desire 11, 52, 92, 96n11, 139; community of 89;
   Graph of Desire (Lacan) 113n3; group 87; and
   Occupy movement 69, 70, 72; political 78, 106,
   122, 123; and politics of resisting subjectivity
   110, 113n3, 113n8
Dillon, M. 15
direct democracy 66, 68, 70, 75
dissociative, motif of 14
divine violence 94, 95
divisibility 15
Domestic Security Alliance Council, US 73
domination, intra-human and inter-species forms 144
Douzinas, C. 103, 104, 105, 106, 111, 112
drive (psychological term) 72
Dublin, Ireland 68, 74, 75; Council of Trade
   Unions 71; *see also* Occupy Dame Street (ODS),
   Dublin
Dundas Square, Ontario 48
Durkheim, E. 87
Duvall, J. 39n3

Eagleton, T. 9, 10, 12, 19, 20, 21
Eastern Mennonite University, Summer
   Peacebuilding Institute 33
eco-feminism 144
ecologism, complex 138
Edkins, J. 13
ego (Freudian theory) 13
Egypt 4, 27, 36, 67, 86, 103, 104, 112; Tahir
   Square 108, 109, 111
Elam, D. 18, 20
Ellis, C. 40n6
Emerson, R. W. 121
Enbridge pipeline project, Canada 45
Enlightenment 135, 143
Eschle, C. 8
essentialism 18, 19
Estrada, E. 28
ethico-religious pacifism 25, 26
ethnographic research, militant 66, 68
Eurocentrism 19
expressive auto-ethnography *see* auto-ethnography,
   expressive

Facebook 50
fanaticism 82

INDEX

Fanon, F. 124–5
fantasy 69–72
Fascism 7, 106
Federal Bureau of Investigation (FBI), US 73
Feldman, A. 92
Fellowship of Reconciliation (FOR) 31
feminism 8, 16, 22n1; eco-feminism 144; third-wave 18, 19; women's liberation 125–6
Ferguson, K. 118, 131n7
festival, image of 123, 125
Fierke, K. M. 83, 84–5, 89, 90, 91, 96n12, 96n13, 97n23, 97n24, 97n25
financial crisis (2008) 1
First Intifada, Israel 28–9
First Nation bands, Canada 49
First Nations Control of First Nations Education Act (FNCFNEA), Canada 59, 62n23
Flannigan, T. 49
flash mobs, Canada 43, 48, 49, 51
Flatirons Mall, Colorado 61n10
FNCFNEA (First Nations Control of First Nations Act), Canada 59, 62n23
Foucault, M./Foucauldian tradition 3, 6, 7, 8, 13, 14, 96n1, 125
Fox, W. 140
France 29, 85
Freud, S. 13, 21, 105, 112
Frost, S. 134
Fukushima disaster, Japan 35, 36
Fukyama, F. 141

Gamson, J. 18–19
Gandhi, M. 26
Gaza Strip 28
Gbowee, L. 37
genealogy, as mode of resistance 13–14
generic left 57, 61n20
Geneva, Switzerland 28
George, D. 45
Giddens, A. 87
Girard, R. 93–4, 97n27
Gitxsan people, Canada 45
Global Anti-War Assemblies 35
global North 67
global ordering 8, 9, 22n1; appropriation by/ reinscription within 6, 7
Goldman, E. 115–32, 140; anarchism of 116, 117–22; deportation of 130n4; Jewishness 127; on Nietzsche 116, 117, 118, 119, 121, 126; self-creation, ambiguities 124–8
Gorbachev, M. 28, 31
Gordon, J. 47
Graeber, D. 123
A Grammar of the Multitude (Virno) 105
Gramsci, Antonio/Gramscian approach 3, 7–8, 9, 25; Neo-Gramscian tradition 6, 7; *Prison Notebooks* 26

Grassy Narrows (Anishinaabe resistance action), Canada 45
Gray, J. 138, 140, 141
Great Peace March for Global Nuclear Disarmament 29
Greece 4, 103, 104; Ancient Greece 109, 113n8; Syntagma Square 106, 107, 108, 111
Greenham Common Women's Peace Camp 122
Green Party, Canada 61n20
Greenpeace 55
Grindon, G. 123
Guattari, F. 25, 26, 40n6, 41n7, 97n15
Guevara, E. (Che) 32
Gulf Wars 31
Guswenta/Two-Row Treaty, Canada 52–4, 53
Gutiérrez, G. 39n4

Haraway, D. 138
Hardt, M. 105
Harper, S. (Canadian Prime Minister) 44, 48, 49, 59, 61n17, 61n23; anti-Harper backlash 56
Haudenosaunee Confederacy/territory, Canada 53
Hegel, G. W. F. 93
hegemony/counter-hegemony 9
Heidegger, M. 21
Hemmings, C. 125–6, 126
heroic death 84
hierarchisation 127
Hirst, A. 3
Hobbes, T. 113n6
Hobden, S. 4
homosexuality *see* queer theory/movements 120
Honduras 28
horizontalism 137
Houen, A. 88
House of Representatives, Permanent Select Committee on Intelligence 27
Hoy, D. C. 22
Hubert, H. 88, 93
humancentric prejudice 137
humanist politics: post-humanist political projects 141–5; post-humanist political theory, varieties of 136–9; resisting challenge of 139–41
human nature 127, 131n7
Huneker, J. 118
hunger strikes 48, 49, 57, 90, 91, 93, 95; Irish Republicans 88–9; and self-destruction 85, 87
Hurst, A. 13
Hussein, S. 27
hybridisation process 137
hyperanalyticism 15
hyperdiabolicism 15
hyperpoliticisation, as depoliticisation 68–9

Iceland 28
id (Freudian theory) 13

INDEX

Idle No More (Canadian political protest
  movement) 3, 43–65; blockades 48, 49, 58;
  blogs 61n12; contributions of 60; Days of Action
  48, 50, 51, 59; educational conference,
  Saskatoon (Canada, 2012) 47–8; events and
  contexts 47–9; extended reach 51; flash mobs
  43, 48, 49, 51; founders 47–8; fragmentation 49;
  hashtag (#IdleNoMore) 47, 48, 50, 51, 58, 60n4,
  60n5; impact 44; as a 'movement moment' 43,
  44, 57–60; origins 43; protests 43, 47, 48, 49,
  52, 61n8, 122; rallies 49, 57, 58; and Settler
  Canadian politics 54–6; social media and online
  organising 50–1; support for 44; teach-ins 43,
  47, 49, 50, 51, 60n6; transgressive actions 43,
  44, 51–4, 55, 59; *see also* Canada; Indigenous
  people, Canada; Settler Canadians
Immigrant Workers' Freedom Ride 57
immobilisation 9, 20
immortality, desire for 96n11
imperialism 19, 32, 92; anti-imperialism 26, 32
India 85
Indigenous Governance Program, University of
  Victoria 51
Indigenous people, Canada 43–4; activism 43, 49,
  51; resistance 49; resistance to Settler
  colonialism 44–7; tactics of resistance 45, 46;
  'thirdspace' sovereignty 44, 52, 54; *see also*
  Canada; Idle No More (Canadian political
  protest movement); Settler Canadians
individualism 121
intentionality, and sacrifice 88
International Atomic Energy Agency 36
International Confederation for Disarmament and
  Peace 28
International Monetary Fund 33
International Network for the Abolition of Foreign
  Military Bases 35
International Peace Bureau 28
International Relations 33, 40, 91, 144, 145
International Year of Peace 29
Interreligious Foundation for Community
  Organization (IFCO)/Pastors for Peace 31, 32
interviews, semi-structured 66, 68
Ipperwash Standoff, Canada 45
Iran 27, 36
Iraq 27, 37
Ireland: Dublin 68, 71, 74; Irish Republican
  hunger strikes 88–9; Peace Park, Cork 66; social
  crisis 92; *see also* Occupy Dame Street (ODS),
  Dublin
Israel 27, 28–9, 37; Boycott and Divestment
  Campaign 35
Italy 113n9

Japan, Fukushima disaster 35, 36
Jasmine Revolution, Tunisia 103

Jaspers, K. 127, 129
Jeppesen, S. 124
Jihadism 97n21
Johnson, J. T. 46
Johnston, D. 48
Jones, S. H. 40n6
jouissance 9, 12, 21, 69
journalist auto-ethnography 39n1
judgment 3
Jun, N. 117

Kamikaze 96n4
Kantorowicz, E. H. 84, 101
Kappo, T. 60–1n6, 61n6
Karman, T. 37
Kateb, G. 96n11
KBG, Soviet Union 31
Keeping Together in Time (McNeill) 124
Kelowna Accord, Canada 56, 61n18
Khomeini, Ayatollah 27
Kilibarda, K. 45
Killian, K. 40n6
King, H. 61n6, 61n12, 61n22
Klein, N. 45, 59, 75
Konstant, D. 113n8
Kundalini energy 33
Kurdistan 37
Kuwait 31

Lacan, J. 21; on desire 113n3; and politics of
  resisting subjectivity 101, 102, 110, 112, 112n1,
  113n1; theories of, and Occupy movement 4,
  66–70, 72, 79; *see also* Derrida, Jacques
lack 79
LaDuke, W. 34
Landauer, G. 117, 127
Larsen, S. 46
Latin America 67
Latour, B. 137–8, 140, 141–3; on fact position and
  fairy position 141–2
law: altercation of 94; institutions of 103; violence
  of 72–4, 94
Lebanon 28
Le Bon, G. 105
leftist movements/politics 9, 10, 44, 61n20, 71
Leitner, H. 57
Lenin, V. 140, 141
Levinas, E. 20
Lévi-Strauss, C. 40n6
liberalism 67
Libya 86
lines of flight concept 41n7
literalisation 15
Living My Live (Goldman) 118
London 123, 124
'Long Cold War' 84

INDEX

Long Kesh prison 92
love 110

Maiguashca, B. 8
Maoism 10, 32
Marchart, O. 13
Marcuse, H. 105, 106
Martin, P. 61n18
Martineau, J. 58, 59
martyrdom 83, 84, 90, 95, 96n11
Marx, K./Marxism 9, 26, 123, 134
mass politics 116
mass psychology 105
Massumi, B. 41n7
materialism: 'massive materiality' 134; new *see*
 new materialism; old 134; vital 136–7, 139
Mauss, M. 88, 93
McAdams, S. 47, 58, 61n21
McLean, S. 47
McNeill, W. 124
McQuillan, M. 17
Merkel, A. 36
messianic vision 12
metaphysics 6, 7, 8, 21
Miami, Florida 32, 38
Michelsen, N. 4
micro-politics of deconstruction 16
micro-violences 22
militarism 17, 26, 118, 124; anti-militarism
 40n6, 119; militant ethnographic research
 66, 68
misogyny 126, 127
Mitchell, S. D. 140
Mobilization for Global Justice 33
modernism, humancentric 141
modes of engagement 49
Mohawk Warriors 45
monks, self-incineration 85
mononaturalism 142
Montreal, Canada 48
morality 119
Moreiras, A. 19
Morgensen, S. 60n2
Morin, E. 140
Morrison, N. 85
Mother Earth (anarchist newspaper) 118
'movement moment', Idle No More as 43, 44,
 57–60; *see also* Canada; Idle No More
 (Canadian political protest movement);
 Indigenous people, Canada
Mubarak, H. 36
multiculturalism 142
multilateralism 142
multitude 104–7
Munich, tomb of the martyrs 84
muscular bonding 124

Musqueam Indians, Canada 45
myth/myth-making 82, 83, 92, 93, 94, 95

Nader, R. 34
Naess, A. 140
Narodnaya Volya (Russian anarchist group) 96n3
Nationalism and Culture (Rocker) 117
nation-to-nation relationships 52
nature 135, 137, 142, 145; non-human 134, 138,
 144, 145; *see also* human nature
naturecultures 138
Navajo communities, American southwest 45
Nazism 106
Neale, J. 39n1
negative dialectics 23n6
Negri, A. 104, 105, 107–8, 110
Neo-Gramscian tradition 6, 7
neoliberalism 2, 67, 70
Netanyahu, B. 37
Network Institute for Global Democratization 35
networks 137
New Democratic Party (NDP), Canada 61n16,
 61n20
new materialism 133; and old materialists 134;
 post-humanist political theory, varieties of
 136–9; 'ten tenets' 135–6; varieties 135–41
newspaper entries, auto-ethnographic method
 26–39, 40n6; circa 1980 26–8; circa 1986
 28–30; circa 1992 31–3; circa 2001 and after
 33–6; circa 2011 36–9
new vitalism 136
New York City 27, 37
NGOs (non-governmental organizations) 33,
 61n20
Nicaragua 28, 31
Nietzsche, Friedrich 4, 21, 22, 115, 120, 121–2,
 124, 125, 127–30, 141; and anarchism 116,
 117, 121; Goldman on 116, 117, 118, 119, 121,
 126
nihilism 9, 123
9/11 terrorist attacks 34
99% slogan, Occupy protest movement 75–7
Non-Aligned Movement 26
non-governmental organizations *see* NGOs
 (non-governmental organizations)
non-human world 134, 138, 144, 145
non-intentionality, as depoliticisation 68–9
Norwegian massacre 37
Noys, B. 16, 22n3

Oakland, San Francisco 66, 68
Obama, B. 56
object petit a (object little-a) 72
Obomsawin, A. 61n7
Occupied Territories, Israel 29, 37
Occupy Atlanta 70

152

INDEX

Occupy Dame Street (ODS), Dublin 68–72, 74, 75, 78, 80n2

Occupy Oakland 71, 73, 74, 78

Occupy protest movement 1, 3–4, 36, 66–81, 108; and acts/decisions 68; anti-state attitude 70; aporias 66, 68, 77–9; challenges of 74–7; decisions and violence of law 72–4; and democracy 77–9; ethic of care 67; fantasy, traversing 69–72; General Assembly (GA) process 70, 71, 76; 99% slogan 75–7; non-hierarchical organising, challenges 66, 71, 74–5; non-intentionality and hyperpoliticisation 68–9; as a political act 68–74; and post-political reformist social activism 68; radical inclusion 66, 75–7; real politics in 66–81; and Socialist Workers Party 71–2; status quo, questioning legitimacy of 69–72

Occupy to Decolonize Oakland 74

Occupy Wall Street (OWS) 37, 70

ODS *see* Occupy Dame Street (ODS), Dublin

Oglala Sioux nation, US 45

'Oka Crisis', Canada (1990) 45

Olsen, S. 73

Ontario, Canada 48; Provincial Police 45

onto-politics 8, 11, 15, 19; of totalisation 6, 7, 20

Operation Desert Sabre 31

Operation Desert Storm 31

organisation, non-hierarchical 66, 71, 74–5

Orientalism (Said) 26

originary violence 72

Oslo, Norway 37

Otherness/'something other' 11, 13, 69, 70, 72

Ottawa, House of Commons (Canada) 48

OWS *see* Occupy Wall Street (OWS)

OWS Journal 70

pacifism, ethico-religious 25, 26

Pahlavi, Shah Mohammad Reza 27

Pakistan 36

Palach, J. 85, 90, 97n18

Palestine 37

Paris 29

participatory action research 66, 68

Pasha, M. 19

patriarchy 118

Patton, P. 14

Peace Churches of Mennonites and Friends (Quakers) 32

peacemaking 47

Peace Movement 26

Peace Park, Cork (Ireland) 66

Pearly Square, Bahrain 113n5

Pearson, C. 26

The People of the Kattawapiskak River (documentary, 2012) 61n7

Perez, R. 129

Permanent Select Committee on Intelligence, House of Representatives 27

Pfeffer, R. 123

philosophical realism 136

Pin-Fat, V. 13

PKOLS (Canadian mountain) 57, 61n19

Plumwood, V. 144

pluralism, complex 142–3

poetics of peace epistemologies 40n6

polis 108

political act, Occupy movement as 68–74

political action, space for 108–9

political activism 68, 108, 113n1

political ecologism 135

political praxis 4, 9, 115, 116; deconstruction as 16–19

political resistance *see* resistance, political

political subjectivity *see* subjectivity, political

political suicide *see* suicide, political

political–theological distancing 84–5

political theory, post-humanist 136–9

politics: attachments, conservative politics of 141–2; deconstruction as political praxis 16–19; in global North 67; humanist *see* humanist politics; leftist movements 9, 10, 44; mass politics 116; micro-politics of deconstruction 16; neoliberal, challenges to 67; onto-politics/ onto-political 6, 7, 8, 11, 15, 19; 'paranoid politics of binarity' 56–7; political acts 69, 70; 'the political' distinguished 13; and political reality 73; post-politics 67, 68, 69, 70; radical 115, 116, 117–18; real, in Occupy movement 66–81; of resisting subjectivity 109–12; of security 15; and self-destruction 84–6; Settler politics, in Canada 54–6; violence of 83; *see also* political act, Occupy movement as; political activism; political praxis; political suicide; political theory, post-humanist; resistance, political

post-colonialism 8, 19

Posthuman International Relations 134

posthumanism 4, 133, 134; critical 140, 143–5; political projects 141–5; political theory, varieties 136–9; *see also* humanist politics

post-politics 67, 68, 69, 70

post-structuralism 10

poverty 120

Powell, C. 34

Prague Spring 85

praxis: concrete 6, 8, 17, 22n2; political 4, 9, 16–19, 115, 116; radical 8

price celebrations 18

Prison Notebooks (Gramsci) 26

problem orientation 135

protests 86, 102, 106; anti-austerity 67, 106, 113n4; anti-nuclear 27, 29, 35; of Idle No More

INDEX

(Canadian movement) 43, 47, 48, 49, 52, 61n8,
122; student protests, Paris (1968) 101, 112n1;
youth 37; *see also* Idle No More (Canadian
protest movement); Occupy protest movement
Proudhon, P.-J. 117
psychoanalysis/psychoanalytic theory 13
purification process 137

Quakers 32
Quang Duc, Thich 85, 91, 92
Queen Elizabeth II Highway, near Edmonton,
Canada 61n9
queer theory/movements 8, 16, 18, 19

Rabaté, J.-M. 103
radical inclusion, Occupy movement 66, 75–7
radicalism, of deconstruction 10, 15, 19
radical politics 115, 116, 117–18
Rancière, J. 40n6
Rapaport, D. C. 84
Reagan, R. 27, 28, 29, 31
Real, the: Real Democracy 78–9; and the Symbolic
70
realism: agential 137; philosophical 136; political
136; speculative 135, 136
reappropriation of resistance 7
Regina, Saskatchewan 48, 51
reinscription of resistance 6, 7, 9
Reitan, R. 3
relativism 9
religious pacifism, and anti-capitalism 25–42
religious sacrifice 88
representative democracy 69, 77
reproductive agency 138
Republican Party, US 61n17
resistance, political 100–14; acts of resistance 6, 7,
8, 102, 103, 107; agent or actor of 6, 7, 8, 9, 12;
analysis of resistance 13, 14; concept 12, 13;
deconstruction, conceptualising as form of 8–12;
everyday forms 8; expansion of study 6–7;
Indigenous resistance to Settler colonialism
44–7; multitude and crowd as spatial political
entities 104–7; subjectivity, politics of resisting
109–12; subject of resistance 7, 8, 9, 19, 20;
violence and political subjectivity 102–4; *see
also* deconstruction; indigenous resistance;
protests; subjectivity, political
Resistances of Psychoanalysis (Derrida) 12
responsibility 72, 91, 96n1, 129, 135, 144, 145;
creative 128; and deconstruction 7, 15, 19;
economic 61n17; ethical 4, 71, 119; fiduciary
61n18; fiscal 56; limitless 20, 115, 116; mutual
76; real 68, 74
ressentiment, in anarchism 116, 117
retrospective semiosis 90, 91
revolutionary communism 25, 26

revolutions 67, 86, 101, 103
Reykjavik, Iceland 28
ritualisation 97n16
Robbins, T. 133, 134
Rocker, R. 117
Rollo, T. 52, 53, *54*
Rorty, R. 9
'Round Dance Revolution', Canada 48, 51
Rousseau, J.-J. 110
Royal Commission on Aboriginal Peoples (RCAP),
Canada 52, 53, 54, 61n15
Rumsfeld, D. 34
Russian Revolution 120, 121, 140

Sachs, W. 144
sacralisation 83
sacrifice/self-sacrifice 20, 82–99; concept 96n11;
logic of 95; meaning 88; sacrificial rite 93;
self-sacrificial subjects 89–90; *see also* self-
immolation; suicide, political
sacrificial system, unity 88
Sadat, A. 27
Said, E. 25, 26
Sands, B. 84, 89, 91, 92
San Francisco, California 32, 66
sans papiers 102, 103, 104, 106–7, 109
Saskatchewan, Canada 47, 48
Saskatoon, Saskatchewan 47
Schmidt, J. 140, 141, 142, 143
Schmitt, C. 84
School of International Service, United States 33
Scott, James C. 8
second- and third-order political critiques/
resistance 6, 7, 14, 15, 17
secular groups, suicidal-like methods 84
security, politics of 15
Security, Territory, Population (Foucault) 125
Seery, J. E. 84
self-annihilation 90, 91, 92, 95, 97n25; *see also*
self-burning; self-destruction, and politics;
self-immolation; suicide, political
self-burning 82, 83, 86, 87, 89, 90, 91, 93
self-creation 115, 119, 121; ambiguities 116,
124–8
self-destruction, and politics 82, 84–6
self-immolation 82–99, 100; political subject of
87–93; political suicide 82, 83, 93–5; politics
and self-destruction 84–6; politics and self-
destruction 82; and protests 86; terminology 87;
see also Bouazizi, M. (self-burning in Sidi
Bouzid, Tunisia)
self-investigation, auto-ethnography 40n6
self-writing, as method 41n6
semiosis, retrospective 90, 91
semiotic capture 82, 89
semiotic contestation 83

INDEX

semiotic functionality 87–8
semi-structured interviews 66, 68
Settler Canadians 43; identity and positionality
60n1; Indigenous resistance to colonialism 44–7;
leftist politics 44; Settler Canadian politics and
Idle No More 54–6
sexual assault 22n1
Shakur, A. 32
Shapiro, M. 25, 40–1n6
Sharp, G. 39n3
Shi'ite guerrillas 28
Shukaitis, S. 122–5
Sidi Bouazid, Tunisia (self-burning by Bouazizi) 4,
82, 83, 86–91, 94, 95, 100, 102–4, 107, 109
Simpson, L. 45, 49, 52, 60
Sirleaf, E. J. 37
Situationist movement 113n2
Six Nations Reserve, Canada 45
Skinny Legs and All (Robbins) 133
social contract 107
Socialist Workers Party (SWP) 22n1, 31, 32, 72,
80n3; and Occupy movement 71–2
social movements 8, 38, 51, 55, 57, 60, 142;
transnational 25, 26
South Korea 85
sovereignty 89, 94, 95, 105; Canada 43, 44, 52, 54;
non-sovereign politicality 83
Soviet Union, Former 31, 85, 96n10
space 108–9
'Space Hijackers', anarchist group 123, 124
Spain 36, 113n9
Spectacle of Defiance and Hope (annual Irish
demonstration) 80n3
speculative realism 135, 136
speech act, and self-sacrifice 89
Spence, T. 52, 55, 58, 61n14; hunger strikes 48, 49,
57
Spivak, G. C. 19
Starcross, L. 118
status quo: acquiescence to 9; questioning
legitimacy of, and Occupy movement 69–72
Stern, N. 143
Strategic Arms Limitations Treaty (SALT) 26
strategic essentialism 19
Straw Dogs (Gray) 138
street, the 101
student protests, Paris (1968) 101, 112n1
subjectification 20; conscious and unconscious
6, 8
subjectivity, political 100, 102; politics of resisting
109–12; post-foundational forms 21;
revolutionary 20; self-immolation, political
subject of 87–93; and violence 102–4; *see also*
resistance, political
subject of resistance 7, 8, 19, 20
sufferance 11–12

suicide, political 83, 93–5; altruistic suicide 87;
suicidal political subject 95; suicide bombs 85,
87, 90, 91, 93
Summer Peacebuilding Institute, Eastern
Mennonite University 33
superego (Freudian theory) 13
Switzerland 28
Symbolic frameworks 69, 70–1, 72, 79
Syntagma Square, Greece 106, 107, 108, 111
Syria 86
Syrotinski, M. 19
Szolucha, A. 3–4

Tahir Square, Egypt 108, 109, 111
Tao Te Ching 138
Tarrow, S. 58
teach-ins 33, 43, 47, 49, 50, 51, 60n6
temporalisation 77
terrorism, political 84; *see also* 9/11 terrorist
attacks
textual activism 17
Thatcher, M. 29
'thing power' (Bennett) 137
'thirdspace' sovereignty, Indigenous 44, 52, 54
third-wave feminism 18, 19
Thomas, J. 39n1
Three Mile Island, Nuclear Station 27
Thus Spake Zarathustra 117
Tibet, self-immolations in 85, 88
Toronto, Canada 48
Toscano, A. 82, 83, 84
totalisation 15, 79; onto-political 6, 7, 20
totalitarianism 84, 106
transgender identity 19
transgression: boundaries, transgressing 51–4; Idle
No More (Canadian political protest movement)
44, 51–4, 55, 59; Occupy protest movement
70–1; tactics 44, 51–2, 55
Tucker, K. 7
Tunisia 67, 112; Jasmine Revolution 103;
self-burning by Bouazizi in Sidi Bouzid 4, 82,
83, 86–91, 94, 95, 100, 102–4, 107, 109
Twin Cities Habitat for Humanity 33
Twitter 50, 59, 60n4
Two-Row Treaty, Canada 52–4

Uebermensch 121
Uehling, G. 88, 96n10
Ukraine 29
undecidability 68, 72, 73
UNESCO 29
United for Peace and Justice (UFPJ) 32
United Kingdom 22n1, 29
United States: American Indian Movement (AIM)
27, 45; American University School of
International Service 33; auto-ethnography 27,

155

INDEX

31, 32, 33, 36, 37, 40n5; Coalition of the Willing 35; FBI 73; Indigenous resistance 45, 46; 9/11 terrorist attacks 34; Occupy movement in 73, 80; *see also* Canada; Idle No More (Canadian political protest movement); Indigenous people, Canada; Occupy Atlanta; Occupy Oakland; Occupy Wall Street (OWS)

unity 14, 76, 88, 105, 106; and singularity 66, 78, 79; unitary subject 128–9

Uptown Centre, Victoria (Canada) 58

USSR (Soviet Union) 31, 85, 96n10

Vancouver, Canada 45, 46

Vaneigem, R. 123

Veracini, L. 60n2

Vessey, J. W. 28

Vietnam 92, 97n25; Vietnamese monks, self-incineration 85

violence 12; and deconstruction 22; divine 94, 95; of law 72–4, 94; originary 72; and political subjectivity 102–4; of politics 83; symbolic 91; *see also* self-immolation; suicide, political

Virno, P. 105

vital materialism 136–7, 139

Wacquant, L. 12

Walker, L. 31

Wall, I. R. 113n7

War on Terror 35

Warsaw Pact 85

war/wars 17, 25, 45, 73, 85, 97n, 143; anti-war groups/movements 26, 27, 28, 31, 32, 35, 40n6, 71; civil war 36; class war 26; Gulf Wars 31; refugees 29

Washington 30, 34

Weber, M. 94

West Bank 28, 37

Wet'suwet'en people, Canada 45

White House, Washington 30, 34

Wilson, N. 47

Winnemem Wintu communities, California 45

The winter we danced (Kino-nda-niimi Collective, 2014 60n3, 60n4, 61n6, 131n6

Wittner, L. P. 39n2

Wolfe, P. 60n1

Women's International League for Peace and Freedom (WILPF) 28

women's liberation 125–6, 127

Worker's World 32

World Bank 33

World Peace Council 27

World Social Forums 32, 34, 35

World Trade Center 34

World Tribunal on Iraq 35

Wounded Knee (US town), Indian occupation (1973) 45

Yasukuni Shrine, Tokyo 84

Yelineck, P. 118

Yemen 86

yoga 33

Young, R. 19

youth protests 37

Zarathustra 121, 122, 128

Zevnik, A. 4

Žižek, S. 37, 101, 102, 103

Zuccotti Park, New York 73